Praise for *Religion*

"Kriyananda has continued to devote h
of his beloved guru, Paramhansa Yogan
ers that petty differences in religious pra
such practices is not a spiritual journey of
interest. His teachings tell us that just the opposite is true, and that radiant
Self-realization fills the heart and actually helps the individual to a more
peaceful and spiritually fulfilling life, and the recognition of the great human spirit in all religions, when Self-realization is practiced."
— Fred Alan Wolf, Ph.D., author of *The Yoga of Time Travel* and
Mind Into Matter

"I avidly read Swamiji's books and consider him one of today's true
spiritual luminaries. This new work helps light our way in this post-
denominational, inclusive new era."
— Lama Surya Das, author of *Awakening the Buddha Within*, founder
of the Dzogchen Center

"Seldom have I read a book like this, a book whose every single word
I can agree with; a book in which every page radiates attention, under-
standing, and wisdom. Truly Kriyananda is a great apostle of divine love
which, as he declares, is the true essence of religion."
— Ervin Laszlo, Ph.D., author of *Quantum Shift in the Global Brain*, and
Chaos Point: The World at the Crossroads, founder of The Club of Budapest

"This extraordinary work by beloved Swami Kriyananda is a very special
gift for the soul, offering us remarkable spiritual insight and deep wisdom.
This is such a wondrous contribution to all of humanity! Just at the right
time, too, as we move into a period of great change, and confront all of the
personal and global challenges that go with that. Endless appreciation to
Swamiji, by whom we continue to be bountifully blessed!
— Neale Donald Walsch, author of *Conversations with God*

"Kriyananda has intimately and fully explained how we . . . have entered
a "New Age." . . . of energy exchange, energy transference, and most im-
portantly . . . energy expansion. Kriyananda takes the reader on a journey
through two centuries—from some of the beginnings of this "new thought"
within Sri Yukteswar's exciting writings in *The Holy Science* through the
further intrinsic thoughts of Kriyananda's guru, Paramhansa Yogananda,
and up to the present time—with the much-needed explanation of how . . .
simply and effectively . . . each one of us has the capability, the intelligence,
and the opportunity to become enlightened. . . . Kriyananda . . . shows the
reader that . . . the eternal truth is "love," which in its highest form is
energy, is God—and since each soul is a part of that energy of God, one's
true status has been and ever will be, a holy state of being."
— Rev. Paula T. Webb, author of *An Independent Prosperity*, founder
of The National InterFaith Council

"*In Religion in the New Age*, Swami Kriyananda. . . . brilliantly explores the essential trends of the unfolding age of energy and explains how they will affect us, and future generations."
  —Richard Salva, author of *Soul Journey* and *Walking with William of Normandy*

"Kriyananda's newest exposition—a collection of deeply personal and insightful essays—is more than a book, but rather a guide for the coming year. 2008 was the most tumultuous period in recent memory and has shaken the citizens of the world into a new reality; one they never thought could happen. The joyful Truth of the situation we find ourselves in is that it was always known, always evident, always part of our evolution. This Truth is well understood by those in tune with the cyclical nature of the cosmos.

  "By bringing the remarkable predictions of the famous sage, Sri Yukteswar, and the practical wisdom of his most potent disciple, Paramhansa Yogananda, to the pages of this book, Swamiji has once again opened the door for the modern reader to discover the truth of his nature through the ancient wisdom of the yogis . . . a wisdom that is now available to all who seek it."
  —Yogi Amrit Desai, author of *Amrit Yoga and the Yoga Sutras*, and *Kripalu Yoga: Book I and II*

"Kriyananda, a modern sage, has once again written an illuminating yet practical spiritual masterpiece. This fascinating book takes a look at the New Age and how we can best embrace both its challenges and possibilities for spiritual awakening. A timely and much needed outlook."
  —Rev. Justin Epstein, Unity Church of Hilton Head Island.

"I love Kriyananda's new book *Religion in the New Age*. It is a brilliant star, offering the perfect illumination to navigate one's life by."
  —Vaishali, author of *You Are What You Love* and *Wisdom Rising*

"Kriyananda's book of essays brings new light to the text of the Hindu sage, Sri Yukteswar's *The Holy Science*. It provides current analysis that supports the thesis of Sri Yukteswar regarding the ancient yuga system of historical interpretation. He also offers insightful and personal anecdotal essays on a widespectrum of spiritual and societal subjects, bringing his considerable intelligence and intuition to bear. His personal accounts with Paramhansa Yogananda bring us closer to this yoga master, whose work and teachings are still relevant through the life work of this dedicated disciple and swami. A worthy read that will shed light on issues from organizational management to loving relations, self-esteem to the remembrance of God as the source of all inspiration and insight."
  —Mike Ellison, President Unity Temple of Santa Cruz

RELIGION
in the NEW AGE

And Other Essays for the Spiritual Seeker

Swami Kriyananda
(J. Donald Walters)

Crystal Clarity Publishers
Nevada City, California

Crystal Clarity Publishers, Nevada City, CA 95959
Copyright © 2009 by Hansa Trust
All rights reserved. Published 2009
Printed in Canada

ISBN: 978-1-56589-236-1
1 3 5 7 9 10 8 6 4 2

Cover illustration: Dana Lynne Andersen
Title of illustration: Gaia
www.awakeningarts.com
Cover design: Renee Glenn Designs
Interior design and layout: Crystal Clarity Publishers

Library of Congress Cataloging-in-Publication Data

Kriyananda, Swami.
  Religion in the New Age and Other Essays / Swami
Kriyananda. — 1st ed.
    p. cm.
  ISBN 978-1-56589-236-1 (trade paper, indexed)
  1. New Age movement. I. Title.

BP605.N48K75 2008
294.5092 — dc22

                                   2008040415

800.424.1055 or 530.478.7600
f: 530.478.7610
clarity@crystalclarity.com
www.crystalclarity.com

CONTENTS

PREFACE
HOW I MET MY GURU

I was desperate. I had been born into a well-to-do home, and I was accustomed to Western conveniences, the American way of life, Western social and moral values. I had no reason to doubt that I could have a successful life by those standards. All my friends expected to achieve material success, to have good marriages, happy homes, a comfortable lifestyle in a well-to-do suburb. I lived in Scarsdale, New York, one of the wealthiest suburbs in America. I was miserable!

"What is it all for?" I kept asking myself. What is money but a burden, forcing one to earn more and more simply to keep afloat? What is marriage but bondage to ego-fulfillment? What is a nice home but a glorified chicken coop where people wait for the butcher, death, to chop off their heads, pluck them clean, and put them in the oven? What can this world give me of happiness itself?

I looked about me and saw no one really happy. Worse still, I saw no one willing to face that all-important question: What is life's purpose? What is it all about?

I was desperate. *I had to know God*. The churches, unbelievably, spoke of Him almost not at all. Everyone seemed to think it unrealistic for anyone to seek Him, and impossible to *know* Him. "Don't be a fanatic!" I was solemnly advised whenever I spoke of my longing to know God. No one I met seemed able to give me the answers I was seeking so desperately. No one I met seemed particularly interested in attaining wisdom.

And then one afternoon, in a New York City bookstore, I found *Autobiography of a Yogi* by Paramhansa Yogananda. In him, I knew after reading only a few pages of this great, living scripture, I had found what I'd been seeking: a true guide.

This was in September 1948. I knew nothing then about the teachings of India. Words like *yoga*, *karma*, *guru*, and all the Indian terms that today are so widely known in the West were totally new to me. Yet I *knew* that this man, Paramhansa Yogananda, had what I sought.

I took the next bus across America, non-stop from New York to Los Angeles. The journey lasted four days and four nights. When I met him, the first words I addressed to him I had never imagined myself addressing to anyone. I said, "I want to be your disciple!"

And so, truly, my life began. He accepted me at that meeting, and said to me, "I give you my unconditional love." I was overwhelmed. He asked me if I would make the same commitment to him. How could I not do so? He asked me to give him my unconditional obedience. Despite my desperate sense of need, I had to be sincere. "What," I asked, "if I ever think you are wrong?"

"I will never ask anything of you," he replied, "except what God tells me to ask." Gladly, then, I gave him that promise. Never thereafter did he disappoint me. Far from making me an automaton in my obedience, obedience to him greatly strengthened my own will. In his guidance what I found above all was an ever-increasing sense of inner freedom.

I'd had no idea what it meant to be a spiritual master. I'd had no idea such persons existed. For I knew nothing of saints and gurus; I was a complete greenhorn. My ignorance may have helped me to this extent, at least: I had nothing to *un*learn. In Yogananda, however, I found a greatness I'd never dreamed existed. It was like living in the very presence of God.

I don't mean to say his every utterance was like some grave pronouncement from a mountaintop. He was delightfully human. Not that he displayed any human flaws. What he showed me were the highest potentials of human nature. He was humorous, always natural, yet also inwardly somewhat remote, as though living in perpetual awareness of God's living presence within him. Gazing into his eyes was like catching a glimpse into infinity. I never saw in those eyes the slightest hint of ego-awareness, likes or dislikes, desires or aversions: only constant bliss and loving compassion.

He wore his wisdom (as I wrote in my autobiography, *The Path*) like a comfortable old jacket: with perfect ease. In his presence, however, I felt constantly his emanations of divine joy and love. He lived ever in an inner, higher world.

He also demonstrated to me again and again an intimate knowledge of my own nature. One day he amazed me by saying, "I know every thought you think." If ever, in meditation, I held a thought that needed to be corrected or "fine tuned," he would say something about it to me the next time I saw him. Often (if others were present) he would give only a subtle hint, which I alone would be able to understand.

And he guided not only by words, but by inspiring me from within with ever-deeper insight into myself. How can I describe what it was like to live with him? The short confines of a mere preface incapacitate me.

I have been his devoted disciple ever since that day, September 12, 1948—at the present date, nearly sixty years ago. It has been the greatest blessing of my life. I live only to serve him and his mission. For that reason alone have I done all the work some people marvel at: the teaching, the books, the music, the number of communities I've founded.

For that reason alone I moved to India, in my late seventies. It has been my honor and my joy to be able to serve him wherever he has sent me—including now, finally (perhaps), in India, the land of his birth. As my Guru was Indian by birth, so do I feel at least partly Indian myself! As my Guru—whom I consider my spiritual father—was Bengali, so do I myself feel, at least in that sense, Bengali.

I pray that this book reflects at least a small portion of the wisdom I have gained from him.

Part One

RELIGION IN THE NEW AGE

INTRODUCTION

In these pages I aim to show how a spiritual mission, regardless of its name and tenets, can be made to relate to the needs of all humanity.

Paramhansa Yogananda prophesied that some day the purpose of all religions would be accepted as being one and the same: Self-realization. Included in that understanding would be a sense of the non-sectarian fellowship of all truth seekers. His own mission, as he stated it, was above all to teach "the original teachings of Jesus Christ, and the original yoga teachings of Krishna." He stated, further, that he had come to unite all religions in an understanding of their sublime and high purpose. His mission, to show the underlying oneness of two great religions particularly, may therefore be seen as symbolic also, being meant to demonstrate the underlying oneness of *all* religions, for humanity everywhere seeks the same eventual fulfillment: bliss in God. Self-realization—the realization of God as the indwelling, blissful Self of all beings—is then, in the broadest sense, the true goal of all religions, and is also the deepest desire in every human heart.

The great master in his teachings also drew to a focus countless truths that have been expressed diversely through the ages. He showed that the highest wisdom has always contained the same essential truths, the first of which is that all men are rays of the one Divine Light, and the second, that man's ultimate destiny is, of his own free will, to merge back into that Light.

For this reason, in my book *Revelations of Christ, Proclaimed by Paramhansa Yogananda*, I proposed that this highest truth be called "*Sanaatan Dharma*, the Eternal Religion," for in all the universe this cannot fail to be one, supreme truth: union with God, the fundamental reality of all existence.

Yogananda presented a way of life that was unitive—one that would make spiritually relevant every aspect of human life: business and the art of self-support generally; marriage; education; the fine arts; self-expansion through service to others; and the supreme art of how to live happily in this body.

Finally, he proposed a lifestyle designed to enable people everywhere to incorporate their varied pursuits into a harmonious, God-centered existence. Through the years that he taught in the West, he urged his audiences to adopt this life-style by gathering together and forming what he called "world-brotherhood colonies." I was blessed by him to be able to found the first Ananda World-Brotherhood community, in 1968, on what are today some 1,000 acres of land near Nevada City, California. At present there are seven functioning examples of this ideal, all bearing the name, Ananda, in various parts of the world.

The sheer breadth of the Master's vision, and its practical relevance to the needs of our age, demonstrate that he was, in the fullest sense of the expression, a World Teacher, and not the guru only of a particular group of disciples. In fact, he'd been sent to be the way-shower for a new age, and the savior for "many millions," as he put it, who would tune into the divine ray he had brought. For mankind now stands at the dawn of new awakening into a globally heightened, spiritual awareness.

Swami Sri Yukteswar, the guru of Paramhansa Yogananda, stated in his book *The Holy Science* that the whole of mankind has arrived, scripturally speaking, at a new age. The earth entered this age in the year 1900, after an interim, or bridge (*sandhya*), of 200 years during which time the new rays gradually increased in strength. The ancient teachings of India gave this age the name, *Dwapara Yuga*.

The first of four *yugas*, *Kali* (the dark) *Yuga*, was an age when most people perceived everything in narrowly fixed and material terms. Men needed inner as well as outer forms. Outwardly, they thought more easily of solid objects than of seemingly insubstantial gasses and air; and inwardly, they felt more comfortable with carefully formulated dogmas and fixed ideas than they would have been with abstractions like relativity, let us say, or subtle distinctions of conscious and subconscious. Organizationally, they were comfortable with firm structures, preferring everything to be established and in its own place. They believed the universe to be cozily geocentric. God, to them, was a bearded old man seated "somewhere up there" on an eternal throne of judgment. The conception of the earth as flat made it easier, of course, to visualize heaven as literally high up in the sky above them.

Dwapara Yuga has already brought greater fluidity to people's consciousness. This is an age, above all, of energy-awareness. Many people, aware of something new stirring around them, and a new awareness within them, welcome it exuberantly as though it were bestowing on them unbridled license to indulge to excess in everything they like.

In the fine arts (painting, sculpture, and music), traditional forms have been cast aside in favor of the grotesque, the trivial, and the blasphemous. In children's education, experimentation has brought more confusion than enlightenment. The same may be said of people's understanding of morality, and of correct social behavior.

Thus the term, "New Age," is also viewed with anxiety by "old fogies" who still adhere to old traditions. In fact, what we are witnessing is a struggle between old ways—which once seemed "carved in stone"—and a new, more flexible spirit that is striving to find its own clear self-expression.

This struggle between the old and the new, though still somewhat amorphous, is in evidence everywhere. We see it also in religion: in the struggle between those who cling to traditions of the past and those who reject all tradition as antiquated. To the religious traditionalist, the mere hint of a new age "sets his teeth grinding."

For Moslems, the cornerstone of whose religion is the saying, "There is no God but Allah, and Mohammed is His prophet," no other way is acceptable.

For Christians, time itself is measured from the birth year of Jesus Christ. Fundamentalists especially are convinced that the world is fast approaching the "end times" supposedly predicted in the Bible, and associated with the Second Coming of Christ. Among Moslems also, there are some who believe that something approximating those "end times" is fast approaching.

Naturally, a world view in which mankind, after centuries of relative darkness, is postulated as being poised and ready to soar up into new realities is fiercely rejected by anyone who believes that the past two thousand years virtually defined the term, "Christian enlightenment."

Much of the present antagonism on the part of orthodoxy toward the "new age" is due, I think, to the arrogance of some who have embraced it mainly for its novelty. For "new age," as a concept, appeals especially to the young, whose tendency in any case is to reject the old. Many scientists, too, have arrogated to themselves the role of "heralds of a new wisdom," basing their claim not on any suggestion of being, themselves, better human beings, nor on any but the thinnest hope that their discoveries will someday produce such human beings, but on the simple fact that a few scientists (the very few real pioneers) have discovered unexpected facts about the universe.

Writers on philosophy since Einstein have had a heyday with the theory that morality, far from being absolute ("all things are relative"), may even, with a little manipulation, be discarded altogether.

"Avant-garde" artists of all kinds, again, having milked the "new age" concept for every ounce of its shock value, offer nothing to replace the rubble created by their iconoclasm, which still litters the countryside.

And self-styled trend-setters, finally, have no clear notion as to where, why, or how to direct people's attention. They offer only trivia—or, worse still—blasphemy in place of the worthwhile and the meaningful. Indeed, I personally have reached the conclusion that anyone who follows the dictates of "style" reveals himself as someone lacking taste of his own.

The public, quite naturally, is bewildered. Nor is it surprising that many people today gaze back for comfort to past traditions which, to them, are at least recognizable. The relativity of time which Einstein claimed has not, after all, thrown anyone's clocks out of kilter. Scientific discoveries have altered no fundamental *human* reality. Works of art may titillate or outrage a few people, but the meaninglessness they suggest neither inspires anyone nor offers any hope of new insights to come. Indeed, the most that the dogma, "art for art's sake," can ever accomplish is to inspire a certain smugness on the part of those who accept it, and who consider themselves favored with insights that are unavailable to the "*canaille*."

What is most notable about the times we live in is that, in every field of endeavor, human perceptions are expanding, and new windows opening onto the vastness and subtlety of the universe. The need is growing in human hearts everywhere to make sense of these insights. We cannot simply reject them. Nor can we merely embrace them in the exuberant manner of adolescents, welcoming them for their shock value. We must assess them, and do our best to understand what implications they have for human life.

We must accept first, of course, the simple fact that these new waves of insight *are*, in fact, unprecedented. We must also transcend any fear we may harbor that eternal values are being threatened. Indeed, Truth cannot be a house divided. Self-proclaimed "wisdom," moreover, that is rooted in neither Truth nor tradition, is almost always mere superstition.

In this essay I propose to explain at some length what Sri Yukteswar said and meant about the new age, and his reasons for claiming that we have entered it already. I will present facts in support of his statement, which he himself could not have presented back in 1894, when he wrote his book, for the simple reason that science had not yet made the discoveries that were to justify his claims.

The first part of this essay will present the general basis for Sri Yukteswar's predictions, and will explain at some length what is implied by the term, "new age." The last part will focus more specifically on Paramhansa Yogananda's mission in this age.

One of the results of the new awareness of energy that is flooding our planet is that people are being challenged to assume more personal responsibility for their lives. In a sense, certainly, religious organizations may continue to obstruct the spread of true, inward religion. I shall also show, however, how religious organizations also can prove beneficial and expansive to this new awareness, in the spirit of *Dwapara Yuga*, and how Paramhansa Yogananda himself set the tone for this new type of religious organization.

CHAPTER ONE
ARE WE LIVING IN A NEW AGE?

That we live in a new age seems an incontestable fact. Almost everything nowadays, especially since the beginning of the twentieth century, has proclaimed the newness of this age as a fact.

In 1899 Charles Duell, the director of the U.S. Patent Office, is said to have written to President William McKinley recommending that the office be abolished. "Everything that can be invented," he stated, "has been invented." At that time, virtually every invention that we associate with modern civilization was either unknown or in such a rudimentary state of development as to seem, today, either comical or endearingly quaint. The world at that time had no paved highways, no speeding cars, no airplanes. It lacked a veritable host of other items that have become commonplace in our age: radio, television, voice recorders, refrigeration, washing machines, computers—to name only a few things that we today take entirely for granted.

The greatest change that has occurred has been in our perception of reality. This change began with the discovery, barely ten years after Sri Yukteswar published his book, that matter is actually composed only of vibrations of energy, a discovery that has forced the conclusion that energy is the reality behind everything man-made that we see around us. This reality underlies not only material things, but also institutions and ideas.

A number of people still claim that when the oil resources of our planet eventually become exhausted, we'll be thrown back to medieval times. Those forecasters of gloom overlook something important: It would be impossible for man at this stage of his development to turn back, for the simple reason that the world has become not only energy-dependent, but also energy-*conscious*. We today perceive everything in terms of energy.

It wasn't the discovery of oil that gave us the modern age. It was an already-manifesting awareness that *energy is a reality*. Energy-consciousness, in the first place, was what led to oil's discovery.

My father, an oil geologist for Esso, was posted by his company to Romania. He told me that oil was first discovered seeping out of the ground in that country—an oddity that had been occurring for centuries, but that had long been considered only a nuisance. When energy itself became recognized as a global need, oil was recognized as crucial to civilization's further development. Men like my father were sent to Romania and elsewhere to help develop those resources.

Whenever mankind is ready to take a new step in his advancement, that step will—indeed, *must*—appear as if "out of the blue." Penicillin, a product of bread mold, was unheard of as a medicine until mankind was ready to discover its practical uses. Every new step in civilization's advancement may have developed from facts that had been staring everyone in the face for centuries. It wasn't so much the new discoveries which produced the change as the fact that man was ready to make use of those discoveries. Once mankind was ready, the discoveries became not only possible, but inevitable.

The shock waves generated by the realization that matter is only a vibration of energy have led some physicists to suspect that energy, too, will in its turn prove to manifest even subtler realities.

Ancient Indian tradition gave the underlying concept the much simpler name: consciousness.

A New Age? Traditionally, the chronology of civilizations has been reckoned from earthly events: from the birth of Jesus Christ; the death of Buddha; the emigration of Mohammed to Medina; the assorted reigns of kings and emperors. By any objective reckoning, however, the time through which we are now passing is so radically different from any previous one that it seems reasonable to define it for all mankind as a *New Age*.

For new scientific insights are threatening to grow to the dimensions of an avalanche. In view of this fact, it seems pointless to try to reconcile present times with past history.

The old order began crumbling centuries ago, even before the increasingly powerful onslaughts of modern science. The first sledgehammer-blows, delivered in the West, were soon felt throughout the world. The new spirit of inquiry gave birth to the Italian Renaissance, to the Protestant Reformation, and almost simultaneously to the voyage of Christopher Columbus to the New World and the consequently "shocking" revelation that the world is round.

The same spirit led to other discoveries, including the fact that high civilizations co-existed with our own, and that still others, at least as high, existed in ages past. Western civilization, clearly, is far from unique. To the extent that it is special—and the people of certain other, older cultures may have defined us as "those revolutionary Western barbarians, shaking up everything!"—Western science has merely anticipated findings that were bound to be made anyway. The major blows to tradition came, certainly, through the findings of Kepler, Copernicus, Galileo, and Newton. They were followed by a swelling number of scientific pioneers, most of them Western, whose findings fundamentally changed man's approach to reality.

Indeed, for more than a century now it has been almost a fad for thinking people to challenge the validity even of traditional morality.

Science has given us an entirely new way of looking at matter, at life—at everything! Whereas in the past it may have sufficed in the West, particularly, to reach conclusions by logic, the criterion for acceptance today is *experience*—which, scientifically speaking, is to say, *experiment*. The German philosopher Georg Hegel stated, "All that is real is logical, and all that is logical is real." On this premise virtually all of Western civilization rested.

What, indeed, is one to make of the discovery which resolved the long-standing debate as to whether light is a particle or a wave? The answer? It is both!

What, then, of even subtler, more abstract questions such as the existence of God? Back when logic ruled Western thinking, scholastic theologians stretched the unprovable to the point of absurdity by arguing logically the question, How many angels could stand together on the head of a pin? Modern science refused even to consider such questions, dismissing them not necessarily as absurd, but as imponderable.

Interestingly enough, that decision led eventually to serious consequences. For, having avoided all seemingly imponderable questions for centuries, scientists ended up demoting them finally from irrelevance to non-existence. The modern "scientific solution" to the question about the existence of God was reached—however, and of course—by default, not at all by the vaunted scientific method.

The new approach to reality, based on demonstrated facts, has created an upheaval in people's thinking, and has produced a profound sense of confusion. A story—no doubt apocryphal, but nevertheless suggestive of confusion as to what does and does not constitute proof—illustrates delightfully the ensuing bewilderment. A Hindu in the Indian city of Benares is said to have assured an American tourist, "With all the archaeological investigations that have been conducted in my country, not a single wire has been discovered. This *proves*," he concluded triumphantly, "that in ancient India they had the wireless!"

Nevertheless, the new ways of thinking, based on experiment, have come to stay, and need, therefore, to be understood. Nothing in the scientific approach to reality says that man must limit himself to experimenting with material instruments—particularly now, when matter itself has been found to consist only of vibrations of energy.

Formal religion—not the high spiritual teachings of Krishna, Buddha, and Jesus Christ, but the outward forms that clothe religion everywhere—no longer holds deep appeal in the minds of growing numbers of thinking people. There remains in many such people, however, and perhaps more insistently today than ever, a deeply felt need to understand what life is all about. I number myself among them, at least in my past. I had a deep longing for that inner security which religion ought to bestow. Lacking today is a perception of how to fulfill that need by bringing it in line with present-day understanding.

Old-fashioned ways of looking at life and of expressing oneself no longer exert, these days, the same appeal as they did in their own day. We are, for one thing, immersed in the ebb and flow of rapid movement and instant communication. The old ways were more leisurely than ours are today. Yet, beneath their longer, more placid rhythms, old human realities were basically the same as today's. The present hustle and impatience are merely garments that cover a human nature basically the same everywhere, even if people no longer display courtly manners or conscious elegance in their speech. Thus, there remains a need to understand motivations which people often hide, even from themselves.

Is mankind, as many aver, sliding rapidly into moral chaos? Or is this age simply more challenging in the demand it makes of all men to live more energetically? If this truly is a new age, fresh ways of thinking must be sought for whatever deeper insights they may provide into reality.

What faces us today is much more than a revolutionary perception of the universe. It is, potentially, a deeper perception of divine truth itself. The change in thinking that mankind is undergoing is not limited, moreover, to any nation or culture: it is worldwide.

To begin with, it seems reasonable to say that, whether we like it or not, the times we live in are indeed different—radically so—from any within known history. Consider only a few examples:

In literature, everyone writes in greatly shortened sentences. Reviews of Jane Austen novels of the early 1800s often praise her style; yet who today could write that way even if he wanted to? It is more than the fact that we no longer use quill pens, fountain pens, or even typewriters. Computers now enable us to set down on paper our most fleeting thoughts in the full knowledge that it will be easy to correct and polish as we go. We don't even need, if a page contains a mistake, to type out the whole page laboriously again. A simple change, and our electric printers give us the new page within seconds. Even our thoughts race ahead of us at a speed that might have been unnatural, and perhaps impossible (judging by the way people seem to have spoken), in Austen's day.

In the composition of music, computers have made it possible to write quickly and legibly while remaining in the natural flow of one's inspiration. Music synthesizers, too, have obviated the need to learn to play many instruments, and have thereby opened the field for composers to remain even more completely in the flow of the inspiration they receive.

The same may be said of countless other fields of endeavor. In business, it is now possible to conclude trans-oceanic agreements with a single telephone call. Gone is the need to write long letters, then wait months for a reply. On the other hand, if a face-to-face confrontation is required, one can hop on an airplane and arrive at one's destination in a few hours—or, if physical contact isn't necessary, convey one's thoughts by a variety of methods: fax, e-mail, and direct communication by video phone. So far-reaching in their impact are these changes that one no longer needs to affirm that this is a new age. The facts stare one in the face from virtually the moment he awakes every morning.

Is there, then, some explanation for these revolutionary changes?

Interestingly, an explanation was published more than a century ago, in 1894, before any shift toward energy-consciousness was even suspected, and five years before the director of the U.S. Patent Office is said to have written the President recommending that his Office be abolished. In a sense, indeed, that recommendation was valid, for everything that could be squeezed out of old ways of doing things had, quite possibly, been manifested already. Virtually every invention that has been made since then has been powered by energy. The old ways were formally buried in the year 1900, with the beginning of the new age.

The task facing mankind today is to understand even better the implications of this new energy-consciousness.

CHAPTER TWO
THE AGES OF CIVILIZATION

As I said earlier, Swami Sri Yukteswar, a man with exceptional credentials as both a scholar and a sage of deep wisdom, wrote a book toward the end of the nineteenth century titled *The Holy Science*. In his book the author stated that, according to the ancient system of chronology once used in India, our earth recently entered a new age called *Dwapara Yuga*, which was defined by a heightened awareness of energy as the underlying reality of the material universe.

His book described that chronology, and showed it to be based not on earthly events, but on astronomical data. Sri Yukteswar corrected mistakes that had entered subsequently into the ancient system, which had occurred, he explained, during the time-period when our earth was passing through the darkest of four ages, called *Kali Yuga*, an age that brought confusion to human understanding.

There is obviously some sense in basing a system of chronology on astronomical data, provided one really can do so. One wonders, however, how a periodic decrease and increase of mental clarity can be attributed, as Sri Yukteswar claimed, to such phenomena. At first glance, to the rational mind, basing its thinking on so-far demonstrated knowledge, the proposal seems preposterous! One convincing factor would be whether, in defiance of all reasonable expectations, the testimony of history substantiated that ancient belief. Otherwise, how in the name of sanity could an idea that challenges the wildest fantasies of science fiction even possibly be justified?

Modern materialistic science insists on a number of premises, among which might be listed the following:

    a) There is no God; there are only mechanisms (though this last assertion has already been disproved).

    b) There is no immaterial soul.

    c) There is no life after death.

    d) Consciousness itself is only a product of brain activity.

    e) Computers, or something like them, will someday be capable of creating *self-conscious*, artificial intelligence.

These dismal claims are made, or at least endorsed, by many of the leading and most highly intelligent men and women of our day. Their conviction has, moreover, been growing for several centuries, to the point of having become virtually a fixed dogma.

Some years ago I read of a prominent professor of psychology who made it a practice to tell his students at the beginning of each school year: "I request any of my students who believes he possesses a soul please to park it outside the door before entering this classroom." The remark got repeated annually because, one assumes, it always received a gratifying titter.

Cracks, however, have begun to appear in the seemingly solid façade of traditional science. Physics, long at the forefront in that formidable march, has recently begun to branch out into lines of inquiry that include the possibility of consciousness itself being the bedrock of reality, and not merely an intriguing product of a sophisticated network of nerves in the brain.

Indeed, if complex electronic mechanisms alone could produce consciousness, how is one to explain the obvious fact that even the earthworm is conscious? This simplest among all visible creatures is, indeed, sufficiently *self-conscious* to wriggle away from any perceived threat, such as the prick of a pin.

The evidence mounts all around us that consciousness itself—and, still more challenging to scientific dogma, *self-consciousness*—is a basic reality underlying the universe. Such, amazingly, was the claim made in ancient India: namely, that all Creation is only a dream in the consciousness of the Creator. Modern physicists are beginning more and more to suspect that, as Sir Arthur Eddington put it, "The material [here, I paraphrase] of which the universe is made begins to look suspiciously like mind stuff." And Sir James Jeans, the prominent British physicist, wrote in *The Mysterious Universe*, "The stream of knowledge is heading towards a non-mechanical reality; the universe begins to look more like a great thought than a great machine."

Indeed, common human experience, too, has always inclined toward this suspicion—as, for example, in the oft-heard exclamation "Am I really awake, or am I only dreaming?" Doesn't everyone experience, sometimes, a vague doubt that the solid-seeming reality of his daily existence is only a figment of his imagination?

The alternatives before us are absolute: Either nothing is conscious, or everything is conscious, or in some way manifests consciousness. Does this seem too bold a statement? Please reflect, first: Were nothing conscious, how could the question even be asked? Could it be asked unconsciously?

Such would be an unconscionable postulate! On the other hand, assuming the existence of consciousness even in ourselves, where did this consciousness come from? There had to be a Supreme Source. Brains cannot *produce* consciousness; they themselves have to be the product of consciousness.

God, the Supreme Source, can have had nothing out of which to produce His Creation except His own consciousness. Before Creation there was nothing. ("The earth was without form, and void, and darkness was upon the face of the Deep." Genesis 1:2) There was either nothing at all, or there was Absolute Consciousness. Something could not emerge out of nothing. Therefore, everything had to emerge from consciousness. Everything is, in fact, a vibration of consciousness. Even the rocks, far from being solid, are vibrations of conscious energy. Even the rocks possess, to however slight a degree, some awareness.

Since it takes consciousness even to address this question, we may safely insist that the second of our alternatives is the correct one: Everything is conscious. Much ancient wisdom supports this conclusion. And it will have to be pointed out that religion, too, given this insight, will need to be seen in a new light. More on this point later, however.

Meanwhile, is it not at least conceivable, from the conclusion we've just drawn, that there may exist vast and *diverse* currents of energy flowing in the universe? This cosmic possibility takes us far indeed from the narrow view championed by most of modern science, much of which still hopes to pry out every mystery of the universe with the heavy crowbar of a mechanistic outlook.

Ancient India—in common, in fact, with a surprising number of other ancient civilizations—taught that the earth passes through successive ages. India claimed that the earth's movement through space is submitted, in the process, to a succession of influences of varying intensity which affect the consciousness of its inhabitants.

It is fairly obvious that awakened and focused mental energy does make for brighter intelligence and keener understanding, and that weak energy accompanies a duller intelligence. In any work that I myself have done, I have always noticed that my output was greatly influenced by the amount of energy I was able to raise to the brain. If I was sleepy or mentally foggy, I more or less had to postpone my labors.

The present age of rapidly increasing energy-consciousness, which has greatly affected also our speed of physical movement, seems to be producing not only the haste, impatience, and superficiality of our times, but also its creative output.

To return to those old traditions: Ancient India—indeed, as I stated before, this truth was hinted at also in many ancient countries and civilizations—taught that the earth passes in cyclic succession through ascending and descending ages and produces, alternately, increasing and decreasing mental clarity. Western scholars, quite understandably, make short shrift of those traditions. But then, it must be considered also that we are in an ascending age, and have just come out of a time of relative darkness from which we must draw whatever glimmers of understanding survive to the present day. Recent history (from 500 A.D.) covers a fairly straight line of ascent toward the modern world, and what we consider ancient history (say, the one or two thousand years before that) covers what might be called the "dying gasp" of the great, ancient cycle.

Swami Sri Yukteswar, however, gave surprisingly scientific support to the theme he presented. It is interesting to consider (again) moreover, that India's was by no means the only civilization of ancient times that had this, or very similar, traditions. Indeed, careful study shows that the traditions were, in one form or another, virtually worldwide.

What India claimed was that the earth passes through four ages, alternately advancing and declining: *Satya Yuga* (also called *Krita Yuga*), a spiritual age; *Treta Yuga*, a mental age; *Dwapara Yuga*, an age of energy; and *Kali Yuga*, a dark age. *Kali Yuga* was held in Indian tradition to be a time of general spiritual ignorance, when mankind as a whole is confined (I use the present tense to indicate indefinite perpetuity) in what I might call the "straitjacket" of matter-consciousness. *Kali Yuga*, according to Sri Yukteswar, is the age from which mankind, in the upwardly ascending cycle, has only recently emerged.

Other very ancient civilizations, all of whose traditions were recorded during the last *descending* cycle, gave various names to these four ages. The Egyptians called them the ages of gods, demi-gods, heroes, and men. The Greeks named them the golden, silver, bronze, and iron ages. This is not the place to enumerate all those traditions, but it is interesting to note that all of them believed that mankind had descended, in historic times, to the lowest age, when the actual tradition was, to our present knowledge, recorded in writing.

People nowadays, when they read of those old traditions, dismiss them condescendingly as myths. They comment—usually somewhat cynically—on any claims (mistakenly) made by modern Indians that we are now in the darkest age. One can imagine someone in Brooklyn saying, "So what else is noo?" In India, too, it is believed—of course!—that we still live in the lowest age. What better (the modern skeptic concludes) could those primitive historians have bequeathed us?

Sri Yukteswar, on the other hand, announced (as I said earlier) that the world quite recently, in 1900, actually left the dark age, or *Kali Yuga*, having passed through a 200-year "bridge," or s*andhya*. The year 1900 saw us fully entering the second and higher age of *Dwapara Yuga*. This age, the one we are now in, is predicted to last a total of 2,400 years.

After *Dwapara* (which is comparable to the bronze age of the Greeks, and to the heroic age of the Egyptians) will come *Treta*, the silver age or age of "demi-gods," which will endure a total of 3,600 years. Finally we'll come to *Satya Yuga*, the golden age, named also "the age of the gods." *Satya Yuga*, the last ascending age, will last a total of 4,800 years before the earth commences its downward swing again.

Of immediate interest to us nowadays is the fact that Sri Yukteswar described *Dwapara Yuga* as an age of energy. In the ancient Egyptian tradition, too, the next higher age is an age of heroes, a description which suggests energy also. And the Greek tradition of a bronze age suggests copper, of which bronze is an alloy. Copper, as we know, is the element used for transmitting electricity.

Interestingly, certain ancient artifacts and *bas relief* sculptures, discovered in various parts of the world, suggest that ancient man may actually have known and used electricity. There is, for example, the wet cell battery that was discovered in the Baghdad museum by the German engineer and archaeologist, Wilhelm König. That relic supposedly dates back to 248 B.C. There are *bas reliefs*, again, in the ancient Egyptian temple of Dendera, which depict what look very much like electrodes and plasma discharge tubes.

In India, the presently accepted tradition (which has filtered down to us through the dark age) is that we are still in *Kali Yuga*. According to that current reading of the texts—a reading disproved with cool logic by Sri Yukteswar—mankind is, relatively speaking, not much beyond the beginning of *Kali Yuga*, and is destined to sink ever more deeply into the mire of ignorance and moral degradation which are the signs of this age. The prospect is worse than gloomy. Things will continue, according to that interpretation, to worsen for another 427,000 years, at which point, some believe, the world will be annihilated. (Others believe that *Satya Yuga*, the spiritual age, will reappear once more in its full glory at the end of *Kali Yuga*, to re-initiate the downward descent from "edenic" idyll to Satanic darkness.)

In contrast to those dour forecasts, Sri Yukteswar sounded a very different and cheerful note. He found a serious flaw that, several centuries earlier, had crept into the reckoning regarding the very ancient *Yuga* system. The flaw itself, he said, was a product of *Kali Yuga* ignorance.

The true duration of *Kali Yuga*, and of each of the other ages, is, Sri Yukteswar proclaimed, much briefer than those impossibly long time spans allotted by present convention. Instead of a 432,000-year total for *Kali Yuga*, the dark age lasts, as I said, only 1,200 years. In the year 1600 A.D., the earth began to emerge from *Kali Yuga* into a one-hundred year "bridge," or *sandhya*, completing its emergence in the year 1700 A.D.

As the night stars pale before the slow approach of dawn, so the final century of *Kali Yuga* saw the weakening of its rays before the approach of *Dwapara Yuga*, the age of energy. In 1700 A.D., the earth experienced the first pink clouds, so to speak, of *Dwapara Yuga*. Another two hundred years were required for these new rays to increase in strength to the point where the full sunrise of *Dwapara Yuga* flooded the earth. The age of energy had dawned.

What makes Sri Yukteswar's analysis particularly fascinating is that it corresponds so amazingly well with innumerable objective facts, including more recent discoveries of science that were unknown at the time he wrote his book.

At the time of that writing, science had yet to learn that matter is a vibration of energy. Even more astonishingly,

Sri Yukteswar's description of the universe—since then scientifically verified in numerous details—was completely unknown to the astronomers of his time.

He stated that the galaxy is energized from its center—what he called its "grand center"—or, citing the ancient texts, the *Vishnunabhi* or "seat of the creative power, Brahma, the universal magnetism." Sri Yukteswar described the solar system's movement within the galaxy at a time when no one had any idea that our solar system moved at all. He described the energizing effect from that "grand center" on the solar system as we approach closer. It follows that the effect, as we move away again from that center, must gradually weaken.

His book, *The Holy Science*, was written and published near the end of the nineteenth century. It was some ninety years later that astronomers finally discovered a gigantic outpouring of energy from the center of our Milky Way galaxy, as also from the centers of other galaxies. Today, the debate still rages over what this massive source of energy may signify. Science, of course, can only measure perceivable energies, and is therefore aware only, at present, of solid-seeming realities and of the grosser kinds of energy. Spiritual energy is beyond the reach of any instrument.

At the time Sri Yukteswar wrote, scientists already knew something of the stellar movements. They had no idea, however, that these movements occurred independently of our sun. They believed still, in fact, that all the stars revolve about our sun, which the astronomers considered the largest body in space. They had no notion that our own star system is only one of many such systems, which have been defined since then as galaxies. The truth hadn't yet occurred to them that the Milky Way is simply our own galaxy seen edgewise from our position near the edge of it. They had no idea of the vast distances between the stars. Most astonishing of all to us today was their belief that the sun was the center of the whole universe—and of a relatively small universe at that. Even today, astronomers are skeptical of the possibility that there may be life on planets elsewhere in space, though that skepticism itself is waning rapidly.

It was only in 1918 that the American astronomer Harlow Shapley found that the sun is only the center of our little solar system. And it was not until after 1924, when Edwin Hubble demonstrated that the so-called nebula in Andromeda is in fact another galaxy, that the truth began to dawn on astronomers that the Milky Way must be a galaxy also.

When I was a schoolboy in England during the mid-1930s, I joined a few friends in founding an astronomy club. It was wonderful for us to contemplate the recent finding that there were two, and perhaps even three(!) other galaxies besides our own in the universe. Today, barely a half-century later, over 100 billion galaxies are known to exist, and I can't help suspecting that astronomers have simply stopped counting.

Sri Yukteswar explained that, as the sun moves in an orbit of its own within the galaxy, it approaches closer to, then recedes from, the galactic "grand center." During its approach, powerful rays of energy emanating from that "grand center" energize the solar system, and thereby energize human consciousness also, enabling humanity in general to comprehend on an ever deeper level the workings of the universe. As the sun and its solar system recede from that "grand center," the general awareness of mankind will grow progressively dim and less capable of comprehending the universal laws, until matter will assume again, for mankind, the nature of an absolute reality in itself, forever solid and immutable.

Energy is what stimulates consciousness. Hence the correlation between mental energy and genius. High mental energy is a universal sign of high intelligence. The opposite is true also: Low mental energy is the infallible accompaniment of stupidity.

During *Satya Yuga*, humanity as a whole is able to perceive all creation as being composed of "mind stuff," even as Sir Arthur Eddington suspected. When that golden age comes, the majority of mankind will realize that the universe is simply a projection of the Divine Consciousness.

By contrast, the human race as a whole, during *Kali Yuga*, is incapable of perceiving matter except as the senses reveal it. People are forced, if they consider the point at all, either to attribute consciousness to material causes or to view it as wholly separate from and quite unrelated to matter. God, in the dark age, can only be considered, as theologians today still describe Him, as "wholly other."

Sri Yukteswar's amazing insights, partly but not wholly drawn from his study of the ancient texts, revealed universal realities that, at that time, were not known even to advanced scientists. His knowledge is impressive enough in itself to command a respectful hearing. It must be conceded, however, that certain aspects of his explanation have yet to be scientifically verified.

He claimed, for example—again, on the basis of those ancient texts—that the sun, in addition to its known revolution around the galaxy (astronomers calculate one of these revolutions at approximately two hundred million years), moves in a secondary revolution within the galaxy around its own stellar dual. This dual has yet to be discovered. It is interesting to note, however, that astronomers are in fact becoming more and more intrigued by the possibility that such a dual may exist.

Several years ago, articles appeared in newspapers in America and abroad quoting the suggestion of a number of astronomers that there may actually be a sister star to our own sun. Such a dual, they stated, would explain certain eccentricities in the movements of the outer planets of our solar system. It is well known of course that many stars do have duals. If a sister to our sun were discovered, it might well turn out, the astronomers stated, to be what is called a "dark" star.

Sri Yukteswar claimed also that the time span for each orbital revolution of the sun around its dual is 24,000 years. He explained that this revolution coincides with one complete precession of the equinox—from 0 degrees Aries backwards through Pisces, Aquarius, and so on, ultimately returning to 0 degrees Aries again.

Since the precession of the equinox is an unfamiliar phenomenon to most people, let me explain it here briefly.

The sun, the moon, and the solar planets appear to us to be circling the earth. Of course, only the moon really does so, but to the human eye they all appear to move around us—and it is appearances which concern us here. Behind those moving planets, as a sort of backdrop to them, are the seemingly motionless constellations, or signs, of the zodiac. Each constellation consists of a configuration of distant stars which, in aggregate, have been long believed to emanate certain psychic influences. Modern astronomy accepts these constellations as mere conveniences; it doesn't believe in cosmic influences. The constellations are, however, a long-established and traditional way of dividing up the heavens.

While there are many constellations, those which form the zodiac, before which the sun, moon, and planets of our solar system appear to move, are only twelve in number.

The moment when the sun crosses the equator, moving from the southern to the northern hemisphere, marks the beginning of spring. This "vernal point" occurs on or about March 21st of each year. The degree in a sign, or constellation, over which the sun happens to be passing at that moment alters slightly with each year as the true vernal point moves backwards a fraction of a degree. Present ephemerides, which show the positions of these bodies, always show the vernal point as 0 degrees Aries. That is to say, the vernal point is supposed to occur at the beginning of the constellation Aries. In fact, however, that position is only a convenient fiction. Every year, for the past fifteen hundred years or so, the vernal point has been moving fractionally backward through Pisces, which is the sign immediately before Aries. In another 300 years, roughly speaking, it will reach 0 degrees Pisces, upon which it will begin its movement back through the sign of Aquarius. This is why people often refer to the present time as the Age of Aquarius, though they "jump the gun," since the sun has yet to reach that point on the vernal equinox.

Astronomers claim that the equinoctial precession requires about 25,800 years to complete its revolution around the zodiac. Their explanation for the precession is based on the Earth's slight wobble on its axis. Sri Yukteswar, instead, connected the precession to the sun's movement around its dual. No one so far has made a serious attempt to compare these divergent phenomena, partly because the very movement of the sun around a dual still remains to be proved. Perhaps the discrepancy between the astronomers' 25,800 years and Sri Yukteswar's 24,000 is due to variations in the speed of precession. Or perhaps these explanations simply describe two parallel, but distinct, phenomena. In any case, 24,000 years was the figure Sri Yukteswar gave, basing his conclusions on that ancient tradition.

It must be admitted that Sri Yukteswar's explanation, taken all together, reveals a level of information that was so far in advance of anything even dreamed of by scientists until very recently that his system deserves serious consideration. Certainly it would be churlish at this point, and on the basis of many still-unresolved questions, to dismiss as "mythical" everything the ancient texts proclaimed. To do so would resemble a modern accountant sneering at the abacus—not because the abacus is slower or less accurate than our modern adding machine (the abacus has been shown, in the hands of experts, to be quite as fast and every bit as accurate), but simply because the abacus is "old-fashioned."

Sri Yukteswar stated that the solar system, in its orbit around our solar dual, is presently moving toward the "grand center" of our galaxy. Here, again, the extent of his knowledge is nothing less than astounding.

Astronomers, even after their discovery that the Milky Way is, itself, only one galaxy, had until quite recently no idea where the center of our galaxy is located, nor in what direction, relative to that center, our sun is moving. Only well into the twentieth century was it discovered that the center of the galaxy lies in the constellation Sagittarius, and that the movement of our solar system is in the direction of a constellation about 50 degrees from Sagittarius, named Hercules. Needless to say, on an elliptical orbit we would not be making a beeline for the galactic center. Hercules fits in very well with the concept of an elliptical movement generally directed toward Sagittarius.

Once again, Sri Yukteswar's explanation has proved uncannily accurate.

His explanation of gradual change from high to low ages, revolving in a never-ending cycle, is more reasonable than the conventional one of unilateral descent (which, again, is at variance with the Western notion of unilateral *ascent*. Indeed, the conventional explanation in India has no logical backing whatsoever).

What reason can be given, indeed, for the supposedly abrupt change from *Kali Yuga*'s stygian darkness to *Satya Yuga*'s shining enlightenment? As for the claim that, at the end of *Kali Yuga*, the world will be destroyed, this claim rests shakily on another ancient tradition that a planet is destroyed for only one of two reasons: that its inhabitants become either all good, or all bad. No tradition, however, claims that the cycle of *Yugas* will end so soon.

Nature itself, moreover, supports the concept of cyclic reversion. From what we can observe of Nature's workings, its movements are always cyclic. Day fades through twilight to darkness; night's darkness returns to the light of day, but not abruptly; rather, it returns through a graying dawn. The weather warms slowly from mid-winter, with its icy winds and snows, through the pale greening of spring, to the heat and warm colors of summer; it then cools through the season of autumn's falling leaves to the freezing ice and snows of winter again.

The moon, too, waxes, wanes, then waxes full again in endlessly repeating cycles. And life itself appears on earth, stumbling and helpless at first, then gradually assuming the full power of maturity until, having reached its peak, it fades to old age and then dies—to be born ever anew in endless cyclic repetition. Even the sunspots are cyclic, with their eleven-year periods of maximum and minimum activity.

Similar examples might be cited endlessly: the rise and fall of civilizations; the orbiting of planets and comets around the sun; the emotional ups and downs of sentient creatures. Contrary to the limited mind-set of *Kali Yuga*, no natural development is ever really linear. In some cases, of course, it may appear so—for example, when a surface is so broad that it cannot be encompassed at ground level. Mankind during *Kali Yuga* believed that the earth is flat; it was only toward the end of ascending *Kali Yuga* that Christopher Columbus proved it, in fact, to be round. Interestingly, it was at approximately the same point during *Kali Yuga*'s descending arc that knowledge of the earth's roundness appears to have been lost.

Euclidian geometry, with its straight lines and flat planes, was for centuries considered the last word for measuring physical reality. By contrast, scientists today claim that the universe is ruled more by spherical geometry than by Euclidian geometry. It is the spherical form, indeed, which is dominant in Nature.

Even the most advanced discoveries of modern science may turn out to be old stuff, well known to humanity long ago. Evidence is being unearthed constantly that ancient civilizations, some of them as advanced as our own (and others perhaps more advanced), existed in the past. A growing body of evidence indicates that atomic power may have been known in ages past;* that the early Egyptians, Indians, and other ancient peoples had flying machines; that mankind may actually have traveled to other planets; and that ancient peoples were capable of projecting images to great distances, even as we do today with television.

All this material comprises a body of evidence too startlingly different from presently accepted assumptions, and still insufficiently abundant, to demolish the model that archaeologists, for more than two hundred years, have been

---

*   Large tracts of vitrified sand have been found in the Gobi desert and elsewhere, resembling in every way the effect of atomic blasts in the Nevada desert. There are descriptions, moreover, in the ancient Indian epic, the *Mahabharata*, of a "terrible" weapon very similar in its effects to modern atomic blasts. The *Mahabharata* also, along with other ancient Indian texts, describes machines that flew (*vamanas*, they were called), and tells in some detail how those machines were constructed. A considerable body of modern literature on these and similar subjects is available to interested readers. Some of these books are, of course, more, and others less, objective and reliable. For many years I myself wanted to research such a book. The quantity of published material already available, however, has become so vast that one would have at this point to make it his life's work to enter this field in a responsible manner.

painstakingly creating of the past. Though this new material must still be labeled "fringe data," its sheer volume is gradually growing to such an extent as to be embarrassing to orthodox thought. It is drawing into its sphere of influence, moreover, a swelling list of respected researchers.

Sri Yukteswar stated that, after 1,200 years of descending *Kali Yuga*, the earth, in 500 A.D., reached the point farthest from the galactic center. (To be exact, he placed that date at 499 A.D. He himself, however, rounded out this figure to 500 A.D. so as to make it easier for people to match the ancient system with the one widely in use today. The discrepancy of a single year didn't strike him as significant.)

In 500 A.D., then, mankind reached its lowest point of intellectual, moral, and spiritual decline. 500 A.D. was followed by another 1,200 years of ascending *Kali Yuga*, which brought humanity to 1700 A.D. and the beginning of *Dwapara Yuga*. A one-hundred-year transition period, from 1,600 A.D., covered our emergence from *Kali Yuga* proper. Another two-hundred-year transition period, into *Dwapara Yuga* proper, brought mankind fully, in the year 1900 A.D., into the present age of energy. The twentieth century saw finally the true beginning of *Dwapara Yuga* proper.

Thus, we stand today at the early part of what is, in fact, a new age. This age of *Dwapara* will endure in all (including the 200-years transition periods into and out of it) for 2,400 years. Fortunately, the higher ages grow progressively longer. While *Kali Yuga* lasts only 1,200 years (including its transition periods), *Dwapara Yuga*, the age of energy, lasts 2,400 years; *Treta Yuga*, the mental age, lasts 3,600 years (with two 300-years transition periods); and *Satya Yuga*, the spiritual age, lasts 4,800 years (with two 400-years transition periods). These 12,000 years, in all, form the ascending arc of the cycle.

At the highest point of *Satya Yuga*, the process is reversed. The earth then passes, in descending order, through another 4,800 years of *Satya Yuga*; 3,600 years of *Treta Yuga*; 2,400 years of *Dwapara Yuga*; and 1,200 years of *Kali Yuga*.

Such, then, is the ancient system. We are at present, according to Sri Yukteswar, in a new age based not on any earthly event or life of some important person, but, quite impersonally, on the sun's movement within the galaxy.

He suggested that the human race recognize this fact of a new age by instituting once again the universal chronology. What, indeed, could be more reasonable or appropriate? To give the year we presently know as 2000 A.D. the name, *Dwapara* 300, would be an affirmation that we really are in a new phase of history, and that the time has come for mankind to try to understand both earthly events and universal realities in subtler, energetic relation to human affairs.

The present year, then, is not 2008 A.D. Following the chronology proposed by Sri Yukteswar, it is 308 *Dwapara*.

CHAPTER THREE
WHAT IS HAPPENING TO OUR PLANET?

Few people, even among those who most sternly resist the thought that ours is a new age, will deny that we live in critical times. One has only to listen to popular music to feel its ever-quickening pulse and heavy beat.

It is revealing to trace the recent development of this music, from the stately minuet of the eighteenth century through the more exhilarating rhythm of the waltz ("shockingly sensuous" people considered it when it first appeared), to the nervous excitement of the jazz age, after which came the heavy self-affirmation of the forties—the era of the big bands. Then came the era of "rock 'n' roll," with sounds suggestive of a mood of increasing violence, anguish, and outrage. The process has continued, toward ever-increasing violence and cynicism. There's no point in saying, "It's only a matter of taste." Popular music reflects not only taste, but mood.

The past 200 years demonstrate what sweeping changes have taken place in public attitudes. Popular music says it perhaps better than any other medium. It declares boldly that we are living during a time of tension, of inner and outer conflict, and of nearly apocalyptic fear.

Small wonder that religious fundamentalists look on these as the "end times" which, according to them, were predicted in the Bible. They see nothing good to be hoped for from this new age. It takes time, however, for sweeping changes to take place. It takes time for them even to be noticed. Once they *are* noticed, they commonly evoke a variety of reactions, both positive and negative, which may only confuse the issues and delay the formation of a clear understanding. Indeed, change never comes either quickly or easily.

Let us step outside the present, then, and view the changes we are contemplating as historic events. We'll pretend for now that we are already in the future—in, let us say, the twenty-third century A.D., or, to be properly futuristic, in the sixth century of *Dwapara*.

Kali Yuga was, as history makes clear, a time when human consciousness was hemmed in by the conviction that matter is, so to speak, concrete and absolute. People were committed to that view of things, and could not easily understand things in fluid terms.

In religion, a truth was acceptable only if it could be clothed in firm dogmas. The universe, even to the scientists of those times, appeared to be a giant mechanism. The divine realms, if accepted, were visualized as static, not dynamic—like crystal images frozen in eternity, with the Lord seated on a throne (possibly of marble), in eternal judgment.

In society, too, things and people were assigned their proper places. People had defined positions, and were in turn defined by those positions. A king was a king, not a normal human being, acting out his regal role. A peasant was a peasant, and if anyone ever thought of him purely in human terms (in general, the upper classes viewed even his intelligence with condescension), he definitely was considered to belong—at least in the eyes of his social betters—to a lower order of humanity. Even as recently as a few years ago a friend of mine in Naples, Italy, remarked about someone who owned a restaurant, expostulating with a suggestion of outrage, "But I knew him when he was only a waiter!"

Gradually, in time, the fogs of *Kali Yuga* lifted. Old forms began to lose their former definitions, as stars do at the approach of dawn. *Dwapara's* influence began to filter down into the world, and into human consciousness. Soon a few precocious spirits began to make startling discoveries. They learned that the earth is not flat, as everyone believed, but round. Copernicus, in the early sixteenth century, proposed that the sun, not the earth, is the center of the universe. Copernicus was later supported in his theory by Galileo, Kepler, and Newton. Copernicus, however, created the first storm of protest in orthodox (and particularly in church) circles, where it seemed the very foundations of religious truth were being threatened.

The seventeenth century saw the end of the night of *Kali Yuga*. Fixed notions regarding the natural order, based on the syllogisms of logic, lost their grip on humanity and got swept away on tides of a more realistic, scientific outlook. Dogmatic assertions gave way to the desire for personal experience as the only valid guide to truth. The ramparts of many established assumptions were breached, year after year, by the steady cannonades of new discoveries. The eighteenth century is looked upon as "the age of reason"; it would be more "reasonable" to call that age "the dawn of common sense, based on experience."

The high walls of habit, however, which for so long had enclosed people's thoughts protectively, thereby excluding broader views of reality, were not so easily demolished even after they'd been breached. In the seventeen and eighteen hundreds—the period which Swami Sri Yukteswar described as the *sandhya*, or transition period, into *Dwapara Yuga* proper—there lingered a tendency to view new theories and discoveries with suspicion, and even with hostility. That resistance still awaits its final dissolution under the full rays of *Dwapara*. Indeed, what could be more natural? The dogmatic tendency is not dead even in scientific circles. We are dealing here also with human nature.

William Thompson Kelvin, the nineteenth century British mathematician and physicist, could never accept Maxwell's electromagnetic theory of light for the reason (he said) that he couldn't make a mechanical model of such a universe.

Kali Yuga is only slowly relinquishing its hold on people's consciousness. Fresh, *Dwapara Yuga* energy has been employed to reinforce old and still-lingering *Kali Yuga* attitudes. People have taken the increasing energy they've felt within them, and directed it outward toward plundering our planet's riches rather than toward working with Nature in reciprocal harmony.

Meanwhile, the more sensitive spirits of the nineteenth century—artists, poets, and composers, for example— decried the ascendancy of materialism and dreamed nostalgically of what they visualized as simpler, more natural times. Hans Christian Andersen, mocking the absurdity of this romantic dream, wrote a tale about a man who found himself transported back from the nineteenth century to the Middle Ages. Andersen described the poor fellow's disillusionment on finding nothing but muddy, dark streets, grinding poverty, and countless material inconveniences. His story made its point very well, for when one is without all material conveniences and labor-saving devices, and has no respite from dawn-to-dusk material bondage, he is plunged deeply into matter-consciousness.

And yet the poetic spirits dreamed on, not realizing that their very dreams were animated by the new rays of energy that would eventually liberate the human spirit from the very materialism they deplored.

Generally speaking, the new awareness has inspired in mankind a new desire for self-expression. Never again will people be bound necessarily to hereditary positions with which they feel no inner resonance. Here too, however, change is coming only haltingly. Under the lingering rays of *Kali Yuga*, these new trends in social awareness took the form, for a time, of mass movements. People thought rather in terms of quantity than of quality. Mass uprisings, revolutions, and new social philosophies with invented slogans like, "Power to the People!" (rather than the more enlightened concept, "Power to the Truth") were signs, simply, that people were still thinking institutionally, and did not yet dare to think for themselves.

The nineteenth century saw what was widely touted as the triumph of materialism. In fact, what was really happening was that *Dwapara* energy, filtering into people's consciousness, was for a time energizing the old ways of thinking, including the old hypnosis that matter is the "bedrock" reality of everything. *Dwapara Yuga* merely animated those concepts for a time, before shattering them altogether.

The fact that morality, too, was portrayed so rigidly and self-righteously during the Victorian era was due simply to the increased energy, held fast for a time to traditional notions of what constituted right behavior. This increased animation from within was only a herald of the time when those fixed notions would be shattered by the new rays of energy. People gradually felt the inspiration to adopt more fluid and energetic ways of relating to one another—ways, above all, which demonstrated more love, compassion, and all-inclusiveness.

L et us now, having taken a brief backward glimpse at those former trends, return to the present. People, though still decrying the general decline in morality, are becoming increasingly conscious of the need for greater personal responsibility. Jean Paul Sartre, who claimed to find in nihilism the very definition of personal enlightenment, declared gloatingly that life no longer has any purpose or meaning. Yet for all that he sought also *within the individual* his clues to any possible meaning.

Seen from every angle, the mood of our times may be described as a crisis of faith, gradually resolving itself into the higher energy that goes with personal integrity. People have yet to realize that the seeds of a deeper faith have been sown already, and are even now thrusting green shoots up into the air, welcoming energy and making possible a greater understanding.

Conflict inevitably rages between *Kali Yuga* attitudes, still seen as right and good by unthinking and excessively conventional people, and the more "*Dwapara*" attitude which the freer spirits being born today embrace as their path to personal liberation. Conventional minds turn back for support to old texts and old authorities. In most cases, however, the support they claim to have found is simply a matter of wishful interpretation. Jesus Christ himself, whose teachings they so often call upon to combat science, encouraged his followers to embrace the truth—and not dogmatically. "Ye shall know the truth," he declared, "and the truth shall make you free." (John 8:32)

The conflict between the old rigidity and dogmatism of *Kali Yuga* and the newborn openness of *Dwapara Yuga* seems destined soon to flare into open conflict. We may indeed live to see world wars far more devastating than those in the past, terrible as they were. We may suffer other disasters:

plague, worldwide economic depression, even global cataclysms before human consciousness can be softened enough
to receive unobstructedly the rays of *Dwapara Yuga*.

Earth changes, should they occur, will be Nature's
response to the disharmonious thoughts and energies which
at present rage in human hearts. A slight shift in people's
thoughts and energies, however, if turned in the direction of
greater harmony, would result in worldwide change for the
better. Devastation, on the other hand, should it occur, will
serve to clear the ground, so to speak, for the next season's
crops. Disaster, during this ascending age, will not be total.
Indeed, any change will prove ultimately beneficial.

Essentially, the difference between the mass consciousness during *Kali* and *Dwapara Yugas* was epitomized
by Zeno's paradox of the arrow. Zeno, an ancient Greek
philosopher, argued—how those old Greeks loved a good
philosophical fight!—that it is a contradiction in terms to
refer to the flight of an arrow. The arrow, he claimed, at any
given moment during its supposed flight is stationary at that
point in space: its movement, only apparent, is defined by
an endless series of points along the way. In other words the
arrow, despite appearances, isn't really moving at all! Zeno
was offering, of course, what he knew was a logical paradox. At the same time, however, fluid movement didn't play
a large part of people's awareness in his day. Had it done so,
he'd have been "laughed out of court" immediately.

Plato himself thought one should be able to understand
a truth by merely "talking it out," and thereby reaching
a fixed definition of it.

Zeno, incidentally, offered another logical paradox, this
one as if to forestall the age-old conundrum, "Why does
a chicken cross the road?" (The answer? to get to the other
side, of course!) Zeno squelched the question itself by insisting that a chicken *cannot* cross the road. Why not? asks

Kali Yuga mentality. Because whatever distance the chicken still needs to go, it must first go half that distance. No matter how small the distance still remaining, he must still go half that distance before he can complete the whole. *Ergo*, the whole distance can never be covered! The *Kali Yugi* mentally scratches his head, knits his eyebrows, and in the end declares, "Well, I guess that makes sense. But then, the arrow cannot ever get where it is going, either, so I suppose we're all safe!" *Kali Yuga* mentality can't resolve either paradox for the simple reason that, to its way of thinking, fixed points are natural frames of reference; any movement between them lacks substance, and is therefore difficult to comprehend.

Dwapara Yuga mentality, on the other hand, says, "How can you be so absurd? The *motion* of the arrow, as well as of the chicken, is the reality. The points along their journey are mere figments of the imagination, and have, in themselves, no reality: they are illusions!" In *Dwapara Yuga*, matter itself is understood to be but a wave, or vibration, of energy.

Where *Kali Yuga* can only understand progress in terms of separate stages of movement, *Dwapara Yuga* sees it as a flow.

Kali Yuga sees every reality as compartmentalized, each compartment separate from the others, whereas *Dwapara Yuga* sees reality as an integral whole.

Kali Yuga analyzes and differentiates: *Dwapara Yuga* seeks, beneath all superficial differences, an underlying unity.

Kali Yuga says, "either . . . or"; *Dwapara Yuga* says, "both . . . and."

To *Kali Yuga* mentality, which tries carefully to segregate every concept from every other, contradictions may appear unsolvable. *Kali Yuga* therefore sees no natural connection between a problem and its solution. *Kali Yuga* is problem-oriented, not solution-oriented. Whatever problem is presented to it, it sees as the immediate, and even overwhelming, reality.

Dwapara Yuga, on the other hand, with its unitive view, realizes that everything in creation is balanced by its opposite. *Dwapara Yuga*, therefore, views things integrally, which makes it more naturally solution-oriented. When it beholds a problem, it automatically seeks its solution as the natural companion to the problem. *Dwapara Yuga* is therefore easily able to find solutions to problems that, to *Kali Yuga* mentality, remain insoluble.

Modern science, burdened with increasing complexity, longs for greater simplicity. Its fixation on details is, in fact, merely a carry-over from *Kali Yuga* ways of thinking. Even today, the cutting edge of science is taking man beyond forms to the energies of which all forms are the product.

A struggle is inevitable between fading *Kali Yuga* consciousness and the dawning impact of *Dwapara Yuga*. The struggle can only be temporary, however; it must be resolved in time. Let us look ahead, therefore, to that time—not so distant—when the issues have become clearer. And let us then visualize what that future holds for us.

For future trends, clearly, are already beginning to emerge all around us, and are becoming clearer to those who, to paraphrase Jesus Christ, "have eyes to see."

CHAPTER FOUR
GLIMPSES INTO THE FUTURE

What may we expect in the years and centuries to come? Matter, during *Kali Yuga*, was manipulated by lifting, carrying, or beating things into shape and people into submission. What ruled were muscle and physical power. Even with labor-saving devices such as the lever, the sheer difficulty of lifting or transporting things was daunting; even minor results required major efforts. Popular heroes were men of brawn. A person's importance was seen in terms of the power he exerted over others. His greatness was reckoned in terms of his ability to best people in battle or in other kinds of contest.

Greatness, nowadays, is more often attributed to those who help others: whose ideas are inspiring, who invent devices that reduce the need for manual labor. We no longer stand in awe of those who, like Hercules, can accomplish extraordinarily heavy tasks. I remember, in the 1930s, that it took many men fifteen years, working with shovels, to complete the underpass at the railway terminal in Bucharest, Romania. And when, in the late 1940s in Los Angeles,

California, I helped with the construction of a building, even at that late date we had to mix the concrete by hand. Young people today have no idea how recently big machinery for jobs like that has come into use. Nowadays, however, heavy jobs are accomplished increasingly by machine power, not by manpower.

Who knows what means will be found in future to move heavy objects? Big machinery is the application of Dwapara-discovered energy to *Kali Yuga* know-how—to the lever, for instance, which was invented by the ancient Greek Archimedes. As *Dwapara Yuga* progresses, subtler methods for moving matter will surely be discovered. Authors of books even now challenge the tradition that the Egyptian pyramids were constructed by human muscle alone.

Consider the following possibility: Already matter is known to be only a vibration of energy. In time heavy objects may be moved by sound, or by some other kind of vibration. Indeed, a number of avant-garde thinkers have already pondered mankind's past accomplishments during times when civilization is believed to have been primitive, but when, according to Sri Yukteswar, it was in an advanced age in the descending *yuga* cycle. These writers have suggested, for example, that sound vibrations would explain better than slave labor how the largest, most ancient pyramids were built, and huge stones moved. Fanciful? Perhaps, but again, perhaps so only to *Kali Yuga* mentality. And again, if fanciful, so also was Jules Verne, the nineteenth century French author of science fiction, most of whose "impossible" predictions have been fulfilled already.

Even now, at the beginning of the twenty-first century, we are still very early into *Dwapara Yuga* proper, and have some twenty-one more centuries to go. As energy's potentials continue to unfold to our understanding, mankind will inevitably see wonders that, even today, would seem incredible: wonders that, not many centuries ago, would have sent their inventors to the stake as being "in league with the Devil."

Like the director of the U.S. Patent Office with his rumored proposal that the office be closed (since everything that could possibly be invented had been invented already), a number of scientists today have been saying that we are approaching the end-times of discovery. The universe, they claim, can have few surprises left for us. Yet physics is already moving into hitherto unimagined territory.

What the Patent Office director referred to was mechanical inventions. He can have had no idea of the impact energy would have even on those mechanical gadgets. And what those people in science I've alluded to still affirm is, once again, *Kali Yuga*-type knowledge. It may indeed, from their limited perspective, be true that we are approaching the end-times of discovery, in terms of a purely material universe. The age of energy, however, is already opening up boundless horizons before our gaze, and cannot but continue to do so for centuries to come.

Uncovering matter's energy-secrets will bestow on humanity hitherto-undreamed-of power and freedom. The knowledge that energy is the (still-little-known) secret underlying matter will give mankind unprecedented power to transform and transport material objects. Such developments are sure to have an enormous impact on human life and on the world we inhabit.

It will also force upon us a measure of self-discipline, lest the consequences of irresponsible behavior bring humanity to disaster. Let us for now, then, concentrate on the positive opportunities before us, rather than on their potential pitfalls. And let us cling to the hope—or, rather, to the reasonable expectation—that the rays of energy enlightening the planet, which have produced so many wonders already, will also bestow on mankind the wisdom to handle them safely.

Indeed, the very fear that an increase of power might result in the destruction of the planet is merely a sign of *Kali Yuga* thinking. It was that kind of mentality which inspired the nay-sayers of the past to declare, "If God had wanted us to fly, He'd have given us wings." And in the nineteenth century there were protests from pulpits in the Christian churches against the invention of the umbrella. Priests, pastors, and ministers of various denominations objected that the umbrella was an offense against the Biblical statement, "For he maketh his sun to rise on the evil and on the good, and *sendeth rain on the just and on the unjust.*" (Matt. 5:45)

In an ascending cycle, the human instinct will surely be more strongly motivated to create than to destroy.

What, then, will be the consequences of this new, dawning consciousness, which is bringing to mankind a historically unprecedented sense of freedom? I see three probable trends especially.

Trend Number One

The first trend will be a reaction against complexity, and a corresponding move toward simplicity. At present one still encounters, in every field, an increasingly burdensome number of details. This may be seen in the physical sciences, including medicine. Complexity is rampant in psychology, in education, in business, and in the sheer "business" of everyday living. It is the inheritance bequeathed to us by *Kali Yuga*. Complexity is not a necessary accompaniment of advancing knowledge, however; it is merely a reflection of the kind of thinking that is more concerned with the minutiae of knowledge than with the "arrow-flight" of intuitive wisdom.

The new simplicity, then, will not constitute a return to rustic ignorance. Rather, it will accompany an enlightened awareness, when knowledge is absorbed into an energetic flow of consciousness.

What I am describing is, as I just hinted, the simple flow of intuition. People in future will realize increasingly that, when the flow of inspiration is right, the details seem to have a way of working themselves out, as if on their own. This important truth may be ascribed to an even simpler cause: Energy contains its own intelligence.

In music, it is from such simplicity that haunting melodies are born. Melodies are, in fact, the product of heartfelt aspiration, not of the sophisticated knowledge of musical notation. Folk melodies, indeed, are often far lovelier than those painstakingly crafted by professional composers. This fact explains why so many of those composers have borrowed some of their best melodies from traditional folk music.

In the arts, simplicity (again) means an intuitive flow, which transcends the intricacies of intellectual craftsmanship and emotional, egoic *self*-expression.

In politics, simplicity means having the wisdom to understand that a carefully worked-out treaty can never take the place of genuine kindness and good will.

In business, simplicity means recognizing that more profit results from creative energy than from a detailed analysis of sales statistics.

In medicine, simplicity means encouraging the flow of energy in a patient's body. Only secondarily will doctors of the future concentrate on curing specific body parts.

And in science, simplicity means the knowledge that great discoveries are a product of intuition—very much more so than of encyclopedic knowledge.

In every field of endeavor, simplicity will mean our having to learn less, intellectually, as we tune in more to inspiration. And we'll find that inspiration flows the more freely, the more open we keep our hearts and minds to its appearance in our minds.

Trend Number Two

The second trend will be a renewed emphasis on the individual. Less effort will be devoted to studying man as a social statistic, and much more to bringing harmony into his inner life, and attunement with higher Truth. People will realize in time that even the greatest human achievements can never be greater than man, himself, the achiever. For man is the source of everything he accomplishes. Great achievements, in their totality, can only hint at the potential of all mankind for greatness. The supreme work of art, therefore, will of necessity come to be understood as being man, himself. The highest art, therefore, will be understood to be that of the way to Self-realization.

Thus, complementing the continued quest for outer knowledge and outer dominion will be a return to the simple wisdom inscribed at the Delphic oracle, an admonition recorded in pre-history (perhaps—who knows?—during the last descending *Dwapara Yuga*). That admonition, well-known to us all, was: "Man, know thyself."

Trend Number Three

The third trend will be an increasing demand for quality over quantity. "Bigger" will cease to be equated with "better."

The perception of matter as an absolute reality led many kings during *Kali Yuga* to imagine that the more territory they possessed, the greater they themselves were. An aspect of that thinking was that it encouraged people to view humanity in the mass, rather than in the particular as an aggregate of individuals. It was that thought which led

Karl Marx to exalt the sweating laborer over the visionary and the man of creative ideas. (What, indeed, is the underlying theory of communism but a dying echo of *Kali Yuga*?)

E.F. Schumacher wrote a trendy book a few years ago titled, *Small Is Beautiful*. The name itself helped to sell the book. Increasingly, indeed, in human affairs we see a trend toward miniaturization, and a corresponding rejection of the "bulldozer mentality" which sets material power against inertia in a struggle for conquest by brute force. The future trend will be to adapt to external realities, and not to beat them into quivering submission.

Great shifts in human awareness have always begun with a few individuals who (first) could perceive sensitively the need for a change, and who (secondly) had the energy to dive into that current and the ability to swim with it. Changes in overall human awareness follow such innovations only gradually, usually requiring one or more generations for them to be more than narrowly accepted by a few.

The more fundamental a change, and the more far reaching, the longer the time required, usually, for its universal acceptance. Thus, at least some of the habits of *Kali Yuga* are sure to persist well into *Dwapara Yuga*, and—given the known obtuseness of humanity—may well persist, at least vestigially, into the next *yuga* as well. During *Kali Yuga* there were, after all, a few enlightened souls (Jesus Christ and Buddha spring to mind) whose attainments were of the highest order, though the majority of mankind stumbled in its material blindness. What determines an individual's level of awareness is not only the energy coming to our planet from its galactic environment, but also his own refinement as a receptor of that energy.

Old habits are affirmed most aggressively when confronted by new alternatives. In *Dwapara Yuga*, this aggressiveness is already being animated by the increased intensity of inflowing energy. Thus, even though quantitative thinking is on the wane, we have seen in every field in recent times an exaggerated emphasis on, and an appeal to, mass consciousness: in politics, in social philosophy, in merchandising, in entertainment, in advertising, and even in such fields as education and religion. Nevertheless, the shift away from quantitative and toward qualitative thinking is inevitable.

This increasing emphasis on quality will be like the reverse side of the same coin; it will be a new concentration on the inner man, rather than on man as a social quantum. Scientists have said, "The key to the universe lies in the electron." Modern man will come at last to say, "The key to understanding the universe lies ultimately in man himself, the individual."

Unity in Diversity

Simplicity is rapidly becoming a "must" in human affairs. The flood of information, to which we find ourselves subjected in every field, has reached a point where people feel increasingly unable to cope with its sheer volume. The discovery of energy as the underlying reality of matter will influence the way we process this flood of factual information. Computers will not—how could they be?—be the last word in this evolutionary process.

A multitude of phenomena will be seen as only individual expressions of a unifying flow. In countless aspects of life, people will come to realize—as indeed they are doing already—that to tune in to the flow lessens one's need to be overly preoccupied with the details. It will become increasingly clear that, inherent in the energy itself, there exists a sort of guiding intelligence, rooted in an awareness higher than man's. Our awareness of that higher intelligence remains blocked as long as we allow our attention to be tumbled about by excessively numerous details. The flow will be released when our will power is engaged in what we may describe as the natural rhythms of inspiration.

The problems and obstructions that arise when we deal with inert matter will be transformed into an awareness of the opportunities for success, once we become conscious that we are dealing with a living reality *behind* those appearances of inertness.

CHAPTER FIVE
RELIGION IN THE NEW AGE

Religion today no longer commands the respect it once did, and the reasons for this decline are not difficult to find. Everywhere on earth, people have identified religion with attitudes they have now begun to abandon as they embrace this new age of energy. We are less bound nowadays by form—that is to say, by the conviction that form itself is the definition of substance.

Religion has traditionally been defined by its dogmas and beliefs, and not by such dynamics as the individual's inner experience of peace, closeness to God, and openness to higher inspiration—things which the great scriptures have always held out in loving promise to all mankind. Formal religion has focused its attention on outward worship, to the detriment of the inner spirit of religion which those forms were meant only to express.

In the West, religion (taking its bias from Roman rationalism rather than from the "take no thought for the morrow" dicta of Jesus Christ) has deliberately encased the spirit also in *organizational* forms. As a result, religion has, to a great extent, been suffocated. Wherever organizational forms have been given less attention—as has been the case, for example, with many of the Protestant churches—there has been an unfortunate over-emphasis on religion as a social institution, and an accompanying under-emphasis on its teachings as a guideline to inner, spiritual development.

Of all human institutions, religion has always been the most resistant to change. In conservatism lies its strength, but also its greatest weakness: its strength, because religious teachings express eternal values; its weakness, because those values are betrayed, in a sense, when they are limited to specific outward expressions. It is right not to interpret those values in such a way as to reflect merely passing fads. At the same time, to define them at all means already to interpret and therefore to limit them. No mere expression of an eternal value can ever do it justice.

Human perceptions of truth change, moreover, even though the truth itself remains unchanging. When specific expressions of a truth, rather than the Truth itself, become guiding principles, they become dogmat*ism*. Deeply rutted habits take over, and Truth itself is forgotten. Justification is ultimately found for shrinking revelation itself to fit into the box of an ever-narrower vision.

The weakness of formal religion is that, in the name of perpetuating truth, it buries the truth itself, and confuses even wholesome change with dilution and heresy.

Religion, in its higher aspect of inner spirituality, is God's gift to mankind; it is not merely some wise man's utterance for the good of humanity. During times of great change, including the period through which we are now passing, it is especially important to be guided by higher inspiration. With this purpose have great spiritual teachers come to earth at times of crucial human need. The birth of those great saviors has not been only opportune: It has also been ordained. Buddha, Krishna, and Shankaracharya in the East; Jesus Christ in the West: these men were no mere accidents of history.

At the present time, with the dawn of *Dwapara Yuga*, there is an overwhelming need for a fresh message to be sent from above. If ever God has spoken through His prophets to mankind, now surely is a time for Him to speak again, for man's present need is as great as it ever was. If God truly is our Father, Mother, and Eternal Friend and if we, His children, call to Him from our hearts, He *must* respond. For there are limits to how far this limited intelligence of ours can take us.

To continue that thought: Common sense can convince us of our need to adapt to new realities; logic can facilitate this adaptive process by helping us to see how new discoveries can actively support spiritual truths and not undermine them in any way. Our sense of history, also, applied to this transition period from matter- to energy-consciousness, can show us the directions that religion will probably take, once mankind has adapted to the "rays" of this new age.

Nevertheless, spiritual faith rather than intellectually or emotionally based belief demands some sort of clear sign from above—a sign that we, with our all-too-human understanding, are being guided rightly. Without such a sign, and without such higher guidance, the danger of becoming opinionated is too great. Arrogance is the death of wisdom.

With or without such guidance, we must still continue to use our powers of reasoning to the best of our ability. For God responds to those who do their best with the faculties they possess, and not to those who, out of false humility, suspend those faculties altogether. Wise guidance, my Guru once said to me, is not given to the stupid. Nor is it given to anyone who contracts his energy self-protectively instead of reaching out with it expansively.

With or without higher guidance, then, we should still use our reasoning faculty to understand what we are able concerning future trends. Only thus will we, on our part, succeed in doing our best to adapt to those new rays.

The first point which formal religion, too, must recognize is that we are, indeed, living in a new age of energy. Church teachers and administrators must accept that energy-consciousness is not a mere passing fad, but a matter of actual fact. Short of the kind of cataclysmic warfare that might bomb men back to the caves, energy must be accepted as an enduring aspect of human existence.

Driving the nail in more deeply still, we must accept that energy is the reality and matter, the illusion; energy is the wave, the underlying vibration, of which matter is but a manifestation. Energy is not, in other words, the product of matter: It is its underlying reality.

What does this new knowledge mean to religion? The answer is forced upon us: the result *must be* a more fluid and more individual perception of higher, as well as of lower, truths. For the power of religion to influence mankind rests not in its outwardness—not, for example, in its ceremonies, its dogmas, or its crystallized institutions, but in the indwelling, divine Spirit of which all else is but a manifestation. Truth gave us religion; never could religion alone give us Truth.

The power of religious ceremonies lies in the energy people bring to them by the depth of their, or of the priest's, sincerity. Their sincerity cannot be measured by instruments. Inspiration is spiritual—unseen, but distinctly felt by all who immerse themselves deeply in the spirit of their practice.

I have seen people in church praying, but letting their eyes roam about restlessly as they watched the people coming in and going out of the sanctuary. I once observed a priest reciting the office for the dead while cleaning his fingernails. And I have attended Vedic fire ceremonies in India where the priests merely went through the ritualistic motions, repeating the mantras by rote while glancing about them for others' approval.

The setting sun, as it shines on the clouds in the western sky, irradiates them with color. Once it has fully disappeared beneath the horizon, however, those same clouds look gray and lusterless. It is, similarly, the spirit *behind* religious practices, and not the practices themselves, which determines their true influence.

Religion in the West, and perhaps throughout the world, has tended to focus more on the number of its adherents than on the quality of their worship. Where inner spiritual development has been encouraged — as has been more often the case in India, where religion also has not been organized — it is easier for religious leaders to adapt to the new age of experience over belief, and to recognize the insuperable handicap of blind belief. Ultimately, religion everywhere will have to move toward an emphasis on universal truths over outer forms.

The importance of spirit over form, and of experiment (that is to say, in spiritual matters, of true inner experience) over dogmatic assertions: These are what religion must teach now. Unless and until these principles are given their rightful emphasis, religion must become increasingly irrelevant to mankind. However, it isn't likely that religion will be able to resist such valid expectations for long. For outer religion, too, is a basic need of the heart. Without religion of some sort, the human spirit would shrivel and die. I am confident that mankind will not allow such a thing to happen.

During a visit I paid to Australia many years ago, someone approached me after a lecture and said, "I'm an atheist. Can you define God in such a way as to make Him meaningful to me?" I paused briefly, waiting for an answer from within. Then I replied, "Why don't you think of God as the highest potential you can imagine for yourself?" He was taken aback at first. Then he delivered his verdict: "Yeah, well, I can live with that!"

The human spirit would languish and die if it had nothing higher to which to aspire. Human beings would condemn themselves to apathy and to the gradual decay of all their higher faculties. As Voltaire put it, "If God did not exist, man would find it necessary to invent Him."

Since the human spirit cannot live without religion, people will have to find a way of living with it. The process of adaptation will not mean rejecting, so much as exploring and reconciling, differences between old, dogmatic assumptions and the progressive discoveries of modern science, and the natural demand of human nature for inner peace.

The basic directions in the future—simplicity, an emphasis on quality, and research into our inner being—cannot but be as important to religion as to other fields.

The deepest truths of religion are basically quite simple. They've been obscured by their complex superstructures; we have, in consequence, lost sight of their true purpose. Of all human institutions, religion ought to be the most unitive. Alas, it is, instead, one of the most divisive. People denounce, persecute, and fight wars over their religious differences—all in the name of God who, so they all claim, is a God of Love.

It is surely time, even independent of the rays entering the earth at this time, to explore man's inner relationship with his Creator. Jesus Christ said, "Behold, the kingdom of God is within you." (Luke 17:21) He also said, "Destroy this temple, and in three days I will raise it up again." (John 2:19) The Bible tells us that Jesus was referring not to the temple at Jerusalem, but to the temple of his own body. The inference to be drawn is obvious, for worship is conducted *inside* temples, not outside them. The true goal of pilgrimage is, as the Indian scriptures declare, the "kingdom of God within you": the divine Self. That which matters in religion, then, is neither outer places of worship nor rituals, nor even particular systems of belief (which are, after all, only man-made definitions): What matters is our own actual, direct, inner experience of God and Truth.

According to every saint who has experienced this sublime awakening, God is simple: it is man, with his intellectual justifications, who is complex.

The demands of Truth are simply that religion become once again simple, and no longer weighed down with dogmas, or bewildered by hair-splitting theological definitions. Religion must return to that most basic of all truths: love. It must return to the need of sincere aspirants for direct, personal experience of God's love.

The true spiritual work, then, is not the conversion of others: It is to live with, and to give outward expression to, divine love.

A friend of mine in India once spent the summer at a hill station in the Himalayan foothills. In the bungalow next to his there lived a missionary lady who was the headmistress of a local Christian school. My friend, open-hearted by nature, spoke to her pleasantly every time they met. She, unfortunately, mistook his friendliness for possible susceptibility to conversion. Her response, therefore, was wreathed in smiles. She invited him to visit her school; when he came, she introduced him to her students, and explained to him at length the good work she and her church were doing, and the beauty of Jesus Christ's teachings. To all of these attentions he responded with appreciation.

As it gradually dawned on her, however, that he was not interested in changing his religion, her manner toward him grew cool. The smile faded from her lips; the cordiality, from her voice. The day came at last when she began to treat him like a complete stranger. For his part, he continued to greet her cordially. She, however, preserved a dignified front in return. As a potential convert he had been important to her. As a fellow human being, however, she ceased to find him interesting enough even to greet with cordiality. Clearly, she had never viewed him as a human being with spiritual needs of his own. Now—such, at least, was the impression she gave him—she simply regarded him as a disappointing statistic of church membership.

The emphasis, during *Dwapara Yuga*, will shift from the quantitative to the qualitative approach. It will change from the quest of churches for more converts to an emphasis, first, on people's need for satisfactory answers—even if the questions they ask are "inconvenient" or "difficult"—and then on the needs of the individual, rather than those of any church.

This shift toward simplicity, toward emphasis on the needs of the inner man rather than the demands of any outer church, and, finally, the shift toward qualitative over quantitative solutions, is already creating a demand for religion to meet science with methods of its own for testing and experiencing the truth.

Recent centuries have clearly demonstrated the inadequacy of untested belief. They have justified the scientific method of demonstrating the validity of hypotheses by experiment. People still assume that the scientific method won't work in religion, since religion deals with truths that can't be measured, weighed, or quantified. If such were the case, however, science must be said to be rapidly disqualifying itself, for how is one to measure energy? Measurement has been a useful tool in the sciences, but when one deals with subtle subjects like energy, and still more with consciousness, other standards must be sought.

If religion had nothing more to offer than untested beliefs, it would attract only dreamers. Would anyone go to a gambling casino that had a reputation for never paying its customers? or for fobbing them off with promises of payment "eventually" (perhaps when the sky collapses)? Despite religion's promises of consolation someday (in the hereafter), the churches also fulfill a very present spiritual need. Were such not the case, people would long ago have stopped turning to religion for comfort and enlightenment, even as primitive tribesmen have stopped going to witch doctors once they realized that modern medical doctors could do a better job of healing them.

Religion offers truths that uplift and broaden the human spirit. More even than intellectually imparted truths, religion offers experience. The inspiration one feels while praying deeply can be life-changing. By contrast, the greatest works of art bring inspiration only to the degree that they echo the soul's inner inspiration. Religion alone offers direct soul-inspiration.

An example of the immediacy of the teachings offered by every great religion is the simple, universal admonition: "Do unto others as you would have them do unto you." Religion helps people to be more sensitive to truths in which all can participate. We all belong to the same one, universal reality. "No man," wrote the poet John Donne, "is an island." No one lives utterly alone except as he isolates himself, in his own mind, from other people.

As laboratories are the workshops of science, so human consciousness is the workshop of religion. Religious ceremonies are only projections of man's aspiration to inner perfection. It is on his own thoughts, primarily, that the sincere seeker works. His inner feelings are what he seeks to purify.

It was Jesus who told us exactly that: "Blessed are the pure in heart, for they shall see God." (Matt. 5:8) He didn't say, "Blessed are my disciples," or even, "Blessed are those who accept what I say." He made it clear that salvation depends not on outward affiliation, nor even on mental acknowledgement of the truth, but on one's purity of heart before God whose kingdom, Jesus said, is "within."

A great deal of what religion teaches can be tested and verified. It may ultimately turn out that *all* its claims can be verified. To observe a microbe, what is needed is a microscope. To perceive the Truth, what is needed is the "mind-scope" of a calm mind and heart, which bring to both mind and heart crystal clear perception.

Today, there are two distinct needs in religion: One is to test the scriptures, as Jesus himself in the Bible tells us to do. The other is to develop practical methods for conducting those tests.

Obviously, test tubes cannot be used in the "laboratory" of the mind. The need in this case, then, is methods for attaining calmness and concentration. Meditation is comparable, in this sense, to the science laboratory. Meditation is a means of achieving the mental clarity that is needed for this type of research. The truth cannot be perceived so long as the mind is restless, and its attention directed outward to the senses.

In modern medicine, numerous cures have been adopted from other cultures, where they were found to work. In other fields, too, discoveries that have been made in one culture have helped other cultures. Throughout the world, especially in our modern day, the trend toward cultural cross-pollination has been increasing rapidly.

In religion, unfortunately, claims of exclusivity have caused people to look with skepticism, and even with hostility, upon practices and beliefs that differ even slightly from their own.

In this *Dwapara Yuga*, at last, man's search for spiritual understanding is already taking him in a new direction.

Religion is no longer as dogmatic as it was in the past. Its emphasis, now, will surely become increasingly experiential as it concentrates on the individual's spiritual development. Religion must therefore come to include, among its practices, psycho-physical methods for helping individuals to achieve inner peace and mental clarity. Thus, yoga in all its branches will come into its own.

Inasmuch as yoga deals not only with mental and physical techniques of self-development, but with direct control of the inner energy (*pranayama*, or energy control), it will come to be recognized as an actual science of religion. It will become—I say this with confidence—the human science *par excellence* for the new age. Yoga meditation practices will be used to test the claims of religion by helping people to get in touch with their superconscious, and thereby to be guided by soul-intuition.

It seems obvious to me that the religion of the new age will be directed more inwardly, and less outwardly. The purpose of man's inner research will not be to strengthen his ego, but to trace self-awareness back to its source in Infinite Consciousness. Inasmuch as the ego's attention is usually directed to the body and to the world around it, man's self-definition is derived from these superficial identities: "I am a man, or a woman. I am an American, or a Frenchman, or an Italian. I am . . . I am!"

The ego's grip on human consciousness can be weakened only by contact with a higher consciousness. If we hope ever to achieve a clear understanding of who and what we really are, we must go within, and there explore our deeper connection with that universal energy and consciousness which sustain the world around us.

Jesus said, "Love thy neighbor as thyself." His meaning was that our neighbor is, in a deep, spiritual sense, our *true* and universal Self.

The reality of an island is only superficially the land mass we see above water. Its greater mass lies out of sight, extending underwater in all directions. Therein lies its connection to the earth itself, and to all the other islands in the sea.

The religion of the future will be, as I said, Self-realization. It will consist in realizing that the infinite love and joy of God are our own deepest reality, and that God is our true Self. For even as matter is energy, so is energy, in its turn, only a manifestation of thought. Thought—again in its turn—is only a manifestation of consciousness. And consciousness, in its ultimate refinement, is the Divine Spirit from which all things, all beings, and our very selves were first manifested.

CHAPTER SIX
RELIGIOUS INSTITUTIONS IN THE NEW AGE

The fact that matter is a manifestation of energy doesn't relegate it to non-existence; it only means that the world around us is very different from what it appears to be. Matter has been exalted in people's minds to the virtual status of an idol, claiming, if not their worship, then at least the entire focus of their attention. This exclusivity puts one in mind of the Biblical commandment, "Thou shalt have no other gods before me." (Exo. 20:3) Matter is not a god, of course, but most people view it even today as a fundamental reality. It isn't the task of *Dwapara Yuga* to overthrow *Kali Yuga* realities. New understanding will, however, show them in their proper relation to higher truths.

The same will be the case for the *Dwapara Yuga* perception of Jesus Christ, whom Christians thought to exalt as the only Son of God. In fact, that designation falls far short of his true greatness, which—far from having a limited, human form—is infinite and is, indeed, an aspect of God Himself. What *Dwapara* will accomplish is show divine reality as the *essence* of, and therefore infinitely subtler than, anything the human mind can encompass.

Religion, too, will be transformed to a much loftier vision than man has achieved heretofore. That vision will not be undermined by the discovery that the divine dramas enacted on earth by the great saviors of humanity have been limited in scope, for what they represented was much more than people could even hope to imagine. Nor will religion be weakened by the realization that the Creator of a hundred billion galaxies must certainly be very different from the old man with a flowing white beard that Michelangelo depicted on the ceiling of the Sistine Chapel. Indeed, the Lord cannot possibly be anthropomorphic (having a human form) in essence. Religion, far from being outmoded by the discoveries of science, will only find its teachings translated from an archaic language into one that is alive and infinitely exalted.

People's grasp of morality, too, will undergo radical transformation. Morality is not dead, as so many people imagine. In people's first exuberant realization that nothing is absolute, they came too quickly to the conclusion that one would be perfectly safe in doing anything he liked. In fact, the rules of morality, though relative, still apply *universally* to everyone at the same stage of spiritual evolution. To give an example: Were a worldly person to pray for a healing for himself, he would be right, for at least it would mean a turning to God. For a saint to utter such a prayer, on the other hand, would be wrong, for it would mean descending from the awareness of God's omnipresence and reaffirming his own ego. At his stage of spiritual evolution, he should be offering up his ego completely to God.

Relativity, and relativism in human affairs, are directional. The principles guiding human behavior are not whimsical. Were a lazy fellow one day to declare with energy, "I'm going to go out and get a job, and then work hard to become a millionaire!" everyone, including saints, would applaud. Were a nobler person like Gandhi, on the other hand, one day to make the same announcement, his decision would be met with universal dismay, even by worldly people.

With growing emphasis on the inner man, it will become increasingly clear that the principles of morality are deeply rooted in human nature itself. I've explained this subject at length in my book, *Out of the Labyrinth*, and therefore feel no need here to go into it further. The point is, our understanding of morality, too, is growing under the rays of *Dwapara Yuga*, even if, in the process, the change still entails a certain amount of confusion. Morality is not out of date. It will be seen in time, instead, as the basis for a truly fulfilled, effective, and happy life for both the individual and society as a whole.

The same will prove true for religious organizations. The realization that they are not an absolute good will pass on, after an initial disillusionment, to a more mature assessment of the great good the churches, and religious organizations in general, can accomplish.

The goal of all religious practices is to lift man into the state of absolute freedom in God. At that point he will have graduated from dependence on any religious organization. As a saint in India once put it, "It is a blessing to be born into a religion, but a misfortune to die in one!" Religious organizations can, nevertheless, be a force for great good in the world, provided they keep their spirit expansive and self-giving, that they never place self-interest ahead of their members' spiritual needs, and that they keep service to others as their highest goal.

The degree of an organization's expansiveness or contractiveness determines its state of mental and spiritual health, whether good or bad.

Contractiveness in individuals, as much so as in organizations, leads to exaggerated self-importance and self-preoccupation. Such attitudes show a lack of any true sense of proportion. This is as true for organizations as it is for individuals, since individuals run organizations and project onto them whatever attitudes they themselves have. A self-involved leader will project his contractive attitudes down through every level of his organization, to a point where the entire work force thinks less in terms of any good it might accomplish for others than of the good each worker might accomplish for himself. The general concern of such people is only to create safeguards, for themselves as much as for their organizations. In such institutions, the prevalent atmosphere will be one of fear. Creative initiative will be non-existent.

Rationalizations are generally devised by religious organizations to explain away blatant selfishness. Thus, if creativity is discouraged, the explanation will be, "The teachings must be preserved in their pure form." If anyone demonstrates a generous urge to help others, he will be urged to curtail his impetuosity, the rationale offered being, "The organization must be financially strong, that it may all the better serve mankind." Finally, fear lest the organization lose its precarious balance will mean that suggestions are not even listened to that don't support already-established principles and ideas.

What happens in such religious organizations is, of course, inevitable: spiritual vision is lost sight of in swirling mists of bureaucracy, and is ultimately forgotten altogether.

The cure in every case lies in a change of direction: from a contractive to an expansive flow of energy; from protective attitudes to healthier, more generously sharing ones.

Two principles must be kept uppermost in mind if truly spiritual ends are to be served. The first is, "People are more important than things." And the second is, "Where there is adherence to truth, there is victory."

I first saw this second principle expressed in India. It was the motto of the royal family of Cooch Behar. In Bengali it possessed a special rhythm: *"Jato dharma, tato jaya."*

The first of these principles, regarding the importance of the individual, has been stated many times and in many ways. It was expressed by Jesus Christ in the words: "The Sabbath was made for man, and not man for the Sabbath." (Mark 2:27)

The second principle is more difficult for worldly minds to grasp. People tend to see high principles as a stumbling block to success. As a friend of mine was advised by his father—who no doubt thought to share with his offspring the garnered wisdom of a lifetime—"Son, no one ever grew rich by being too honest." The interesting sequel to that counsel was that every time that same man succeeded by trickery in amassing a fortune, he quickly lost it again.

It is essential, of course, to be practical. There is limited practicality, however, in that very advice. Many people oppose every expansive idea with the explanation, "I'm only being practical." Such people, if ever they find themselves in a position of leadership in an organization, will condemn the organization to mediocrity.

Organization in Nature

An excellent way to learn how to run an organization is to study Nature's way of organizing. Consider the human body, which, like every well-run institution, has its chain of command. The ego works through the will, issuing directives that flow down to the body through nerve centers in the brain and spine. For the body to thrive, its ruling ego, like the chief executive officer of a corporation, must heed the body's needs and respond to them sensitively.

Again, for the body to thrive, its various parts must feel nourished and respected by the supreme "boss," the ego.

The body will languish and will, indeed, be drained of energy if the "boss," neglecting his duty, lives wrongly.

The ego must have a healthy, expansive relationship with the body and, through that body, with the world around it. It must serve a higher purpose than merely fulfilling its selfish desires. When it fails in this duty, it introduces harmful vibrations into the body's entire functioning.

The entire universe manifests the same unifying principles, for the reason that the mechanistic laws governing matter are rooted in spiritual truths. Gravity is a reflection of the highest spiritual principle, divine love. Newton's law of action and reaction is a reflection of the law of compensation, karma. The very ebb and flow of ocean tides manifests the primordial principle of *dwaita* (duality), which, according to the ancient teachings, is the very basis of creation.

The Universal Key

The master key to the laws of the universe is love.
Swami Sri Yukteswar wrote in his book, *The Holy Science*, of the effect of love on the human body: "When love, the heavenly gift of Nature, appears in the heart, it removes all causes of excitation from the system and cools it down to a perfectly normal state; and, invigorating the vital powers, expels all foreign matters—the germs of diseases—by natural ways (perspiration and so forth). It thereby makes man perfectly healthy in body and mind, and enables him to understand properly the guidance of Nature."

Sri Yukteswar explained further the effects of love on human understanding: "When this love becomes developed in man it makes him able to understand the real position of his own Self as well as of others surrounding him."

Paramhansa Yogananda, Sri Yukteswar's chief disciple, taught that the only way truly to understand others is by feeling deep compassion for them in one's heart. Psychoanalysis is usually intellectual, and therefore provides only superficial insight into human nature. Deep insights are possible only with empathic love.

That is why, when Paramhansa Yogananda was once asked, "What can take your place after you leave this world?" he replied with the sweetest smile, "When I am gone, only love can take my place." Love, that is to say, not only for God, but for God in others, in mankind, in all beings: this was his true meaning. As we contemplate the rays of *Dwapara Yuga*, it should be clear that love alone will help us fully to absorb their energies.

Jesus, too, stressed this principle. The Bible mentions certain orthodox people who were watching Jesus critically one day to see if, by healing a man on the Sabbath, he would break the Judaic law. The account goes on to say that Jesus "looked round about on them with anger, being grieved for the hardness of their hearts." (Mark 3:5)

Again, in John 13:35, Jesus says, "By this shall all men know that ye are my disciples, if ye have love one to another."

The Principle of Love in Human Institutions

In a healthy organization, every member, whatever his position in the "pecking order," is considered and also considers himself important to the whole. Even if the organization appears somewhat easy-going with respect to its procedural norms, as long as its basic energy is expansive, and its workers are concerned with serving their members, clients, or patients rather than with protecting themselves from their superiors' wrath, it will function relatively well.

The leaders, too, in a healthy organization are concerned primarily for the well-being of their subordinates, and only secondarily for whatever work they can get out of them. In a healthy society, greater concern is felt at all levels also for the well-being of the social structure as a whole than for the benefits people render to society itself. President Kennedy's famous call to Americans, "Ask not what your country can do for you: Ask rather what you can do for your country," needs elaboration. What you can do for your country should be seen in terms of what your country can do not only for you, but for all its citizens—and, beyond them, for all mankind.

A spiritually unhealthy organization, comparable to an unhealthy ego, is contractive in its energy. The workers fear for the security of their jobs; its leaders fear any possible challenge to their authority; and the organization as a whole, finally, is more motivated by fear of failure than by hopes and anticipations of success. Leaders and workers alike are indifferent to one another's needs, though they will usually disguise their indifference, like icing a cake, with high-sounding, self-justifying phrases.

In a contractive religious organization, one often hears the disclaimer, "Our lofty aims alone are what matter; the needs of individuals are not important." People, in other words, are considered nothing but cogs in a mighty (and of course glorious) machine. Such disclaimers, so far from affirming high ideals, only provide ample evidence that the disease has reached such an advanced state as to be diagnosed as "galloping contractivitis." In such an organization, any lingering enthusiasm in the work force is feared by those in charge, who will often discourage it openly as subversive.

An auto mechanic knows the importance of treating his tools with respect. He will clean and oil them regularly, and will place them away carefully, each one where it belongs. If a mechanic doesn't show such care for his tools, he may safely be described as incompetent.

An organization obviously, then, thrives when its members feel respected, cared for, and appreciated—perhaps even, in a sense, loved. If the organization fails in its duty to take proper care of its own, one may, without fear of misdiagnosis, assume the worst.

Religious organizations in *Dwapara Yuga* are bound to be guided with greater sensitivity. A good leader will try to make his organization an example of the universal law of action: "Desirable behavior brings desirable results." Energy-consciousness, as opposed to matter-consciousness, is therefore destined to shift its emphasis from outer forms to the inner, motivating spirit.

The defects of *Kali Yuga* organizations in general, and of church organizations in particular, are the following:

1) the belief that good form alone ensures the rightness of an action;

2) the belief that more can be accomplished by a leader who imposes his authority over those under him than by one who supports his subordinates and shows them respect, appreciation, and even love;

3) the belief that everyone in a leadership position must know how to handle all situations, and that no one else should even worry about the success of an undertaking;

4) the belief that many rules, rigidly adhered to, are necessary for developing the right spirit; and, finally:

5) the belief that dogmas, rather than kindness, conscience, and charity, are the true essence of religion.

In *Dwapara Yuga*, if one takes the time to study these alternatives he will see everything from a diametrically opposite perspective. *Dwapara* helps a person, in fact, to see his priorities as the following:

1) Central truths can be expressed in many different ways;

2) love is the greatest test of the rightness of an action;

3) wisdom can be the possession of no man, and depends, indeed, not nearly so much on personal talent or intelligence as on receptivity to inspiration "from above";

4) simplicity of heart nurtures right understanding, and too many rules, too rigidly adhered to, produce a calculating and contractive mind, giving rise to deviousness, deceit, and subtly disguised personal ambition;

5) dogmas are the outer raiment of religion, but charity is its driving life force. Dogmas, in other words, are the definition of religion, but charity is its living heart.

If, then, the choice for an appointment to some administrative position in a religious organization happens to lie between someone who is deeply spiritual but who lacks experience, and someone else who is worldly minded but competent, the decision will obviously have to go to the experienced, worldly person. This is, however, only the *Kali Yuga* way of thinking, which views the outer husk but neglects the inner essence.

During *Dwapara Yuga*, it will become increasingly clear that an organization's effectiveness is determined more by its prevailing spirit than by such superficial criteria even as efficiency. Though efficiency is always, of course, desirable, it can serve no useful end if its motivating spirit is murky as to its ends. Efficiency can be learned, but the right spirit can only be inborn, or at least inspired by good leadership.

In *Dwapara Yuga*, the emphasis in spiritual organizations will no longer be on absolute authority, but on ever-increasing understanding and love. Efficiency, though valued, will not be valued over right spiritual attitudes. True insight will be perceived as deriving from divine, not from human, authority. If any particular priest is found to be more saintly than others, his example will cease to be looked upon as a threat to uniformity, but will be hailed as a blessing on the whole church; not an embarrassment, but a model to which all the other priests should aspire.

The lines of authority, likewise, will not be followed so rigidly that high principles become sacrificed to some organizational convenience. If someone in the lower echelons of an organization feels misunderstood by his superior or superiors, those in higher echelons, while giving all possible support to that worker's immediate superior, will also listen charitably to the underling's complaint. A clear understanding of the need for lines of authority will make it possible also to bypass them when necessary, not only by listening to complaints but by working with all the persons concerned to improve matters. Individual needs will be accepted as vital to the morale of the entire organization.

In these last considerations, however, we reach a level of understanding where reason alone is insufficient. Intuition can guide people wisely. Reason, on the other hand, is sure sooner or later to stumble. We return, then, to a point I raised earlier, namely, that some form of revelation is needed at this time, if humanity is to be rightly guided toward the highest potentials that are offered by this new age.

Let us consider whether such guidance is, in fact, presently available. If so, how can we take best advantage of it? Surely what is needed, in religion, is not outer conversion, but a sharing with all of broader, deeper understanding. Such changes are possible within each individual. Conversion should, above all, be to one's own higher Self.

CHAPTER SEVEN
Dwapara Yuga GUIDANCE

S ri Yukteswar, shortly before committing himself to writing his book, *The Holy Science*, prayed that the advances being made by science in this new age might receive the guidance of higher wisdom. In answer to his prayer, God sent him an enlightened soul whom he could prepare for such a mission.

Paramhansa Yogananda was that student. Yogananda, a great master, was given the mission, in part, of bringing the ancient wisdom in its purest essence into alignment with modern knowledge. He was sent, then, to show how those truths could be made practical to everyone in our day.

His mission was not only qualitative—which is to say, to a few close disciples—but also quantitative to a whole civilization. He was sent as a way-shower for all mankind, in recognition of the fact that civilization has at last entered territory that needs exploring in new ways: *Dwapara Yuga*.

One of the patterns of living that Yogananda came to establish was the founding of what he called "world-brotherhood colonies": communities where high-minded people, living together, could bring these new concepts to a clear and easily understandable definition, and subsequently offer them to mankind as a workable model rather than as a merely theoretical concept.

I myself enter the picture because my lot has been to establish the first of these "world-brotherhood" colonies. Ananda World-Brotherhood Village is located in the Sierra Nevada foothills of Northern California, near the twin towns of Nevada City and Grass Valley. In the present year—308 *Dwapara*—there are six branch communities of Ananda: in Seattle (Washington); Portland (Oregon); Palo Alto and Sacramento (California); Italy near the town of Assisi; and what will soon be near Pune, India. The total resident membership of these communities is approximately 1,000. The original community, situated on some 1,000 acres of land, is home to several hundred members.

True to *Dwapara Yuga* principles, however, size is not Ananda's objective. Rather, our aim is to inspire individuals—the more individuals, of course, the better—with new clarity and dedication to their own inner, spiritual development. We seek also to inspire these ideals in people everywhere, regardless of their outward religious affiliations. As Paramhansa Yogananda often put it, "I prefer a soul to a crowd, and I love crowds of souls!"

To put an even finer point on it, instead of being goal-oriented as a community we try to keep our focus on people's inner, spiritual unfoldment. As a saying we have puts it: "The goal of life is not to be goal-oriented, outwardly speaking, but to expand one's deeper sense of BEING to Infinity."

I myself came to Yogananda in 1948 after reading his book, *Autobiography of a Yogi*. I sought him out because of my own deep desire for spiritual insight. I did so also because of a deep anxiety I had for the future of mankind.

For I had realized that humanity, without divine guidance, would never be able to handle the twin threats of moral relativism and a lack of meaningful purpose in life. After reading Yogananda's book, I saw his as a message that was not only the answer to my own personal needs, but also one that was capable of guiding all mankind safely past the ideological pitfalls of our times.

Inspired by Yogananda's vision of spiritually focused communities in this new age, I founded Ananda forty years ago, in 1968, twenty years after I had first met him.

In developing Ananda I have done my best, always, to draw on his example and his way of teaching and guiding others. I have written books to show the relevance of his teachings to numerous aspects of modern life: to marriage and loving relationships; to child raising; to education; to business; to leadership; to the fine arts; to architecture; to philosophy; to communities—indeed, to the whole spectrum of modern life. I have composed songs and instrumental pieces—over 400 in all—to help people tune in to the consciousness behind my Guru's mission. I have helped to establish schools and businesses with the purpose of giving these concepts a solid foundation.

In one important respect, I confess, it seemed to me that Yogananda had not given us adequate guidelines: for the formation of organizations in the new age. Until the actual writing of this essay, nearly sixty years since I first met him, I still believed that he considered organizations to be, at best, only a necessary evil. Some of this belief influenced what I wrote in others of my papers. In an early draft of this paper, too, I stated:

"[Paramhansa Yogananda] himself, as if to emphasize the importance of consciousness over form, never actually gave much energy to organizing his work. Its overriding reality, for him, was his vigorously expansive spirit.

"Sister Gyanamata [I continued], his chief woman disciple, predicted, 'You will never be able to organize this work
so long as he is alive.' Yogananda himself said, 'You all will
have to work hard to organize the work after I am gone.'"

In everything I have done since coming to him, I have
pondered all that he said and did, even down to his small-
est hint. I wanted to draw on my memories of him for their
fullest possible meaning. As the founder of Ananda, I have
considered my own role to be relatively insignificant, for
I saw my job as being rather to transmit to others the
message I had received from that great world teacher.

While writing this essay, therefore, I meditated again on
the example he had set as the founder of an organization
(Self-Realization Fellowship). And I understood, suddenly,
this aspect of his life as I had never done before.

His mission covered a broad range of activities, such
that it would have been impossible for him to limit himself to the usual role of administrator. Nevertheless, he
gave us the guidance we needed to carry on his work along
Dwapara Yuga lines. More than that, by inspiring us to rise
to his meaning, rather than (so to speak) beating us on the
head with what he wanted us to do, he actually established
an ideal for *Dwapara Yuga*-style management.

His own firm commitment to the spirit, rather than to
the form, of his work helped to point us toward a more fluid
and loving approach to organizing than the rigid forms to
which we, as Westerners, had grown accustomed.

To the extent that we failed, the failure was ours, not his;
it was due to our being steeped in old patterns of thinking.
Few of his disciples were ready to take onto themselves his
more fluid kind of leadership.

I remember one disciple telling me, almost in a tone
of bewilderment, how the Master had tried for a long time
to interest him in developing the organizational side of his

mission. Finally the young man, under the impression that he at last understood how to proceed, came to the Master with an elaborate program for how to spread the teachings and bring in more members. The Master was exasperated; his disciple's thickheadedness blinded him to what his Guru really wanted of him. The disciple had thought that what the Master wanted was for him to hustle. Our Guru ended up brushing away the whole program, announcing instead, "When we are ready, God will send to us those whom He wants to help." He forthwith halted all his efforts to work with this disciple in such matters.

It was not the Master's way to dot every *i* and cross every *t*. If he saw that a disciple didn't have the right spirit, he would simply drop the subject. In this respect, too, he demonstrated a basic principle of *Dwapara Yuga* leadership: Don't impose; try, rather, to inspire others *from within* to develop their own understanding.

Here is a further example of the Master's way of working: In 1949 he put me in charge of the monks. I'd been with him less than a year and was fearful of the great responsibility he was giving me—to the point, I'm sorry to say, of doing almost nothing even to declare my position.

A year later he asked me again, and actually told me to organize the monks, who, until then, had never been organized.

One might assume from the fact that he gave me this charge that, after that, he must have devoted many hours to instructing me on how to organize the monks. Instead, as I found he usually did in such matters, he relied on my inner attunement with him to perceive his wishes and carry them out. From time to time he would make a brief suggestion, or offer a cautionary remark. Occasionally he would correct me, if he saw that in some particular I had not understood him rightly. Otherwise, he simply oversaw what I did, with-

out interfering. Every now and then he would express satisfaction, but otherwise he left it to me to do as I felt guided
by him from within. I might add that, toward the end of his
life, he said to me, "You have pleased me very much. I want
you to know that."

Most of his training of the disciples was on an intuitive level. As I organized the monks, it was enough for him
that I grasped the spirit of his intentions, and was in tune
with his inner guidance. From that level of intuitive understanding, he knew that the details would follow as a natural
consequence.

What I have come to realize, then, while writing this
essay, is that organization was important to him, but de-
pended on our understanding of his overall intentions. To
him, the spirit of his teachings was more important than the
forms presenting them. That was why he waited until nearly
the end of his life to request that the monks be organized.
Perhaps it was also why I myself came to him as a disciple
only toward the end of his life, ensuring thereby that I'd
live long enough to bring his ideas to completion. He set the
tone for the right way to organize, but gave priority, always,
to the spirit behind the outer forms.

Again, I think the reason I was destined to come to him
only toward the end of his life (I came in 1948; he passed
away in 1952) was that my own sense of discipleship was
centrifugal, not centripetal: in other words, outwardly directed, from a center of attunement with him. He often told
me, "You have a great work to do." Once he pleaded with
me urgently, "Of the men disciples, apart from St. Lynn
(Rajarshi Janakananda), *every one* has disappointed me. **And
you MUSTN'T disappoint me!**" I vowed inwardly then to
do my best to spread his mission in the right, spiritual way,
and not to focus too closely on him as the Guru, as many
were doing. Others were more attracted to his personality

than to the principles he was teaching. The solution for harmonizing both sides of this equation was, of course, also to go beyond his personality to the spirit which vitalized both him and that mission.

His guidance of me, too, was focused on making me an instrument through which he hoped to help others.

One day, during my first year, I fell into a mood. The next time he saw me a few days later, the mood had evaporated, but he said, "No more moods, now. Otherwise, how will you be able to help others?"

Always, his guidance focused on the inner spirit of what we were doing. Even when we lectured, he told us, "Concentrate on giving people your vibrations. Don't give too much attention to the thoughts you want to express."

There was a time at Mt. Washington (the headquarters of Self-Realization Fellowship) when a skilled worker was badly needed for the print shop. Since this had been a subject of discussion for some weeks, it was with a glow of triumph that I approached the Master one day with the news, "Sir, we have a new man for the print shop!" A young man had come who expressed an interest in this kind of work.

"Why do you say that?" the Master demanded scoldingly. "First, see that they have our spirit. Only then look to see where they will best fit into our work." (Interestingly, this young man proved, fairly soon, *not* to have the right spirit. Evidently, the Master had already known this to be the case. I might add that he hadn't yet met the young man.)

On one occasion I accepted someone for residence in the monastery who even I knew was not ready for our way of life. The man desperately needed spiritual help, however, and was anxious to improve himself. It had meant so much to me to be accepted that I couldn't bear the thought of refusing anyone. The Master, however, seeing him one day for the first time, remarked to me afterward, "I am going to have to give you intuition!"

This principle of doing things by intuition, rather than by reason alone, was important for me in the founding of Ananda, years later. I had to use common sense also, of course, but it became increasingly clear to me that, without intuition, nothing important would ever be accomplished.

One of the instructions he gave me was, "Don't make too many rules. It destroys the spirit." From this single piece of instruction, if from no other, I understood that organization, for him, meant a flow rather than a (perhaps) beautiful, but crystallized structure.

In looking to Yogananda's example for how best to run a *Dwapara Yuga* institution, we must, as I stated earlier, look to the direction of the energy we are setting in motion, rather than to what people commonly describe as the "nuts and bolts" of the institution. In this respect, Paramhansa Yogananda in many ways fulfilled the requirements for leadership in a *Dwapara Yuga* organization.

What was the example he set? First and foremost, it was the expansiveness he expressed in his own nature. Most people experience some conflict between their own expansive and contractive tendencies. If they plunge into a cold stream, they may hastily strike out, shivering, for the shore. In my Guru I observed no such conflict. To those of us who took his expansive nature as our example, that quality in him was a constant inspiration. We found it also, of course, an unceasing challenge.

One evidence of expansiveness in human nature is that it is solution-oriented, and not, like its opposite, problem-oriented. Problem-consciousness is symptomatic of the *Kali Yuga* mentality. Solution-consciousness is typical of the *Dwapara Yuga* nature.

An example of our Guru's solution-consciousness occurred during World War II. Official restrictions were

placed at that time on the construction of any new build-
ings in Los Angeles. Yogananda wanted to construct a new
church in Hollywood, but because of the restrictions was
told he would not be given a permit to do so.

Instead of worrying over the problems raised by what
he couldn't do, he focused on what he *could* do. A solution
soon suggested itself to him.

No restrictions had been placed on remodeling already-
existing structures. The Master therefore sought, and soon
found, the shell of an old building of just the dimensions he
wanted. He had this structure moved onto the Hollywood
property, then proceeded to remodel it.

The neighbors, of course (problem-oriented like most
people), on seeing that gutted shell standing on an empty lot
in the midst of their elegant homes, complained vociferously.
Somehow they couldn't visualize in that shell its artistic
possibilities! Gradually, however, to everyone's amazement,
that dilapidated ruin was transformed into the lovely
jewel that, for many years now, has been Self-Realization
Fellowship's Church of All Religions at 4880 Sunset Blvd.,
in Hollywood.

Expansiveness! Solution-orientedness! Judging a person's
fitness for position by his spirit more than by his already-
demonstrated abilities! Encouraging subordinates to develop
their own intuition, attunement, and understanding rather
than carefully spelling out every move for them! Giving them
a chance to learn from their mistakes! Reviewing an action
after the event, rather than fretting in advance over what
might go wrong with it! Supportiveness! Love! — These were
a few, only, of the ways in which Paramhansa Yogananda
pointed the way to enlightened management in the age
of *Dwapara*.

He showed by other ways also his command of the
needs of management in this age of energy. Of primary

importance, he said, was offering service to others. His mode of dealing with everyone, moreover, was impartial, divinely loving, and equally respectful to all in God.

His concept of spiritual management was top downward, but not in the usual managerial sense. Rather, what this meant for him was giving first priority to Truth and right action. After that followed those concepts which would best express the truth—concepts such as kindness, respect, and a willingness to listen to points of view other than one's own. Next came the search for those people who might be *receptive* to these truths. Last in importance came the organization itself, as a vessel for the truth and a vehicle for spreading it.

People were, to him, more important than the organization. If his teachings were more important to him than the people he was teaching, it was in the sense that he refused to compromise the Truth in order to accommodate people's desires and delusions. Eternal Truth itself, finally, was supremely important to him, above any specific formulation of that Truth.

Chapter Eight
Ananda — A First Step

I have tried in these pages to explain, and also to understand more clearly for myself, Paramhansa Yogananda's example. As I created Ananda, also, I tried always to make it a laboratory for testing and developing his ideas. I haven't meant to say that these ideas themselves are unprecedented, any more than Truth itself can ever be unprecedented. The same thoughts have been expressed many times and in many ways through the ages. What is new today is that these crucial ideas have been presented when the general consciousness of mankind was more ready to receive them.

There are few written rules at Ananda. We try, instead, to work with people as they are, not as any artificial theory says they ought to be. "People are more important than things." It is for the people themselves that the rules were made.

I have always followed to the best of my ability Yogananda's charitable approach to organizing. If a job needs doing, no matter how important it is to the needs of the community, our first concern is for the persons concerned. Only secondarily is our concern for Ananda itself.

The reason for this practice is that spiritual institutions owe their very existence to the desire to help others. Rules are meant for those who can stand up and be counted, and not for some amorphous humanity "out there" which might, perhaps, benefit from them someday, if only Joe and Mary can be squeezed, meanwhile, for everything they have.

At Ananda, if doubts arise as to whether a person being considered for a position would benefit from it spiritually, we seek someone else for that place, even if that "someone else" seems less suitable for the job. For we'd rather see a project fail than have it succeed at any individual's expense. Our projects, consequently, have generally succeeded— indeed, they've flourished, in a field (communities) where the rate of failure, so far, stands close to 100 percent.

In 1980 we bought East West Books, a metaphysical bookstore in Menlo Park, California. The person I put in charge of the store remonstrated with me, "But I don't know anything about selling books!"

"Never mind," I consoled her. "Be a friend to everyone who comes. You will learn what you need to know about books, in time. In fact, your customers will be glad to tell you about them in return for the spiritual nourishment they feel on coming here. Serve them, and share with them God's love."

For some years East West Books was in the top one percentile of metaphysical bookstores in the whole coun- try, and the second-largest-selling bookstore of its kind on the West Coast. Today I don't know the statistics, but I do know that East West is thriving when many bookstores in the country, especially metaphysical bookstores, have gone out of business. One reason for our success has been our principle of giving top priority to the spirit of the people working there—less so than to their demonstrated compe- tence. In fact, competence has usually followed as a matter of course.

Another example of relying on the spirit first, rather than on material needs, occurred in 1976. In that year a forest fire destroyed some 450 acres at Ananda Village and twenty-one of our homes. This devastation might easily have sounded the death knell for the whole community, for we hadn't the financial reserves with which to rebuild, and had no fire insurance. Though generously assisted by donations from friends and various organizations, it took us years to pay off the loss. With a lot of hard work, however, and with joyful faith in God, we did by His grace rebuild at last, better than ever.

During the early stages of the rebuilding process, we faced a moral dilemma. Before the fire, a couple had decided to move away from the community. We had promised to buy their home when the funds to do so became available. This home, too, was destroyed in the fire, and of course we had nothing now with which to buy back that nonexistent structure. Donations were coming in at a trickle, not in a flood. We had the rebuilding of those destroyed homes of our active members to consider. Were we still obligated—such was our dilemma—to buy back that no longer existent home? If so, how soon ought we to do so? Would it command first priority? Or would we be right to delay our repayment?

After consulting the resident members' feelings in the matter, we decided to pay off that couple's home first, from the initial donations we received. "*Jato dharma, tato jaya*: Where there is adherence to right action, there is victory." Our hearts rejoiced in the realization that our homes, and Ananda itself, belonged to God and Guru, not to us.

This belief, inspired by Yogananda's example, inspires in us an awareness that the whole world, and not Ananda alone, is our larger community.

Herewith follows another example of the practical implications of that belief:

The cause of the fire was later discovered to have been a faulty spark-arrester on a county vehicle. This meant we could sue the county for damages. Neighbors of ours, who also had lost their homes, sued and collected. When the news first came out that the county was liable, some of our neighbors phoned us, to announce exultantly, "You'll easily be able to get two million dollars for your losses!" (Ananda had been the biggest loser in the fire.) Two million dollars would have enabled us to rebuild all our homes, and also to redevelop our devastated land.

Instead, I wrote to the county supervisors that we looked upon the county as our own larger community. We would not, I said, be taking out our bad luck on them.

Ten years later, many of our neighbors were still bemoaning the losses they'd sustained in the fire. At Ananda, the very day following the fire we were already pitching in with joyful smiles to clear the land and begin the process of reconstruction. Our joy never left us. In many ways, the fire turned out to be one of our greatest blessings in Ananda's history.

Our deep conviction, justified again and again over the years, has been that when the spirit is truly expansive and self-giving, God Himself—perhaps through the Intelligent Cosmic Energy—always provides.

My very decision to found Ananda was made during a period of my life when my income was less than $400 a month. Friends and relatives ridiculed my ambition as absurd. The inner flow of energy, however, felt right to me. My part in the process was only to put out the highest energy of which I felt myself capable.

The inspiration for this decision was, again, the example I'd seen in Paramhansa Yogananda. One day, during difficult years financially, a visitor had asked him sneeringly, "What are the assets of this organization?"

"None!" replied the Master vigorously: "Only God!"

To raise the money I needed for starting Ananda, I traveled daily from city to city giving yoga classes. Mindful of my Guru's reluctance, years earlier, to charge money for his classes, but recalling at the same time that he'd decided to charge nominally for them once he realized that people appreciate what they are getting only when they give something in return, I charged a token $25 for a six-week course. If any potential student complained that he couldn't afford even that amount, I let him perform some little service in exchange for getting free lessons. He might set up chairs, or perhaps (after I acquired the first Ananda property), work on the land for a weekend. (Strange to relate, it turned out in every case that those who had claimed they couldn't afford to pay demonstrated, later, that they could easily have paid. Nevertheless, I preferred to let them determine their own priorities. My responsibility, as I saw it, was to preserve my spirit of service to others.) As things turned out, God always sent me as many students as I needed to meet my land and construction costs: never more, but always enough.

<hr />

I've already discussed in sufficient detail, for the purposes of this essay, how we have sought to grow by putting principles first, and by keeping always in mind the first principle, "People are more important than things."

One aspect of community life that might seem difficult to develop along charitable lines is that of discipline. Yet a certain amount of discipline is necessary in any institution. For anarchy is not freedom. The more such discipline proceeds from within the individual, however, in the form of self-discipline, and isn't imposed on him from without, the better both for the organization and for the member himself in his relationship with the organization.

Paramhansa Yogananda set the tone in this respect also. He once said to me, "I only like to discipline with love. I just wilt when I have to speak in other ways."

He also gave supreme importance to the individual's free will. "I only discipline those who want it," he told me, "never those who don't."

One might think it necessary sometimes to put organizational priorities ahead of personal needs: to say, for example, "Do it, or else!" This is something I never heard Paramhansa Yogananda do.

On one occasion, before my arrival, a grand opening was planned for the SRF colony in Encinitas, California. Everyone concerned was under great pressure to finish the work in time for the occasion. The public and the media had already been invited. Rev. Bernard himself told me the story:

"I had the all-important responsibility," he said, "of plastering the towers. I'd worked through the night several times, to meet that fast-approaching deadline.

"One final push was needed. My presence was crucial to the completion of the job. On the last day, I failed to show up. When I did finally appear, the Master demanded of me as if scoldingly, 'Where were you?'

"'Sir,' I replied, 'I was meditating.'

"'Oh,' replied the Master, instantly mollified. 'Why didn't you say so?'"

God-communion was the very reason we were there. Never would the Master give precedence to any outer project over that highest priority, no matter how urgent the situation. I should finish this story by relating that the job did—"by the skin of its teeth"—get finished in time.

At Ananda—again following the Master's example—we have always emphasized cooperation over obedience. If anyone shows himself unwilling to do something that has been asked of him, we simply ask someone else to do it.

If the same member refuses a second or a third time, he simply won't be asked again unless and until his attitude changes. For if he won't accept the responsibility of disciplining himself, little can be gained by imposing discipline on him from outside.

When external discipline comes by force or persuasion, it only weakens people and makes them dependent, or, alternately, confuses them and makes them rebellious. Clarity of mind, and inner strength: Both are needed for creating a strong organization—even if unquestioning obedience seems, in the short term, more convenient.

It is important also to see the organization, and the individual's place in it, in terms of energy output. For energy moves in a vortex. Once a positive vortex is created, any negativity will either be converted and drawn in toward the center, or repelled and dissipated.

There are times—and these, too, have come to Ananda— when negative energy must be actively combated. In such cases we've found it better to affirm, and thereby give strength to, positive energy than to energize a negative vortex by allowing ourselves to grow angry over it or to denounce it.

Involvement Management

An unusual feature at Ananda, and one that I hope will someday become widespread, is our practice of managing by direct involvement rather than aloofly, from above.

We call this process "Involvement Management." It is something that has evolved through trial and error over a period of years, and is not the result of an *a priori* theory. There were no community models for us to study at first—none, at any rate, with which I myself was familiar. To me, "involvement management" has always been an important direction for us, and will perhaps be helpful to other organizations too, as mankind progresses further into *Dwapara Yuga*.

For many years before I founded Ananda, I studied other models in history, as well as organizations of our own day, and pondered how those functioned which succeeded best. I observed that high position was often presumed to demonstrate a person's competence for decision-making in every field. *Who* said a thing was considered more important than *what* he or she said.

I also assisted at meetings where those who knew the least about a project often did most of the talking, as if to show that they, too, took seriously their responsibility as members of a decision-making body.

It is important, of course, for there to be leadership positions. When those who hold a high position, however, consider themselves alone competent to determine the outcome of every issue, inevitably their expertise will not in every case be equal to the task of making wise decisions. High position, moreover, invites personal ambition, envy from others, and feelings of self-importance in the person himself. It is important to view these qualities as danger signals in a potential leader, and never to encourage them by promoting such persons.

At Ananda we have, of necessity, a few people in key management positions. Meetings are more frequently held, however, at levels where everyone involved in a project gets to participate.

The important thing is that the energy in every segment of the work be directed in a spirit of unity. Otherwise, nothing will prevent any committee from scattering off in its own direction, destroying in the process the coherence that is so essential to every group project.

Paramhansa Yogananda tried to get people to understand management by involvement, and leadership by attunement with the source of inspiration. Too often, when he placed someone in a responsible position, that person never realized with what a spiritual powerhouse he was living. Often he tried to do things according to his own inner "lights," without much concerning himself about attunement with the Master. Those to whom our Guru gave the job of sharing these teachings with others too often viewed the task as an opportunity for presenting different inspirations of their own.

In a work of such spiritual importance, it is necessary to understand that God sent Paramhansa Yogananda with a divine message to mankind. The more perfectly we can transmit that message to others, the more certain it will be to reach all mankind, as God intended.

No work can flourish with a multiplicity of guiding spirits. Hence the truth of Emerson's saying, "An institution is the lengthened shadow of one man." The logic of this statement, applied to Paramhansa Yogananda's mission, is irresistible: His mission will never flourish unless he himself is held as the source of all its energy flow.

Yogananda knew that after his death his disciples, each one capable of perceiving him only in some one, or in a few, aspects of his many-sided nature, but not in all of them, might be inclined to take his mission in less vital directions. Therefore he told a disciple, "Only love can take my place": Not, "Only your memory of me," nor, "The rules I have written." Love, as the guiding principle for every true disciple, regardless of how differently each one perceives the mission itself, is the true key to its success.

Today, therefore, when two disciples have different interpretations of his teachings or of his personal guidance to them, the key he gave all of us is to place the highest priority on love: to demonstrate our love for and attunement with him by the love we share with one another.

Must we always agree with one another? Ideally so, of course. However, given the fact that people sometimes cannot help seeing things differently, they can still love one another, and simply agree to differ.

Must they shelve their differences, then, in the name of harmony? Again, yes, if possible. But if the differences are so fundamental that it would entail an offense against their own understanding of the truth, then they must, as I said, agree to differ. In this case, they can at least still love one another.

Love is a gift. It cannot be imposed by rule, nor demanded by one person of another. It must be given freely, or else not given at all.

Yogananda showed this spirit by his own life. And he showed how the spirit of love can reign supreme in an organization: by the complete absence of self-assertion; by seeing God in all; by not making the organization an extension of anyone's ego, but seeing all equally as brothers and sisters; by judging no one; and by emphasizing a spirit of service rather than something so often encountered in organizations: a struggle for ever-higher positions of authority.

At Ananda we have succeeded to a gratifying extent in curbing personal ambition. Our method has been simply to emphasize function over position. A person may be relatively new at Ananda, and yet—if he happens to be directly involved in the matter at issue—find himself participating in meetings and helping to make decisions on many issues. By the single device of involvement management, we have eliminated perhaps eighty percent of the infighting and competition that are so common in organizations.

Along with grassroots decision-making, there is always the need for the guidance of authority. These two flows of energy—downward from above, and upward from the grassroots level—need constantly to be kept in a state of balance. If decisions were to get made only at a grassroots level, the result would, of course, be institutional confusion.

Because it is common for people to find themselves caught up in details—to the point of losing touch with the deeper purpose behind what they are doing—we at Ananda have created a safeguard against this tendency. In addition to having a general manager responsible for the *hows* of a decision, we have also a spiritual director, whose responsibility is for the *whethers* of the decision.

The spiritual director's job is to make sure that the spirit of Ananda flows from attunement with the Master's teachings, and from inner guidance, and never from expediency alone. No decision is fully sanctioned unless it is accepted as coming from the special ray of God's grace that has been sent to us by our line of gurus.

The need for attunement with their mission is kept paramount. Ananda is a part of that mission. The mission as a whole, however, is much broader than what we at Ananda define as our own church and community. The mission is to reach out everywhere with love, and not to limit ourselves to the forms by which we express that love. Our solution is to concentrate rather on love itself, and to ask of that love that it flow to all the world, energizing all whom it touches.

Ananda exists for the purpose of serving the larger community of mankind—first of all through its members, and then to those, everywhere, who seek our help.

In *Dwapara Yuga* terms, religious organizations will feel themselves more strongly motivated than they've been in the past by the spirit of love, rather than by any demand for obedience. The emphasis on power and control—so common in the past—will be replaced by an expansive impulse to serve and embrace all mankind in a spirit of kinship in God, and to bless everyone, everywhere, with His love.

Part Two

A MISCELLANY OF ESSAYS

THE FINAL EXAM

The most important moment of life is, in a very true sense, its last moment. For death is when we take our final exam. The thought uppermost in the mind at that time will determine whether our future takes us upward, or sideways, or downward: upward, toward greater spiritual clarity and freedom; sideways, toward further involvement in desires and worldly attachments; or (the least fortunate) downward, toward greater darkness, confusion, and ignorance. The Bhagavad Gita, India's best-loved scripture, says that if our last thought is of God, it is to Him we will go; if that thought is of family and relatives, it is to them we will go; if the last, lingering thought in the mind is of regret for the mistakes we have made in this life, our direction will be downward toward a lessened ability to pass similar tests in the future; and, finally, if that thought is of *attraction* to those mistakes, our downward motion will be farther and more rapid.

"Those who worship the lower gods go to their gods," says the Bhagavad Gita. "Those who worship Me come to Me." This is one of the most important statements in that great and timeless scripture.

Although the time when we approach the end of life is when we should make a special effort to prepare ourselves for life's final exam, we should remind ourselves throughout life of the impermanence of everything on earth. Someday, whether late or soon, we must all confront that moment. Instead of dreading the inevitable, wouldn't it be wiser to accept its inevitability? We should embrace it, then, with an attitude—one that we should hold throughout life—that affirms, "What comes of itself, let it come; and let it come *whenever* it comes."

Foolish indeed is he who lays up for himself treasures here on earth. Money, savings and checking accounts; home;

cherished possessions; family members both near and distant; the reputation, and even the fame, for which we may have labored so assiduously; the pleasures and delights of the senses; our fond attachments to things and to people; familiar scenes and localities; the memory of happy parties and good times; our neighbors and acquaintances, both near to us and distant; the skills we've patiently honed; the language or languages we've spoken; the books we've read; the knowledge we've acquired and stored assiduously on mental shelves; the fond memories we've garnered over the years; dear friends and shared understandings; our unfulfilled hopes; the events on which we now gaze back with nostalgia; the laughter and happy moments; the bright certainties of future fulfillment: All these must be swept away in a moment, as though they had never been.

Has Mozart, relatively little known as he was during his lifetime, realized since his death that the whole world has come to love his music? Does Vincent Van Gogh, who during his lifetime earned hardly fifteen dollars from his great paintings, know now the fabulous worth each one of them has acquired today? How many great men and women of history have become aware, since they lived, of the influence their lives have had on world events? Very few, one suspects. Life is like a tiny puff of wind on a few grains of sand. It may end, moreover, at any moment.

Wouldn't it be a good practice, even now, to prepare for our final "Day of Reckoning"?

Certain practices will help you not only to prepare for that exam, but also to meet your present daily responsibilities most effectively. Such practices will help you also to prepare for what might be called life's "intermediary exams." An attitude, for example, of non-attachment, so necessary for attaining final freedom after death, will also be a much surer attitude for attaining success in this world than would eager anticipation of success, and excessive dependence on results.

Here, then, are a few practices I recommend:

Make it a point, every night before you fall asleep, to check the feelings in your heart. See whether any burrs of attachment still cling there, affixed by desires you may have developed during the day. If you find any such "burr," mentally build a fire and cast that burr into it. Watch with a smile of relief as each burr disintegrates to ashes.

Every time you take a bath, think as you wash, for example, an arm, "This will not be my arm forever. Someday it will be ashes, or dust." And then affirm, "This is not what I am, in my true Self! I am Spirit! I am bliss! I am ever free in God!"

Attachment is not only binding: It is also *blinding*. It stirs up the heart's feelings with emotions of fear, hesitation, and confusion. In anything we do, excessive concern for the outcome of that action saps our energy and concentration, both of which are necessary for success in any undertaking. Non-attachment, far from signifying an attitude of indifference, frees one to devote oneself wholeheartedly to whatever project he attempts. If a person can detach himself emotionally from everything he does, he will find himself capable of living completely in the moment. Everything tried, then, will be done more efficiently.

What is non-attachment? It means not accepting anything as truly one's own. Everything that you may think of as your own is yours *only on loan*. When, nightly, you build that mental bonfire that I suggested, cast into it, *from your heart*, every branch and twig of thought of possessing anything. Try to burst out of the cocoon of self-definitions, of personal associations in life. Tell yourself, "Everything in my life, even my very self, belongs to you, O Lord."

Non-attachment above all means, in a practical daily sense, the principle of *nishkam karma*, defined in the Bhagavad Gita as giving to God the fruits of everything one does, and everything to which one even aspires. However, "giving" is a tricky word. In the sense usually understood, whatever we give, we give *away*. Don't give your life to God in the sense of abandoning to Him all further responsibility for what you do. Act always in a spirit of being committed to what should be, for all that, *impersonal* duty. Thus, when offering the fruits of an act to God, don't relinquish further interest in it, but offer only the outcome to Him, giving Him the final decision in the matter. Meanwhile, *share* with Him everything you do.

When saying "grace" before meals, offer your food up to God not in the sense of giving it away: *share with Him*, rather, your enjoyment of it. When you see something beautiful, share with Him the joy you feel in that beauty. His joy within you will, in time, become your very definition of every experience.

One lifetime passes by so quickly. The wheel of rebirth turns slowly, however, and is studded with nails of sorrow and grief. Many incarnations are required for the soul to pass through this "vale of tears" ere one attains freedom at last in the Infinite. Meanwhile, the Law of Karma works hand-in-hand with another principle: *dwaita*, duality. Every fulfillment is sooner or later canceled out by a disappointment; every success, by a failure; every joy, by a sorrow; every "up" by a corresponding "down." Isn't it ironic, that even after countless incarnations we can never win this game? The sum total of all our striving ends always—must end—in that final cipher: ZERO!

Why cling so desperately to what must be lost anyway? All things pass in time. *You alone, in your soul-essence, are what remains eternally.* Why not live more, *from today onward,* in your inner Self? All else is only a dream. Life follows life, each one seeming so real—until the "grim reaper," death, comes to end it. Death, too, moreover, wakes us only from that fleeting "dream within a dream": it doesn't wake us from the dream of delusion. Why not make a serious effort, now, to awaken from the eons-long sleep of cosmic delusion? Realize that nothing of this world holds any lasting significance—not for you; not for anybody.

Old age, and also lingering illness at any age that bears the possibility of death: these are the best times, for those who have been dilatory in their self-preparation, to start "cramming" for that final exam. At these times, particularly, people may tend to withdraw passively into themselves. In the astral world after death, such a negative withdrawal prior to death produces "postmortem" passivity. If, owing to your good deeds (especially to whatever meditation you've practiced), you are conscious enough to enjoy your astral sojourn, that process of sinking into the death sleep will leave you incapable, even after you've re-awakened in the astral world, of making further spiritual progress there. You will enjoy that existence, if your soul rises, but your sojourn there will endure only as long as permitted by your good karma. You will not be able to engage actively enough in that existence to make a positive effort toward spiritual advancement. Or, perhaps, you will simply not feel the incentive to develop further, since life on that plane will seem to you so idyllic, as a temporary visitor, that you will feel no aspiration toward anything higher.

It may be mentioned here, incidentally, that desires for beautiful and uplifting sensory experiences, such as inspiring music and bucolic earthly scenes, can be fulfilled also in the astral realm.

I once read about the near-death experience of a would-be suicide, who (fortunately for her) failed in that attempt. She revived from that experience, but described a very different world from anything like heaven. Until then, she had always enjoyed "rock" music. During her temporary sojourn in the other world, however, she found herself in a place where the predominant vibration resembled that of rock music. She beheld everyone around her steeped in a self-enclosed darkness and misery. Shafts of loving light from above bestirred one soul or another from time to time. Many, however, had been there in that astral dungeon for a very long time—centuries, even, judging from the clothing they wore.

This woman, after her revival, devoted herself to traveling about, warning people no longer to indulge their taste for rock music. Any music that projects a low vibration—not only rock music, but any dance or other music that emphasizes a heavy downbeat, affirms ego-consciousness. Rock 'n' roll, particularly, vibrates with certain lower astral regions. It is easy to see that indulging the taste for it can suck one down after death to heavily ego-affirming regions.

Enjoyment in the higher, beautiful astral realms also may last for many earth years, even for centuries. It depends on a person's good karma. When this period of karmic respite ends, however, any latent material desires one has will reawaken in him, and will draw him to be reborn here on earth, or on some other planet in the material universe.

A belief common in some parts of the world is that the soul's return to earth can be quite haphazard. One may, according to that belief, be reborn in other-than-human forms: as animals, birds, or even insects. ("Don't for heaven's sake squash that spider: It may have been your mother!") Paramhansa Yogananda, fortunately, declared that the likelihood of coming back as anything other than human is so remote as to be almost discounted, especially by one who is spiritually aware enough to be concerned about this matter. Admittedly, rebirth in a lower form *can* happen, but it occurs only to those with very heavy materialistic karma. When it does occur, the fall, usually, is only for one lifetime, and involves only a short, not a long step downward in evolution.

Deeper falls are much rarer, and occur only in the case of very hardened sinners. Those who are sufficiently evolved to have lived a heavenly existence before returning to earth are reborn into a good family, whose influence will help to hasten the soul's upward evolution.

Every return to human life is, however, fraught with woeful uncertainties. The discriminating person, dreading the danger of any further delay, will do everything he can to break out of his earthly fetters *now* and forever. Indeed, consider just one danger: Even for reincarnated yogis, there is always the possibility of a karmic detour. Consider, moreover, the time one wastes spiritually while passing through infancy, childhood, and adolescence, and afterward perhaps getting enmeshed in further worldly involvements! These alone are major hazards on the course of life! Sooner or later one's good karma draws him back to the spiritual quest, but *how* soon? or *how* late? We have every incentive to start as early as possible, while still we inhabit these present bodies, to prepare for our "final exam."

Throughout life, and particularly in old age or during prolonged illness, but whenever a person feels a special impetus to start "cramming" for his own exam, he can do certain things to make his present existence spiritually fruitful. From this point on, therefore, I'm going to address you, the reader, as much as possible in the second person, for my hope is to inspire you to take very personally the thoughts I offer here.

Check List

1. Life Review: Go over your life up to the present moment. Concentrate on the happy times, rather than on the sad, since positive expectations will be more likely to attract

you to a happy state after death. Still, do not avoid reflecting on the mistakes you may have made. Try, instead, to view those mistakes positively. Bear also in mind the following important points:

a) Feelings of guilt will hinder you from making further progress, acting as affirmations of failure. Cast guilt, therefore, from your heart. You might even say to God frankly, "It's *You* who set up this shadow show! It isn't entirely *my* fault that, through inexperience, I didn't know where the pitfalls lay!"

A certain Catholic saint (I forget her name) had many visions of people "on the other side." Often those she saw, unknown to her, were later verified as having actually lived here on earth. What struck me particularly about her visions was the astonishingly large number who had gone to hell, or purgatory, for what seemed to me trivial faults. Some of them had been nuns on earth, living spiritually dedicated lives. How could such devout souls have possibly sunk so low? That saint said it was because they held feelings of guilt. Yet in each case I read about, the guilt was for some surely minor sin, an example being disobedience to a monastic superior! How could such a "sin" have brought such people of clear spiritual commitment to that low state? The explanation can only be that they'd been so shamed and shunned for their "sins" that they died feeling overburdened by this guilt.

I remember a student of Paramhansa Yogananda's, Mr. Ernest Brockway, a very dignified gentleman, a retired architect. I visited him in the hospital only days before his death. As he lay helpless, his outward awareness waning, I heard him mutter sadly, "I've done many wrong things in my life!" Later I mentioned those words to my Guru, who responded sadly, "He shouldn't have said that."

I have another sad recollection of that hospital episode: a hospital orderly burst briefly into the room, "Is there anything you'd like, Ernie?" To me, a friend of the patient, his name was, "Mr. Brockway." It appalled me to hear him addressed so familiarly by a virtual stranger. It seems to me, as much so now as it did then, that we should all behave toward one another—and toward ourselves as well—with dignity. Are we not divine souls, made in God's image? Our true status is forever holy.

Confession and final absolution may be a good thing, if they leave the penitent feeling truly released from his sins. What worries me about this death rite is that it may leave some persons reflecting on their past sins, newly brought back to their remembrance, and old familiarity with them reaffirmed, rather than soaring in the feeling of mental release. Indeed, is one not likely to think, afterward, "Did I remember to confess *all* my sins? And was I, in every case, sufficiently contrite?" Doing so would make him, again, dwell on negative issues in his past instead of helping him to soar into the inner light.

Surely it is better to make one's confession to God, and to ask *Him* directly for *His* forgiveness. Even then, I wonder how adequate it is to seek forgiveness. God is stuck with us anyway—one might say, whether He likes it or not! We are a part of His eternal consciousness. Why not say to God, simply, "Take me as I am, Lord. I know, now, that I want you alone."

My Guru once scolded a disciple, who then asked him, "But Sir, you *will* forgive me, won't you?" The Master replied with astonishment, "What else can I do?"

One time, fearing the possibility that the soul may experience eternal destruction, I questioned my Guru on this point. His answer was categorical: "The soul is a part of God. No part of God can *ever* be destroyed." The soul simply cannot be damned either, for all eternity! Our final destiny is immutable: Sooner or later, we *must* all be saved, even if it takes us aeons.

OF COURSE God forgives you! Your need is only to forgive yourself!

Go over your past mistakes, then, and mentally offer them up to God. Don't view them as "sins," for they were committed in ignorance of the true state of things. God alone dreamed your existence, and infused into you from the beginning the delusion of ego-identity. View whatever mistakes you've committed as having been made *by Him*, through your own dream-existence!

Here's one way to do it: Think of everything that seems to you attractive. Next, withdraw your energy from that attraction, and concentrate inwardly on the superior appeal of soul-bliss. Bliss is the higher, the true alternative to every outward attraction. In soul-bliss—yes, even in the anticipation of it—notice how sensory attractions, by comparison, simply disappear. You will find it relatively easy, at this point in your reflections, to offer up lesser attractions to God.

If you remember having ever hurt anybody, or perhaps having acted unjustly toward him, mentally send him blessings. Visualize him (or her) floating in the ocean of God's bliss.

If ever you've desecrated your own higher self-image, face that memory frankly, but calmly and dispassionately. Don't seek justification for your mistakes. And don't beat yourself mentally and emotionally for having done wrong. Rather, say to God, "It was You, Lord, acting through my ignorance. Come fully, now, into that experience. I want to share it with You, that I may understand fully that it *was*, really, You: Your energy, which I directed wrongly by my folly. I won't cling to that folly any longer. I release it! I watch it evaporating in skies of Infinite Bliss! Help me to see the truth: Compared to Your light, my folly has been empty darkness, forever foreign to my true Self."

If ever you have spoken or acted inconsiderately toward another human being, even perhaps only in haste, recreate that scene in your mind, and then ask God to bless everyone whom you may ever have hurt. Project rays of love and bliss outward from your heart to all who have ever had to bear the brunt of your anger, impatience, unkindness, or cruelty.

If ever you've held a negative thought toward anyone, send him blessings to replace those disturbing vibrations. Raise your feelings to a level where you find yourself thinking of that person with kindness. Don't imagine it is sufficient merely to *forgive* him, with the lingering thought that he *needs* forgiveness. Send him supportive thoughts, rather, and tell him mentally, "It is your job, not mine, to work out whatever problems you have. For my part, I wish you strength, happiness, and wisdom, for we are fellow pilgrims on the long journey to eternal bliss in God, our common Father."

If in any way you've ever cheated anyone or deprived him of his just dues, ask God to bless that person; send him also your own blessings. It might even help both of you to pray that he be reimbursed out of any store of good karma you have accumulated, yourself.

If ever you've spoken critically of, or mocked anyone, even mentally, offer him now your heartfelt kindness and good wishes for his eventual wisdom and inner freedom.

If ever you've acted in any such way as to cause you embarrassment, laugh happily with God, now, over that moment of folly. Share it with Him as a good joke. Tell Him, "I've learned something from that experience. Please though, Lord, don't let me make such a fool of myself ever again!"

b) Remember this: Every desire must be fulfilled. My Guru once made that statement to me. I asked him, "*Every* desire? Even for something so trivial as an ice cream cone?" His answer surprised me; it was quite definite, delivered without even a smile. "Oh, *yes!*" he insisted. Don't try, however, to search out every fleeting wish you may have had.

(That process might take forever!) Rather, make a sweeping overview of your life, and say, simply, "It is all Yours, Lord. I want only Thee now, nothing but Thee!"

As a new monk at SRF, I heard about a fellow disciple who, at the end of her life, was blessed to be able to linger on consciously for two weeks. That respite gave her the time she needed to review her life carefully, and to let go of everything, mentally. Years later, someone who had known her told me, "I could see her telling herself day after day, 'This desire doesn't matter to me anymore,' and, 'I no longer feel that attachment.' Every day she looked freer, more centered in the Self. At the moment of death she cried out with deep joy, 'Swamiji is here!' [Swamiji was what the disciples used to call our Guru.] At that point, she left her body."

Go mentally over every desire in your heart, and offer it to God. Think of the higher, spiritual counterpart of the fulfillment promised by that desire. If, for instance, you've had a desire for a car, don't merely tell yourself, "I won't be needing a car anymore where I'm going." Say, rather, "Now I will be flying in heavenly freedom through vast skies of eternal bliss!"

If your desire was for—yes, let's say it, for an ice cream cone!—remember these words, addressed to me by Anandamayee Ma (a wonderful woman saint whom I knew in India). Speaking with a radiant smile, as she was giving me a little box of sweetmeats, she said, "*Sabsomoy mishti khao*—Always eat only sweetness!"

If your desire was for a mate, offer that desire up to God and pray for the supreme bliss of eternal union with Him.

If you've ever desired to go anywhere or to see anything, tell God, "Let me soar in Infinity, enjoying Thee everywhere, and in everything!"

If your desire was to do something, tell God, "In infinite consciousness, I will accomplish *everything*!"

Mostly, dwell on happy thoughts. Tell yourself, and tell God, "This life has been a dance in Your bliss. Even the hard tests You've sent me have helped me. I've learned so much from them; I'm grateful for all of them; they have given me priceless insights. But now, Lord, I offer everything up to You. It was Your life I lived, not mine. Let me rest eternally, from now on, in Your love."

2. If you feel any attachments, visualize a cord leading out to them from your heart. With a sharp knife mentally sever that cord, or—if it seems thick—hack at it with an axe. Feel every attachment being cut off, leaving you with the blessing of inner freedom.

3. Dwell on the thought of that freedom: freedom from all delusion, all desire, all attachment, and at last of every self-definition. Above all—if you are able to do so—rid yourself of the thought of any personal, separate, individual identity. You are a ray of God's light. See your little sense of reality becoming absorbed in His infinite bliss.

4. Listen, when you can, to spiritual recordings, whether of music, of lofty, God-affirming mantras, or of God-reminding thoughts. Listen to someone's voice chanting *AUM*, or reciting selected scriptural passages. Select voices that seem, to you, to express higher consciousness.

5. Dwell on thoughts of God's eternal love for you, and for all creatures. Dwell more on His forgiveness: on His utter *acceptance* of you as, through all eternity, His very own.

6. Pray for all beings. Bless them in God's light. Send them His love. Reflect that everyone on earth, no matter how deeply deluded he may be, is, in his own way, seeking eternal bliss. Reflect also that it is *everyone's destiny* to find that bliss, no matter how long a journey it is. *All* beings, equally, are children of the same one Light, Love, and Bliss that Jesus Christ knew, and Krishna (Christna), and Buddha, and all saints and masters. It is the underlying nature of **YOUR OWN, ETERNAL SELF!**

Questions and Answers

1. **Q.** Is the "postmortem passivity" you mentioned necessarily a bad thing?

A. No, not necessarily *bad*. It gives souls the rest and respite they need, if that is all they want. If you want to keep on advancing spiritually, however, your consciousness must be fired with determination. It cannot be passive.

2. **Q.** If someone sinks into a coma, or seems perhaps dead already, might it help him to chant *AUM* in his presence?

A. Yes, definitely. Chant softly, especially in the right ear. Yogananda said the sense of hearing is the last to go. A person may appear dead, but may not yet have withdrawn completely from the body. By chanting *AUM*, or by calling to him in the right ear, you may actually bring him back to life.

Yogananda told of two students of his during his early years in America. One of them, a young woman, died, at least apparently. Her brother, also a student of this path, urgently called to her in her right ear: "Sister, come back! I'm not ready for you to leave me. I need you. *Please* come back to me!"

A minute or so later she actually opened her eyes. "I heard you calling to me," she said, "as if from a great distance!" She continued to live a long time.

3. **Q.** Is there anything else we can do to help someone who is dying?

A. Yes. Place your finger on his forehead at a point midway between the eyebrows. This is the seat of will power, concentration, and ecstasy in the body. Direct energy through your finger to that point, and try to draw that person's energy up in focus there.

At death, people usually sink back passively into unconsciousness. Thus, they leave their bodies, as they first entered them, through the medulla oblongata. Next, they pass through what the Greeks called "the waters of Lethe": forgetfulness of this life. Remembrance may return to some extent later on, but generally speaking people simply pass on from there to a new life.

Yogananda said also that our loved ones may come to us in dreams. He shared with us an account of the mother of a disciple of his who had died of breast cancer. He sought this soul out in the astral world. As he related to us later, "I saw her being led away by an angel. She was pausing for a moment, admiring a beautiful flower. I called to her, and she turned around. At first she didn't recognize me. I touched her on the forehead, and then she exclaimed, 'I remember! I remember! Oh, I'll never forget you again.'"

4. Q. How much effort should be expended toward keeping a dying person alive?

A. It is, of course, right to try to save him. I consider it a wrong, however, to resort to what are termed "heroic efforts" to save people.

My own father suffered a heart attack one year before his actual death. At that time he was mentally adjusted to the thought of going. He said to me, "I've had a good life. I have no regrets. I'm ready to go now, whenever the time arrives."

The doctors, however, then went to "heroic" lengths to keep him alive. That last year, alas, was the most unhappy of my father's life—perhaps the *only* really unhappy time. He could hardly see; his hearing was almost gone; his sense of taste and smell almost vanished. Even his sense of touch was greatly dimmed. How much better it would have been had he died after mentally giving his consent to death!

On the other hand, a friend of mine once asked me, "How much effort should I put forth to remain alive? I feel ready to go at any time." I replied, "Think of what a job it is to be reborn and come back again as a baby, then to grow up, and then take who knows how many years before you remember your spiritual aspiration once again, and decide to take that responsibility seriously. Think of the risks involved, also, of further detours and of consequent pain! I suggest that, as long as you feel able to make a spiritual effort, you do your best to stay alive now and keep working toward your salvation." Fortunately she took my advice, lived several years thereafter, and found that time important for her spiritual growth.

5. **Q.** Many people, when they die, are in great pain. The doctors give them pain medication, but as a result the patients, often, are only barely conscious. Is that a good thing, or a bad?

A. I would say that the greater the extent to which a person is able to retain his consciousness, without requiring sedation, the better.

6. **Q.** What about people who go into a coma before they die? Will they necessarily go out unconsciously?

A. I think it depends primarily on the spiritual effort a person has made during his lifetime. If his effort has been deep and sincere, that final coma will be only temporary, for its cause will be merely physical. As soon as he leaves his body, he will wake up again in his astral form.

7. **Q.** If desires are what bring us back to be reborn on this plane, is it not a mistake also to desire to know God?

A. Of course not! Uplifting desires cannot hold one down. It is desires for the things of this world that keep one bound. Non-egoic desires are called "desireless desires"; they help one to free himself from ego-consciousness, lifting him toward freedom in God.

It is bondage to ego that makes one's desires wrong. They also strengthen one's overall delusion. Specific desires, moreover, determine to a great extent one's next state of existence. As Yogananda put it, "If you die with an attachment to curried food, you may be reborn in India. If as you leave your body you hanker for apple pie, you may be reborn in America." He was speaking also, of course, in a spirit of light humor as well as seriously.

I remember seeing a friend eating curry who had often told me he didn't like it. He explained to me quite seriously, "Master said if we like curry we'll be reborn in India. I'd like to be reborn there, so by eating I'm trying to overcome my distaste for it." I commented, "Such things are determined by many factors. I wouldn't place so much emphasis on this one factor alone!"

8. **Q.** What effect does grieving for a departed person have on his soul?

A. Grief is born of attachment. It can hold the soul back and keep it tied to this earthly plane of existence. Try, instead, to help others on their way by sending them blessings and love, that they soar in divine freedom.

9. **Q.** Will the disciples of a true guru see him on the other side?

A. Our Guru said to a group of us one day, "Those disciples who stick it out to the end—not for just 'sticking it out,' but for the love of God—I myself, or one of the other gurus, will be waiting to welcome them on the other side."

10. **Q.** Is it a good thing to donate one's bodily organs to help others who are still living?

A. In a somewhat abstract sense it would be, of course, a good thing. Death, however, is a sacred occasion. I myself would not want anyone "mucking about" with my organs at that time. A dying person's consciousness doesn't withdraw immediately from his body. The fact that his physical organs still have sufficient vitality in them to be useful to someone else means that the life force has not yet fully withdrawn from them.

11. **Q.** Which is better: cremation, or burial?

A. Generally speaking, cremation is better. In fact, it actually happens occasionally that people return to outward awareness after they've been buried. Think of the horror of waking up in your own coffin, underground! The expression, "He would turn over in his grave if he heard that," is based on the actual fact that corpses have sometimes been found, on exhumation, to have turned over in their graves.

The mother of Robert E. Lee "died" temporarily when still a young woman. The coffin in which she'd been placed was still above ground when she returned to outward consciousness. Beating desperately on the wood, she was heard and hastily rescued. It was, in fact, *after* that event that she gave birth to Robert.

Cremation helps also in breaking attachment to the body. On the other hand, it is better not to cremate enlightened saints. Their physical bodies retain high vibrations that will help anyone praying to them later at their tombs. My Guru said Lahiri Mahasaya's body should not have been cremated, even though he was a householder. (Usually, the bodies of swamis are buried, the rationale being that they've been "cremated" already at the time they took their *sannyas* vows of renunciation.)

12. **Q.** I know suicide is considered a sin. Are there any extenuating circumstances when it might be a virtue?

A. Of course there are! A person may sacrifice his life for a high cause, or to save others, or in expiation for some sin he himself has committed. This last rationale, however, should be reserved for persons of spiritual realization. And it depends always on the motivation behind the deed.

13. **Q.** Can it help those who have died to pray for them?

A. Indeed, yes. It may be good also to pray *to* them. I recall a time, years ago, when it had been my intention to pray for my departed mother on her birthday. When that day came, however, I suffered a sudden episode of very rapid, irregular heartbeats. I found myself praying *to* my mother, instead of *for* her. Help came inwardly, and instantaneously. My mother was a very spiritual woman, but I believe that others who have gone before us may be able to help us also, if we will but ask them.

14. Q. Should one, especially as one grows old, be vigilant about superficial distractions?

A. Yes, certainly so. Many old people waste their days before the television, or playing cards. Television is especially pernicious. I myself never watch it. The thought of all those worldly personalities invading my home and my consciousness with their foolish opinions, attitudes, and vibrations: what an absurd distraction! Yogananda referred to television, in fact, as "satanic."

⸻

In summation, two things will help you especially to prepare for your "final exam":

First, try to avoid as much as possible anything that might have a downward, or even a distracting, influence on your mind. Avoid especially things that might draw your thoughts into negative thoughts and emotions, and toward worldly desires.

Second, surround yourself as much as possible with uplifting, God-reminding influences.

If you follow these simple rules, you will pass your exam with "flying colors" and will find, in doing so, your portal to eternal freedom.

Understanding People

In today's highly mobile world, so many things—places, shops, people—are known only in transit. As people change their homes, their work, and even the cultures surrounding them, it is becoming increasingly rare for them to have intimate relationships with other human beings. Even families often get widely dispersed around their own country, or around the world.

My own parents lived for fifteen years in Romania; I myself called that home for the first thirteen years of my life, though I was also sent off to school in Switzerland for a year and a half, then to England for two years. Meanwhile, we visited relatives in America every three years or so, and they too lived in several parts of the country.

At one point in our adult lives, I lived in Los Angeles; my next younger brother lived in Danbury, Connecticut; my youngest brother lived in Houston, Texas; and our parents lived in Cairo, Egypt. Such is indeed becoming ever-increasingly the normal pattern of life for the world in which we live. Such is this new age of technology.

Even in India, where I now live, I never any longer hear the question I used to be asked when I lived here nearly fifty years ago, "What village do you come from in America?" It is assumed, for one thing, that I probably come from a city, but even that isn't the question. People ask me now, most broadly of all, "Where do you come from?"

And I have to answer, "I'm not sure! Really speaking, I'm a citizen of the world, though the passport I hold is American."

How, given this increasingly normal situation, can we have an in-depth understanding of one another? Our grocers, our shopping malls, our delivery men—almost everyone we meet in our daily lives changes every few years, and for many even every one or two.

A woman, some decades ago, traveled from London, England, to visit the saint Ramana Maharshi in India. She said to him, "I've come a long way to see you!"

"You haven't moved at all," was his startling reply. "The world around you has moved, but your own center has never changed."

Indeed, such is the deeper reality of everything. Centuries ago, people believed the earth to be not only flat, but the center of whatever else there was in the universe. Then Copernicus, and, later, Galileo discovered that our Earth revolves around the sun. Thereafter, and until near the beginning of the twentieth century, people believed that the sun is the center of whatever star system the universe contains. And then, in the twentieth century, astronomers found that all the stars we see at night comprise only the stars nearest to us in a single star system, and that other such systems exist in the universe. When I was a child of eleven, attending school in England, a teacher told me with awe, "Do you realize there are two, and maybe even *three* other whole star systems in existence?!" To both of us it seemed beyond belief.

Nowadays, however, we know that there are some *one or two hundred billion* such systems, which we today call galaxies, and that our own solar system spins around the very outskirts of our own "Milky Way" galaxy.

All this has made man seem very small—indeed, insignificant—compared to the immensity surrounding him. Constantly being uprooted from home and environment has brought us all, increasingly, a sense of our own minuteness, and also our solitude not only in the universe, but on this comparatively little planet of ours, the Earth.

At last, now, we find ourselves returning to what Ramana Maharshi said to that woman: that she hadn't even moved, since she was the center of everything she experienced. This is an ancient teaching in India: "God (and all manifested reality) *is center everywhere, circumference nowhere.*" God creates in a way mankind cannot: *from within.* Man, by contrast, is forced to create from without. But God starts with a little seed, then expands outward from that point. Plant fibers are hollow at their center, permitting the life force to flow through them to their farthest extremities.

Mankind, similarly, is being returned forcibly to his own center of being. Yogis and other mystics tell us, "Go within, if you would know the truth."

We must go within even more especially if we would know ourselves. If we would understand others, moreover, we should make an effort to relax, first, at our own center, and then to try to relate to others each at *his own* center. We can understand everything better, the better we understand ourselves. We can even learn new languages more easily if we try first to understand them *at their centers, from our own centers.*

In my own lifetime of considerable travel, I have had to learn some nine languages, of which I have lectured in five or six. My way of learning them has been, first, by thinking of myself as belonging to those countries. I was merely "brushing up," so to speak, on what were, for that time, my own languages. Strange-seeming sentence structures no longer seemed strange to me, for I sensed as if intuitively their inherent logic. Attunement with the mental outlook of those peoples made it relatively easy for me to imitate their accents—so much so, that the natives of those countries have often assumed I was their own countryman.

With other people, then, the way to understand them deeply is to relate to each of them *at his own center.*

Other tricks for understanding people are easier to adopt in this age of great mobility, where so many relationships are, perforce, transient. Let me list a few:

1. Never judge anyone. Accept all as they are.

2. Realize that each person has a duty to change and improve himself. To do so is not *your* responsibility.

3. Love them as extensions of your own self. We may think of each person as specializing, on behalf of the whole human race, in being, simply, himself.

4. Develop a sense of humor, first as regards your own foibles, and second as regards the foibles of others.

5. Don't accept error when you see it, but accept simply that people do make mistakes. (Haven't you yourself made a fair share of them?) Thus, love people not *for* their faults, but in spite of them, and because everyone is trying, each in his own way, to find his way around or out of his own pits of error.

6. While relating to others at their centers, see their faults and difficulties with sympathetic understanding. Then, if you are so inspired, *encourage them from their own point of view* to change and improve themselves.

7. Look upon other people as friends and acquaintances of yours whom you may have known in past incarnations, and some of them perhaps closely and dearly. It is, indeed, probable that you have known many of them before. For we live a vast number of lives on earth (and also, my Guru said, on other planets in the universe). For myself it often seems, when I am in a crowd, that everyone is an old friend of mine.

8. Whether or not they are your friends from before, God in His infinity is omnipresent. He therefore resides in everyone—*as* everyone See all whom you meet as expressions of our one common Father/Mother God.

9. Be strict in practicing the moral principle of *ahimsa*, or harmlessness. Never wish harm to anyone or to any crea-

ture—nor even (if you are deep in this practice) to any *thing*. Automatically, as you continue this practice, you will find yourself wishing everybody well.

10. Never covet another's property. Wish everyone happiness in his possessions, and in his ideas and inspirations.

11. Dismiss from your mind the thought of personal attachment to anything. Thus, when dealing with others, you will find you have no ulterior motives to warp your understanding of them and of the situations involving you and them.

12. Never view anyone with the thought of needing or desiring anything from him. Give him perfect freedom, mentally, simply to be himself, and to be complete in himself.

13. Be ever truthful and sincere—first of all with yourself, and then with everyone you meet.

14. Live in the thought of God's loving, blissful presence within you. Next, try, when in the company of others, to share with them His inner bliss.

15. Never tell yourself, regarding anyone else's shortcomings, "I could *never* be like that!" The sad fact is, you could be. We *all* have the potential to be like anyone on earth, from the most debased to the most saintly. Every delusion to which mankind is heir is, symbolically at least, the error of every human being. Be compassionate, therefore. Pray inwardly to God never to let you fall into that error again. For who knows what mistakes you may have committed yourself—perhaps in the far distant past.

16. Smile at others when it seems right to do so. Smile *with* them, not only *at* them. Let your smile be not only with your lips, but from your heart. Let it rise from there to shine out through your eyes.

17. Laugh *with* others, never *at* them.

18. When others grieve, never withhold your sympathy from them, but, instead of grieving with them, try to give them your heartfelt joy.

19. When others tell you of their troubles, try gently to steer them in the direction of finding possible solutions.

As you follow the above principles, your own inner understanding may suggest to you countless other ways of recognizing your own broader reality, which dwells within other people also. Seek ways, then, to befriend and help them. All creatures, indeed—each one in his, her, or its own way—are parts of your own one, greater Being.

THE GREAT DELUSIONS

Delusions are not, from a spiritual viewpoint, those individual aberrations which sometimes get one committed into a mental asylum. Personal mental twists of that kind might rather be called "illusions." Delusions, on the other hand, affect a wide range of humanity to the point where they are all but universal. There may exist planets in the universe on which the residents are so sane that a vast majority of earth's inhabitants would, by comparison, be considered crazy! With nearly everyone around us crazy in some way, however, we must simply accept that this world is, itself, a kind of madhouse!

A delusion, then, is a widespread misperception of the actual state of things. Purely subjective delusions may, as I've said, be called instead, by contrast, *illusions*.

A delusion signifies addiction to anything that promises happiness or fulfillment of some kind, but that always ends by bringing disappointment. Delusions are consistent in one thing only: They invariably break their promises.

In America many years ago I met a man from Calcutta who remarked to me, "Americans pride themselves on their freedom from superstition. But can any superstition be greater than this one, which I find almost universal here: the expectation of deriving happiness from mere things?" (Nowadays, unfortunately, that "superstition" is rampant in India also!)

What I have called the Great Delusions are classically three in number: wine, money, and sex. To that standard grouping I am inclined to add another two: the desire for power, and for fame.

Wine includes any intoxicant whose effect on human awareness is depressing or deadening, and addictive. "Wine" doesn't include medication—anaesthesia, for example, which is necessary in operations—nor the medicines people take to reduce severe physical pain. Even pain medication, however, can become addictive if its use is prolonged. That is its chief danger in every case. *Addiction* can occur even with pain killers (this is certainly true of intoxicants) and is the most particular danger of drinking any form of alcohol. Moreover, although some people claim that marijuana and various other hallucinogenic drugs are non-addictive, indulgence in them carries with it at least the danger of psychological addiction.

Anything that dulls one's awareness should, if possible, be shunned by all who aspire to superconscious awareness and inner, soul-freedom. What makes such things delusions is that they promise escape from reality by numbing one's awareness of it. Such a "way out" is no better than the legendary way of the ostrich, which is said to hide its head in the sand at any approach of danger.

People will often, for the same reason, seek refuge in sleep. Some people, again for the same reason, commit suicide. In every case, when people try to escape objective reality by merely avoiding it, they must return sooner or later to the very circumstances which they hoped to escape. Intoxicants, however, since they *are* (as the word implies) toxic, reduce one's ability ever to relate realistically to objective circumstances. For when people recover from their alcoholic hangovers, they find themselves *less* able than before to cope with their difficulties, which they must still face.

The spiritual path, on the other hand, far from being an escape *from* reality, offers the only way out of Delusion itself, and *to* the only abiding reality there is.

Many people, of course, take alcoholic drinks not to deaden their awareness, but simply to be sociable, or for the stimulation they say it gives them. J.C. Bose, the great Bengali scientist, noted that the effect of poison, too, though it kills when taken in larger doses, may be stimulating if taken in small amounts. Any stimulant, however, since it is imposed on the body from without rather than generated inwardly by an affirmation of will power, brings one under the sway of duality. In its outwardness it is a part of cosmic law, which governs the manifested universe. Raising one's spirits by artificial means leads *inevitably* to their becoming correspondingly *lowered*, later on. As with every emotional "high," artificial stimulants cause—they cannot but do so— a neutralizing "low" afterward.

It is a mistake, therefore, to take alcoholic drinks even socially. And although the negative effects of light drinking may not be immediately noticeable, they will become so, in time. It is well, therefore, to heed from the beginning the wise counsel of sages, rather than cater to passing social fads. Reflect on how enslaved most of society is by countless misconceptions concerning the right way to live.

A student of Paramhansa Yogananda's heeded for a time the Guru's counsel that she give up drinking alcoholic beverages. After a few weeks, however, finding it socially inconvenient to abstain from alcohol altogether, she began drinking a little beer or wine at parties. A few weeks later, after church, she saw the Master again. He looked at her sternly and, without preamble, said, "I meant *all* alcoholic beverages!"

There is another point to keep in mind: Anyone who was addicted to alcohol in his last incarnation may, in this lifetime, find himself plunged into that addiction with the very first alcoholic drink he ever takes. (Medical doctors have noted this fact, although, of course, they attribute it to some "chemical imbalance" in the body.)

Intoxicants of all kinds promise something they *never* deliver: higher awareness, relief from (or immunity to) suffering, and happiness.

A number of ways might be suggested for overcoming alcoholic addiction. Most of them lie outside the scope of this article, but one brief story might be helpful. It concerns something else that Paramhansa Yogananda said: "If you have an addiction to any false pleasure, substitute for it another habit that will give you greater and truer satisfaction. If you've developed a taste, for example, for bad cheese, develop an opposite taste for good cheese!"

I met a man many years ago in San Diego who told me an interesting story in this regard. "I used," he said, "to be an alcoholic. When I met the Master (Yogananda), I was inspired under his tutelage to seek God. Hoping for the best, I took Kriya Yoga initiation from him. My friends made fun of me for doing so, saying, 'How can you make this important commitment, when you can't even commit yourself to staying off the bottle?' I answered them, 'I can't help my addiction, but *at least* I can, at the same time, do something positive to offset it.' And so, as I sat down each day for meditation, I would hold my Kriya beads in one hand, and a glass of whiskey in the other. Finally the day came when, halfway through my Kriyas, I thought, 'I'm getting so much satisfaction from doing Kriya, what do I want with this silly drink?' I put the glass aside, and have never touched another drop of alcohol since then."

⸺◈⸺

The next of the Great Delusions is money. Money is not, as tradition tells us, "the root of all evil," for we need it in countless situations of life. In this sense, indeed, money itself may be called (again to use an expression of Yogananda's) a "necessary necessity." We should try, therefore, to make good use of it. Money itself isn't the problem. Rather, people's problem is their *desire for money*. This desire may indeed be called "the root of all evil."

Money never, *in itself*, gives happiness. In itself, indeed, money isn't even attractive—especially after it has received too much handling! Happiness can't be derived from anything we buy with money, either. The desire for money itself is a principal delusion for the simple reason that it offers endless opportunities for satisfying the desire for everything we hope (falsely) will bring us happiness.

Rich people, unless they are free from personal attachment to wealth and use their money primarily to help others, are seldom happy. Indeed, they have been found statistically to be less happy even than poor people. The possession of wealth opens up the possibility of "satisfying" an almost limitless number of desires. The rich person is likely to devote himself to looking around for "what more" possessions and exciting experiences he can accumulate to make him even happier (though happiness, so far, has already eluded him completely!). The law that governs desires was put succinctly by my Guru: "Desires," he said, "ever* gratified, are never satisfied." The converse is true also, though less absolutely so: "Never gratified, ever satisfied."

———※———

What about the third of the Great Delusions: sexual desire?

Sex attraction was placed in mankind by Nature to ensure the continuation of the species. The sex nerves are located at that part of the body (the bottom of the spine) where two important spinal nerves, the *iḍa* and the *pingala*,

---

* In the sense of "always."

conjoin. In the practice of Kriya Yoga, the devotee learns gradually to neutralize the flow through these superficial outward nerves. If the descending current through *pingala* can be drawn inward as it reaches the base of the spine, and from there brought upward through the deep spine (the *sushumna*), true spiritual awakening begins. Otherwise—and this is true for the great majority of people—that downward current through *pingala* coincides with a more superficial sense of withdrawal into the ego-self. The downward movement coincides with disappointment, or with the feeling of wanting personal reassurance, comfort, and satisfaction.

Any withdrawal into one's egoic self acts as a stimulus, at that point, to the sex nerves. It is no accident that people tend to enjoy sex at the time also when they are preparing to fall asleep.

Interestingly, masculine energy is more specifically related to the rising energy through *ida*, and feminine energy more to the descending energy through *pingala*. Thus, in the Biblical story of the Garden of Eden, it was Eve who tempted, and Adam who responded to that temptation. Had her energy flowed inward into the deep spine, instead of outward in dualistic reaction to Adam, the two of them would have continued to live in the inner paradise of soul-consciousness. Instead, because most women try to draw men's attention to themselves, and because most men respond by letting themselves be drawn (to be fair, it is often the men themselves who extend the first invitation), the dance of duality continues. Duality is indeed, as I said, the basis on which the entire universe was created. *Maya*, too, makes women specially attractive to men, and gives men a different appearance to which women, too, are attracted.

What is delusive about sexual attraction, as such, is above all its reaffirmation of ego-consciousness. Men and women, feeling a natural attraction to one another, and trying to attract each other as their sexual opposites, hold particularly to the thought, "I—you." That thought "I" predominates, of course: "*I* want something from *you*." For the devotee, who wants to know God, ego is the supreme delusion he needs to overcome. Ego is the post to which every other delusion is tied. As long as we engage in any activity, even if only of thought, and do so with ego-commitment, we will find it difficult to escape from ego-consciousness.

Most people, of course, are not prompted anyway by high spiritual aspiration. Even so, they must face the fact that, until ego-attachment is overcome, it will pursue them throughout their lives like a veritable Hound of the Baskervilles, and will bring them constantly renewed suffering.

Sex is, indeed, the greatest delusion of all. Indulgence in it is physically and mentally debilitating—especially so for men, but also, in time and particularly with over-indulgence, for women. It keeps one's energy firmly locked at the base of the spine, whereas the universal ideal for humanity is to raise the energy toward the Christ center between the eyebrows. The higher one's consciousness is centered in the spine, the greater one's inner contentment, freedom, and happiness. Sex, however, binds people's consciousness, in a way that no other delusion does, to constant thoughts of lower fulfillment, even if the possibility for such fulfillment occurs only intermittently.

It has been said that the average person thinks in one way or another about sex at least once every five minutes.

Sexual indulgence prematurely ages people. It prevents them from exercising fine discrimination, and from enjoying finer esthetic pleasures. Worst of all, however, as I said, it binds people firmly to the post of ego-consciousness.

The difficulty involved in overcoming sex-consciousness is more than compensated for by the freedom attendant upon inner conquest. The benefits that result from this conquest are:

a) greater energy;

b) greatly increased inner happiness;

c) great inner freedom;

d) better health;

e) much greater mental clarity;

f) an ability to give love equally to all; and

g) joy.

How can one overcome this natural urge? Not by shame, nor by disgust or any other negative attitude toward it. One must learn to see it as a perfectly natural function, placed there by Nature to ensure the continuance of the species. Indeed, were it not for the urge itself, no one would feel any attraction in what would seem in that case an undeniably sordid activity. The way out of it, however, is first to think of it as a holy act—one, however, which can be transcended by even greater holiness in the thought of God.

The next thing is to be more impersonal in one's behavior toward others, especially those of the opposite sex. I have said elsewhere in these essays that to be impersonal does not mean to be cold. One can be very kind in one's treatment of others, wishing only the best for them. The important thing is not to want anything from them for oneself.

The next most important thing is to recognize and accept that a natural magnetism exists between men and women. It can affect them, in one another's company, even if they are physically blind. The principal conduits for this magnetism—principal, because they awaken awareness of it most instantly—are the eyes, and the sense of touch. It would not be realistic to tell men and women to stop mixing with one another, though this is possible, and indeed ideal, for monks and nuns. However, if anyone wishes to rise above this instinct, or at any rate to keep it under control, he should avoid gazing too closely into the eyes of persons of the other sex.

In countries where an exaggerated effort is made to keep women segregated from men—in Arab countries, for example—all the reports one reads is that enforced segregation only fans the flame of desire. It is much easier to keep the natural sex impulse under control if one allows a little steam to escape out of the boiler, so to speak, by treating it naturally, without undue emphasis.

One may, and in fact many do, scoff at the existence of this attraction simply because he (or she) meets so many of the other sex who exercise for him/her no attraction at all. Nevertheless, and even if one feels no attraction for most such people, one must beware the fact that an affectionate relationship may exist from past lives between certain people. That sense of special bond may awaken within him (or her) at any time.

Is there an age when the attraction is, or becomes, lessened? My Guru said, "No age. It is always present, until with God's grace one has truly overcome it." A sister-in-law of mine once mentioned to me that her little daughter, aged about three, had a special giggle she reserved just for little boys. And old people, even when the instinct has become physically dormant, still often show a special affection for young people, especially, of the other sex.

Avoid especially, therefore, the common practice of hugging others or of otherwise touching them unnecessarily. A hug may be only a sign of friendship, but why express feeling for anyone through such a volatile sense: that of touch?

Only as one advances spiritually does he or she find complete immunity, and even then one must be careful until the state of *nirbikalpa samadhi* is attained.

Only persons of really base consciousness, of course, see sexual attraction solely in the light of the physical act itself. Most people mix comfortably with everyone while seldom holding such a thought. Still, one who wants to rise above an attraction which in any case increases ego-bondage in everyone, should be inwardly aware of the power of this delusion.

The best way, for most people, is to limit the field for themselves by monogamous marriage. Only when one can mix with relative freedom from any thought that sexual differences exist does he find it easy not to be drawn downward by this universally "greatest delusion," as my Guru called it.

—⊷—

Beyond these three Great Delusions, there are other major ones that might be included. Supreme among them is the craving for power. What makes this craving a delusion is, again, the accompanying affirmation of ego-consciousness. *All* delusions, indeed, endanger one's peace of mind, strengthen the ego, and deepen one's sense of isolation from others and from any sense he might otherwise have of support from the universe. The desire for power may be less obvious than the first three Great Delusions, but with many people this desire, too, is obsessive. Indeed, in our present technological age, the desire for power is, if anything, growing in strength as the number of opportunities increase for achieving it.

Power might be compared to the manipulation of chessmen on a chess board. There is this important difference, however: a chess player may preen himself on winning a game, but the manipulation of people from one post to another awakens also in the manipulator the thought of *controlling* them. This thought obliges one constantly to reaffirm his own egoic consciousness.

A true leader views his position as an opportunity to *serve* others. He therefore identifies himself with those whom he leads; the thought of serving them lessens any sense of separation from them that he may feel owing to ego-consciousness. If, however, a person exults in exerting power over others, he will *necessarily* think in terms of forcing them to obey him. This expansion of ego-identity is quite the opposite of the spiritual practice of expanding one's consciousness to a sense of oneness with all humanity and with all life. Power perforce, therefore, increases a person's ego-consciousness, and makes it all the more difficult for him to broaden his spiritual identity.

<hr>

Last, I'll mention a delusion that is actually three delusions in one—"packaged" together, so to speak. They come under the general heading of dependence on the good opinion of others. This little bundle of delusions combines the craving for recognition, for fame, and for worldly prominence. Anyone who harbors any of these three cravings will seek support from others for his ego, rather than developing confidence in his own inner Self.

To be centered in the inner Self is the spiritual ideal. To base self-recognition, on the other hand, on the opinions of others is to build a house on shifting sand. The opinions of most people are wrong, anyway! The greatest error in courting their good opinion lies in the fact that such dependence strips away any solid basis one might have for self-understanding. Even when others are right—and especially where their opinions of you yourself are concerned—you should depend even more on your own self-perception before God.

"Praise," Yogananda used to say. "cannot make me any better. Blame cannot make me any worse. I am what I am before my conscience and God."

All delusions suggest distorted images of reality. Worst of all, they make us look for fulfillment to means that always prove to be, in the end, mere shadows. My Guru added this admission, however: "Even shadows may entertain." Still, shadows lack substance. While watching them, we should keep in mind that we are really only entertaining ourselves.

TRUTHFULNESS

"Cretans never tell the truth," was a remark once made by a visitor to Paris. "I ought to know: I am a Cretan." This statement reminds me of the classical Labyrinth in ancient Greece, where lurked in wait the fearful Minotaur, hopeful of seizing and devouring its victims. That maze, too, was on the island of Crete. The statement I've just quoted suggests a different kind of labyrinth: a conundrum from which there is no escape.

Truth does suggest, for many people, a maze of hypotheses, conundrums, and false leads that end always in a blank wall. As Pontius Pilate put it, "What *is* truth?" (John 18:38); his implication was that Absolute Truth probably does not exist. I remember, however, Paramhansa Yogananda's comment on that statement. It especially intrigued me, for to him it demonstrated only the shallowness of pride. Reason, indeed, without the addition of intuitive faith, *is* shallow and *does* induce pride. Any attempt, moreover, to find truth in this world of relativities leads inevitably to the conclusion that nothing, not even the most hypothetically fundamental scientific discovery, can be absolute.

Just consider the following points: This man may be better than that one; if any particular man out of a given lot, however, is the best, who is to say that there will be no one else anywhere, in any other lot, even better? Who can affirm that anyone, in any field, is supremely, absolutely, and unsurpassably the ultimate best?

Again, John may declare, "I am perfectly well!" No one, probably, including John himself, would quite know what he meant by "perfectly," but in any case, it is certainly never possible to be *absolutely* well. Who knows what microbes may be biding their time within even the healthiest body, waiting to wreak their havoc eventually? Harold

Horsey may be a better polo player than Peter Pawn, but Peter, on the other hand, may be able to best Harold at chess. Abstractions like love may not be susceptible to comparisons, but how, in this imperfect world, can even love be expressed absolutely? How can happiness be absolute? Can contentment? In this realm of relativities, it is impossible for *anything* to be absolute.

In this way many people try to justify the outright lies they tell. I caught Jean Paul Sartre in just such a lie,* as I explained in my book, *Out of the Labyrinth*. On the other hand, some lies (not Sartre's, however, who favored the "big lie") might indeed be, in some cases, "perfectly" justifiable. Paramhansa Yogananda offered a few hypothetical situations:

"Suppose," he said, "someone were to approach you and ask you to swear on every scripture you considered holy never to repeat what he was going to tell you, and suppose you consented. Suppose, further, that he then announced, 'I just put a rattlesnake in So-and-So's bed.' What would you do? *Of course* you should reveal such an unholy secret! Not to do so would be sinful. And even though it would also be wrong to break your promise, it would have been still *more* wrong to make it in the first place, without knowing the merits of what you were being asked to conceal. To be faithful to such an oath would only compound your mistake."

Again he said, "Suppose someone were to come rushing up to you pleading for sanctuary, and you hid him in a closet. And then let us say that the men chasing him came to you and demanded to know where he was, or in what direction he had fled. To clarify the issue still further, let us say that

---

* He stated, "Mankind is radically free," and then, making not the slightest effort to prove his premise, went on to make arguments for an entire volume of further unsubstantiated (and "unsubstantiatable") claims, ending by repeating his first claim, "Thus, we see that mankind is radically free."

those men were criminals, and the man to whom you'd granted asylum was innocent of wrongdoing. What would you do?

"Your priority, most certainly, should be to protect the innocent man. In this case—as, of course, in almost all cases—you'd be right to honor your word to him. Your solution, therefore, might be simply to point silently left or right, indicating he'd gone off in that direction. If pressed further, it would even be within the bounds of truthfulness to answer, 'I don't know.' (After all, you couldn't possibly say *exactly where* he was! He might be on the left side of that closet, on the right side, or at the back of it!)

"It would even be justified, as a last resort, to speak an 'unfact,' since this would still, in a deeper sense, be true, or at least not *adharmic* or ethically wrong. You would be morally right, then, in actually *saying to* them, 'He went in that direction.'"

In the story as Master told it, the man who betrayed his supplicant in the name of truthfulness was punished, after death, for having told what was a fact. It had been, in the higher sense, an untruth: harmful, not beneficial. As punishment, the man was given the choice of spending time in hell with ten wise men, or in heaven with ten fools. His sin was that his betrayal of that supplicant had resulted in the man's death.

The Indian scriptures state, "If a duty conflicts with a higher duty, it ceases to be a duty." In God's manifested universe, relativity rules. This being the case, one might wonder why Yogananda even bothered to take issue with that question of Pontius Pilate's ("What *is* truth?"). It can only have been because Pilate presumed to give more importance to reasoning than to the intuitive ability, latent in everybody, to perceive the fundamental Truth of the soul. Isn't this, indeed, what materialistic science does all the time?

People who depend too much on reasoning proclaim boldly that Absolute Truth does not exist. They are, however, merely skating about on the surface of reality. Even

scientists, mistaking endless categories of fact for fundamental truths, are blind compared to the deep wisdom
of great saints and masters, whose realization of Divine
Consciousness as the essential reality is both a fact and a
truth, and one that can be *personally experienced* by all. It is
only, as Yogananda pointed out, in this world of relativities
that there are higher and lower *levels of* reality, and therefore,
in a sense, of truth. The higher truths are those over which
the veil of *maya* (delusion) is thinner and more transparent.

"If you visit a sick friend in the hospital," Yogananda
said, "and find him looking ghastly, ought you to tell him
he looks as though he were at the very portals of death? To
make such a statement might discourage him to the point
where he could actually worsen and die. On the other hand,
even if death does seem to be approaching, ought you to
tell him with a 'beamish' smile, 'Gee, Tom! You're looking
great!'? How could you sincerely make such a statement?
Probably—assuming that you are a sensible, kind human
being—you'll find something positive to say. If you can't
do that, then you'll avoid the subject altogether and tell him
simply how glad you are to see him, perhaps also assuring
him of your prayers. Again, you might say, 'Well, Tom, you
might be a lot worse!' [That is what my Guru once said after
entering the monks' dining room one day, and finding it in
an appalling mess: 'It might be worse.']

"You might even tell him," he said, "if you could do
so sincerely, 'You have it in you to get completely well!' It
would even be good—and, indeed, truthful, provided you
could speak with spiritual power—to voice an *underlying*
truth by affirming the man's soul-potential. Thus, you might
declare with deep concentration, '*You are well!*'"

I used to enjoy, as a child, proposing self-evidently ridiculous reasons to support arguments I knew were obviously
false. I did so not to persuade anyone of the truth of what

I was suggesting, but only to underscore my own awareness of the tricky nature of reason itself. By the same token,
I never accepted reasoning alone as a final proof of anything.
I did, however, accept valid *authority*. Above all, I believed
in the intuitive feeling of "rightness" in my own heart.

In a debating society that I joined temporarily in
college, I won my first (and only) debate by challenging my
opponent for having supported his argument by quoting the
mere opinion of someone who, though famous, lacked any
qualification as an authority on the subject we were debating.
(Our debate was, however, my "swan song" in that society,
from which I soon resigned, for I myself didn't believe the
side I'd been assigned to debate, and was uncomfortable
over my victory.)

When I was a child, I might have said (but—cooks,
please note!—did *not* say!), "Don't give me spinach to eat.
For, consider the expression, 'green with envy.' This means
that green, being the color of envy, may even induce that
quality in people. The darker the green, moreover (and obviously), the more intense the envy. Besides, the slightly bitter
taste of spinach only suggests that any envy it infuses in one
will be all the more bitter. Do you want your son to grow up
bitterly envying others?"

Of course, I wouldn't have believed my argument, and
I knew my mother would have known I didn't believe it.
I would simply have been "having fun." But there was
a serious side to my playfulness. It helped me to keep alive
mentally a distrust of reasoning itself as a final arbiter in
any discussion. "Logic," as the inventor C.F. Kettering put
it well, "is an organized procedure for going wrong with
confidence and certainty." To my mind, an argument had
to go beyond "making sense." (Mother once wrote to our
governess from Italy, where my parents were on vacation,
"Please tell the boys to be good, and that will make everyone

happy including me. Don [meaning me] is sure to find a flaw in that argument, but you might try it, anyway!")

Years later, when I read *Autobiography of a Yogi*, I found in it many accounts of miracles which were utterly beyond anything I'd ever experienced, heard of, or even imagined. The book itself, however, felt so *right* to me that I took the next bus across America and offered myself as the author's disciple. He accepted me, resulting in a complete change in my life, one which, in sixty years, I have never questioned or regretted.

Patanjali, in the *yamas* (the proscriptive principles) of his *Yoga Sutras*, had an interesting way of counseling aspirants to be truthful. Instead of saying, "Be truthful," he wrote, "Avoid *un*truthfulness." What this phrasing of his advice emphasized was that everyone would be truthful naturally if he had no reason to conceal the truth. In other words, it is not so much that truthfulness is a necessary virtue as that *un*truthfulness is a fault to be *avoided*. Truth is what *simply is*. The only thing, therefore, that might make a person want to avoid telling the truth is a penchant for deception, especially for self-deception: for hiding from whatever *is*.

Let us examine a few of the ways in which people often deceive themselves even in the supposed name of truth.

A common tendency is to tell unpleasant truths about *other people*, while "revealing" only *pleasant* truths about oneself. This tendency received a kind of special sanction during the time, years ago, of Werner Erhart's "Self-honesty" programs, called, "EST." A student of EST in Honolulu once told a friend of mine that he wanted to "confront" me about some failing in the way I lead Ananda that, he felt, I needed to address. When finally we met, he made a point of telling me the mistake I was committing. As things turned out, I instantly saw the merit of his advice, and thanked him accordingly.

Well, this wasn't at all what he'd wanted or expected! What he'd anticipated was the ego-satisfaction of a triumph over me! He spent another hour belaboring the issue from every possible angle. At last I said, "Listen, I agreed with you. I also thanked you for your advice, and I intend to follow it. What more do you want from me?"

I've seen another common tendency: that of expressing the truth rudely and unkindly. The thought behind this tendency seems to be that the truth itself naturally *is* abrasive. Why so? Truth is liberating. Speaking the truth abrasively becomes, for such people, a mere "ego game."

When I first lived in India many years ago, I met not a few people who, under the influence of Mahatma Gandhi's noble truthfulness, overlooked the fact that Gandhi himself was always gracious and respectful to all. My Guru taught us to speak what he called "the *beneficial* truth." Sometimes, of course, frankness is necessary even if it must be expressed bluntly or caustically. Still, no one should ever be completely frank with others until he has overcome any tendency in himself to *want* to hurt. All of us want our advice to be *effective*. This usually means that any truths we utter should be expressed usefully, which usually means also, tactfully. My Guru, whose entire life was devoted to helping others, never tried to beat anyone down.* Even when he had to deliver a scolding, what I saw in his eyes was regret. Normally, he was sensitive and diplomatic—so much so that, if he'd forgotten someone's name, he might ask gently, "What is your *full* name?"

If, moreover, our commitment to truthfulness is sincere, we will naturally be more interested in understanding *ourselves* than in pointing out the defects of other people.

---

* Though sometimes he had, for the disciples' sake, to affirm his position as the guru. Dr. Lewis told us about one time when he and Mrs. Lewis were out driving with Master. Master opened a back window. Mrs. Lewis—like her husband a disciple of many years' standing—leaned over silently and closed it. Yogananda, just as silently, opened it again. This wordless tussle repeated itself several times more, until Mrs. Lewis finally gave up! (Yogananda said that she, in a previous life, had been Queen Elizabeth I, of England.)

Absolute Truth does exist. Its domain lies beyond the surging ocean of relativity. Truth is the ultimate essence of all that is. It is *Satchidananda*: ever-existing, ever-conscious, ever-new Bliss. That essential Truth cannot possibly be painful, for it is the very nature of the true Self. In that Self, nothing external can ever affect us. In our egos, on the other hand, there is no limit to how many things we may find hurtful, depending on how we define their influence on us. Suffering comes to us to the extent only that we want things different from what they are. Almost anything can cause suffering to the ego. We may define even a weekend of fresh air and sunshine amid the beauties of Nature as sheer misery, if we have been looking forward to spending these days in a crowded hall packed tightly with hundreds of noisy people jostling together and shouting merrily about some glitzy "event."

The ego is everlastingly the first, the most constant, the most consistent, and the greatest obstacle to our getting even a glimpse of divine bliss.

When we speak the truth, we should bear in mind that no *high* spiritual truth *can ever be* anything but beneficial. Truth, as I said, is liberating! Therefore did Jesus say, "Ye shall know the truth, and the truth shall make you free." (John 8:32)

In an interesting story by Arthur Conan Doyle, a man is killed in a car crash. An old friend of his from many years ago meets him as he lies there, and says to him, "No pain, of course?" The victim, in surprise, answers, "None."

"There never is," his friend replies. Then the accident victim, remembering something, exclaims in surprise, "But—you're dead!" The reason he felt no pain was that he himself was "dead."

Nothing that is painful to your ego can affect your soul. If a hurt to your ego can nudge you toward self-liberation, then, instead of resenting it, you ought to be *grateful*! From that higher point of view, it would even be quite appropriate (though perhaps unusual), to respond to every insult, every slight, every misunderstanding by saying, "Thank you!"

Truthfulness depends, in this world of relativities, on many factors. Facts are not necessarily truths, even in a relative sense. There are higher and lower truths: deeper potentials, for example, in ourselves and in others than present realities. By divine realization, those potentials can be made dynamic to our consciousness. Thus, those latent potentials might well be classed with truths.

To say, then, "I am well," when you know you're actually rather ill, may be a wholesome affirmation, and may be true by very reason of its wholesomeness. It is something I told myself a few years ago, after major heart surgery. As a result, I was home after four days instead of the predicted two weeks.

Here is an important point to bear in mind: If you feel in yourself the slightest tendency to want to correct others, try instead to ferret out *in yourself* what it is that makes you *want* to point out their weaknesses. Don't share with anyone, necessarily, the self-discoveries you may make, for (as my Guru said) someone might someday, in a moment of anger, hurl your self-revelation back at you and perhaps discourage you thereby from trying to become better. Ask yourself, however, "Isn't it more important, and more conducive to my own happiness, to work on improving myself, and therefore to come just that much closer to Bliss itself?" Let the world totter on as it will: you'll never be able to change it or anyone in it, by criticism. Isn't it a big enough job, anyway, simply to improve yourself?

That was above all what Patanjali meant by advising the spiritual aspirant to develop truthfulness by the avoidance of *un*truthfulness. Don't hide from unpleasant realities in yourself. The more you try to conceal from yourself your own faults and weaknesses, the more you'll *only lead yourself into fogs of self-deception.* And the greater the self-deception, the more it will blind you to the underlying reality of your very being, which is Divine Bliss. On the other hand, the better you succeed in accepting yourself *as you are*, and in facing every flaw in your nature *for what it is*, the easier you will find it to improve yourself, and, ultimately, to attain spiritual perfection.

Outwardly, there are also immediate and practical benefits to be derived from truthfulness. For one thing, everyone will naturally trust your word. For another, by strict truthfulness (of thought above all), one's mere word (as Patanjali implied, and as Yogananda stated), becomes "binding on the universe."

This, then, is the essence of what it means to be truthful: I, you, and all manifested beings are integral parts of the vast network of existence. We see ourselves, in our egos, as separate and distinct entities. John, to his own self-perception, is not at all the same person as Joe. Animals are not vegetables; vegetables are not minerals; and even animals and minerals are not often mixed together with greens in a salad.

Musical instruments require a sounding board. Singers use their bodies as resonant "chambers" for the vocal tones they produce. Similarly, when we habitually speak the truth, we find support from the very universe for our concentrated utterances.

Habitual liars, on the other hand, develop in time a certain thinness—perhaps even in the timbre of their voices, but always in their ability to accomplish anything effectively. What one might expect, in other words, to come out as a sort of vocal thinness may emerge instead as a kind of vague mental focus, indicating lack of support from a clear conscience. Interestingly, one does sometimes find people trying to compensate for this lack of inner conviction by loud bluster and bravado. Certain signs betray them, however. For example, they will talk *at* you, not *with* you. It is as if they wanted to exclude you (and any part of objective reality) from some reckoning they wish to avoid. In most cases, the sensitive ear will detect their lack of sincere commitment to truth. The self-betrayal will be either in their tone of voice, or in the vagueness and lack of clarity in their way of self-presentation. If you question their truthfulness, and are willing to confront them on the point (usually, it isn't worth the bother to ply them with incisive questions), they will insist on their own integrity.

Truthfulness, on the other hand, carries with it both conviction and clarity. Its vocal expression will give no hint of protestation, no attempt to persuade or to exaggerate.

The simple truth will be told plainly, but it need not be stark. People confuse truth with dry, rational definitions. The underlying truth of everything, however, is ultimately Bliss itself. There is plenty of room, here, for poetry and *feelingful* statements of truth at all levels without exaggeration. John Keats, in one of his famous poems, lamented, "There was a rainbow once in heaven. Now it is listed in the catalogue of common things." The *sheer poetry* of truth is something seldom considered. It is nevertheless, however, a reality.

The most important thing is not to wish that things were other than they are. This resolution requires both an attitude of non-attachment and an ability to accept reality even if it is not entirely pleasant to the ego.

There is one danger attendant on trying to tell the beneficial truth. Some people make that intention an excuse for telling the merely *convenient* truth—the "benefit" being, of course, to themselves. They may even excuse such feeling in the name of what they tell themselves is a *"higher"* truth—that is, those aspects of truth which will benefit one cause, even if they might harm another. The detective's classical question, *"Cui bono?"* or, "Who benefits?", must be asked here. If your "higher truth" benefits you but may harm someone else, hold that "truth" *more than* suspect! A true statement must be beneficial to everyone concerned.

To discriminate as to whether something you want to say or to accomplish truly *is* beneficial, rather than merely convenient for *you*, hold the thought contemplatively up to the Divine Will itself, asking, "Is this (contemplated thought or action) *Your* will?" Accept wholeheartedly any impartial guidance you feel from God. By following this course religiously, you will never go wrong.

John Keats wrote also: "Beauty is truth, truth beauty, — that is all ye know on earth, and all ye need to know." There *is* something beautiful in the expression of those truths, even, from which one tends at first to recoil in dismay. For everything, in the overall scheme of things, balances out. Today's pain becomes tomorrow's pleasure. Today's sorrow becomes tomorrow's joy. Today's failure becomes tomorrow's triumph. The beauty in this ineluctable fact lies not in those happier outcomes, which must always change back in time and become their opposites. It lies, rather, in the final realization that, through all the ups and downs of life, it is really only *ourselves*, within, that we've enjoyed! That same underlying Self, moreover, is with us always. Whether we revel in a delicious banquet, or find ourselves rushed off to the hospital to get our insides removed, *there is, literally, no difference whatever* to the underlying reality of Who we are, and in what our deepest experience of life consists: *Satchidananda*, ever-existing, ever-conscious, ever-new Bliss.

Live always in that inner bliss, and nothing will be able to touch you, ever. Let your truthfulness be above all an outward expression of your own, inward, ever-blissful nature.

Only Love

One time my Guru was standing in the driveway at Mt. Washington with a small group of monks. I was about two meters from him. As I stood there, I thought, "He's over there, in a particular location in space. Yet at the same time his spirit is also here inside me. How can I understand that in Spirit he is not limited: that he isn't merely 'over there,' but everywhere?"

As I was wrestling with this thought, he walked over to me and, with a quiet smile, handed me an apple.

Obviously he had read my thoughts. Was he merely teasing me? I think not. I think a deeper lesson was involved here.

I had been telling myself, "He is pure Spirit." In effect, I had been mentally denying his humanity. What he was subtly telling me was, "You must come to that deeper reality *through* my humanity—as you now know me, in other words, and not by denying that humanity."

Philosophically it is right to say of the guru, and of every Self-realized master, "He isn't human only; he is the Infinite Self."

Indeed, I recall another strange incident, which I described in my book, *The Path*, when I was new on the path and intrigued by the whole idea—completely new to me—of astral entities and astral possession. I still recall the dream I had that night. I was at a party, talking casually with a few unidentified friends, when all of a sudden I remarked to them, "It is time for me to go and meet a disincarnate spirit." I left that room, and entered another one, which I still remember clearly. It was empty of any furniture; the floorboards were bare. I stood in the center of the room and declared, "All right, come on. I want to see what this business of astral possession is all about."

All at once I felt a presence entering me. The cosmic *AUM* sounded all around me, but it wasn't a pleasant sound. It seemed, rather, to resonate with some lower astral sphere to which the soul I had called must have belonged.

And then I felt myself being sucked out of my body, out the window, and into what seemed a gray mist. The doubt seized me: Was I in danger of losing consciousness? At this point I decided I'd gone far enough. Though I tried to return to my body, I found this attempt a struggle. Rather than risk going any farther with this crazy experiment, I called out urgently to my Guru:

"Master!"

Instantly I awoke. The unpleasant sound ceased. I was again in normal, outward consciousness.

The next morning, Gene Haupt, one of the monks who lived downstairs in the main building, told me, "I was sleeping last night when I heard a loud pounding on my door." In astral experiences of this kind, I've been told, the knocking sounds like pounding over the whole door. In this case, that was what it seemed to be.

"Hello! Who's in there?" roughly demanded a loud, coarse voice.

"Me," came the fearful reply.

"**WHO?**"

"G-g-Gene!"

"**WHO?**"

"G-g-g-Gene Haupt."

"I don't want you," thundered the voice. "I want Don Walters." Gene heard footsteps stamping toward the door to the outside. The door opened, then slammed shut. My room was in a separate building on the same grounds. It must have been moments later that I had my own strange experience.

Later that day I spoke of this episode to Master. He questioned me further, then said, "Don't worry about it. Such experiences occur sometimes on the spiritual path."

I was not to be put off, however. How could he have responded so instantly to my plea, and then, later that day, ask for details about the experience? "Sir," I said, "didn't you *know* about it?"

Almost brusquely he replied, "When you become one with God, you *are* God."

What an unexpected reply! And how different from the impression Tara later tried to convey of him, when she edited something he'd said to me about a saint he'd seen in vision at Encinitas. What Master had said was, "Where God is, there His saints come." Not wishing him to appear boastful to readers, Tara had changed that statement to read, "Wherever *a devotee* of God is, there His saints come." (Italics mine.) However, *I'm* a devotee of God, and I cannot in any way claim to have been so "pestered"!

Indeed, there are two aspects to spiritual truth: impersonal of course, in cosmic consciousness; but also very personal. Arjuna, after being blessed with the divine vision of Krishna in the Lord's omnipresent aspect, begged to behold his guru once again in the human form he so loved. Krishna, moreover, acceded; he did not say, "Haven't you yet understood? I am not that human form *at all*!" God's impersonality is not such that it inspires one to see all beings as insignificant parts, merely, of an infinite whole—as little ants, so to speak, rather than as individual, self-aware beings. His impersonality consists, rather, of not wanting from us anything but our love. His is a *giving* love, not one that draws from us selfishly to Himself. His love is like that of a mother who, on seeing her child fall, hitting its knee, and knowing that this fall means very little in the child's overall existence, nevertheless expresses sincere sympathy and does her best to comfort the child. The mother accepts as real the little one's experience at the moment. At the same time, she encourages it to broaden its awareness, and to embrace a broader reality. "Come on, darling," she may say, "you'll be all right in a few minutes."

This is what I mean by saying that there is also a very real, human aspect to our relationship with God. It is also why we need a human guru: We come to omnipresent God *through* a guru. That is how we come clearly to understand how all-encompassing is Divine Love itself.

I have known disciples to scoff at the human side of their relationship with the guru. They seem to be saying, "That isn't really what it's about *at all*." Philosophically they may be right. It was what I was trying to do that day in the driveway. Certainly, the goal of the path is to merge in Infinite Spirit. Yet I have also noticed that disciples with this mentality don't make the best devotees. They tend to be dry in their feelings, somewhat distant, and more locked in their egos. I hope I was none of these. For I have also noticed that such disciples, in their attunement with the guru, seem to be rather *less* in tune with him than *more* so—something I certainly didn't want, and for that reason, I think, Master gave me that gentle reminder.

Master, in giving me that apple, was subtly implying, "Love me, not *in spite* of my human nature and personality, but *through* them."

As Sri Yukteswar wrote in his book, *The Holy Science*, the devotee cannot advance a single step toward God until he develops *the natural love of his heart*.

It is through love of the guru, in his perfection as a human being, that human beings can come most easily to understand the love of God, who is beyond every human perfection.

THREE BENEFITS FROM USING INCENSE

Incense is used traditionally in religious worship. Though to some people it may perhaps seem a little too "churchy" and ritualistic, in fact it serves three very valid purposes — not only for church services, but for personal meditation and devotional activities.

The first of these purposes addresses the fact that sensory disturbances often intrude on the mind in meditation. They may do so especially if they obtrude brokenly or randomly on one's senses, as with traffic noises or people shouting and babies crying in nearby houses. Those sounds can be reduced and even eliminated altogether if they are smoothed out by the continuous flow of a more soothing sound. Traffic noises, for instance, dogs barking, airplanes passing overhead, or people talking or calling to one another, which may intrude on one's concentration, can be either reduced or virtually eliminated by the single, continuous sound of running water in a brook, from a waterfall, or of ocean surf.

I used to find whenever I visited the SRF Lake Shrine in Pacific Palisades, California, that the sound of traffic on the long curve Sunset Boulevard makes as it flows down around the property on its way to the Pacific ocean was kept at a distance in the sunken garden next to the museum when I meditated there. I could listen to the pleasant sound of a continuous nearby waterfall. Soon, I would forget about all sounds, as if I were sitting in the stillness of a desert.

I also found, whenever I visited our oceanside hermitage in Encinitas, that meditating near the bluff and listening to the soothing surf as it rolled onto the beach below made meditation much easier than in the men's ashram, which was situated on a street corner, surrounded by the distracting noises of traffic and people.

One can produce soothing sounds also artificially, by softly playing recordings of ocean surf, waterfalls, rainfall, or running brooks.

Incense serves a similar purpose. Often, during meditation, the nearby odors from such things as car exhausts, food cooking, cigarette smoke, or even upholstery in the room where one sits can be distracting to the mind, and indeed may also awaken mental associations that have nothing in common with the mood of inner upliftment. The gentle, pervasive scent of incense can help to block that often-bewildering diversity of smells, smoothing them out into a single, prolonged, and continuous sensation that itself, especially with repeated association, becomes uplifting. Gradually that one, overall scent becomes an aid, not a distraction, in directing the mind one-pointedly toward contemplating higher realities.

A second benefit from incense is one I've already hinted at: The sense of smell is said to be the most memory-stimulating of the five senses. How often does the smell of something become immediately associated in our minds with some memory—perhaps from years ago, perhaps even from our early childhood. The regular use of incense during devotional and meditative practices gradually causes an association of that scent with those practices. Thus, the scent helps one to return more instantly, without effort, to an uplifted mood.

The third benefit is more particular. During the yoga practice of watching the breath, the best place to concentrate on the flow of breath is the point where it enters the body. I don't mean the nostrils, but rather where the breath enters the head. This point is, of course, quite close to the point between the eyebrows, the *Kutastha* center recommended in yoga teachings as the best point at which to focus one's concentration.

The benefit of an awareness of the scent of incense at that point is that association of the scent itself with devotional upliftment helps one to keep his mind focused on the breath entering and leaving the body.

In ways such as these, the senses, though in themselves a distraction to meditation, can also become an aid to one's efforts at concentration.

WHY I LEFT COLLEGE

I realize that a college degree is important for most people in their adult life. It is important to whatever employment they seek. It is important also for the general respect, or lack of it, that others give them. Swami Sri Yukteswar (my Guru's guru) insisted that his disciple—who became world-renowned by his monastic name, Paramhansa Yogananda—get a B.A. degree. When I myself told my Guru that I hadn't completed my education, he lamented, "Why does Divine Mother always do this to me?" Yet I must add that I, personally, have never had any reason to think that getting a degree might have helped me, whether in my work of teaching, leading others, editing, or writing. Neither have I felt that it might have helped me personally to gain particular respect from anyone. Nowadays, of course, I do have the credentials of my actual accomplishments. Even before I'd done anything worthwhile, however, no one ever asked me, as a condition for any recognition at all, whether I had finished college.

My reasons for leaving college might be considered only personal were it not for the fact that I feel strongly that those reasons underscore a great need in the modern system of education.

I left college with only six months to go. After that, I would presumably have received my B.A. degree. I left not because I wasn't interested in learning, but because I wanted to learn something more *valid*, or at least more pertinent to what I myself was seeking in life. Indeed, I have often said that my true education began only *after* I left those "hallowed" walls.

What I wanted was eternal truth. I wasn't preparing for commercial employment, nor for any post in government, school, or other kind of paid position. I didn't expect ever to have to worry about these things, and was willing to live on almost nothing. In fact, my father remembered wryly that he had offered me, at the age of sixteen, to buy me a tuxedo, and that my answer had been, "Don't bother, Dad; I'll never need one. In fact, I'm never going to earn enough money even to pay income tax." This prediction proved justified when I became a monk, at twenty-two. What I wanted was a deeper understanding of life itself. I wanted to grow in wisdom. I wanted an answer to my deeply personal search in life: how to find lasting happiness.

And then, if I found any truth that might be worthwhile to others, I wanted to serve them by sharing what I found.

I fully realize that formal education is not normally, and indeed cannot be, geared to such ends. Most people consider it a means to obtaining better employment. Others, even if their desire is to obtain general knowledge in science, history, or the arts, see that acquisition in more worldly terms. Nevertheless, I cannot help thinking that education should be geared also toward *understanding* life: what it is all about, where all of us are headed, how we can live wisely and happily. I don't think people should be left to stumble upon these things on their own later on in life, perhaps only after much suffering and also, perhaps, when it is too late to change.

I remember my class on philosophy at Brown University. The professor didn't seem to think it proper to offer us any value judgments of his own. He would ask us our *opinions*, and then say (for instance), "Thank you, Mr. Walters. Now, what do you think, Mr. Brown?" This suggestion that crucial matters of life and death are matters of mere opinion exasperated me so much that I ended up taking poetry books to class, reading them surreptitiously whenever I thought I could get away with it. To me, the issue of what is true or false has always been crucial to living itself. It distressed me, then, to see such issues as these being treated as matters of mere guesswork.

In literature class we were given works to study without any discussion concerning what made one work of literature in any way *valid* or great, whether artistically or philosophically, and another work either less so or completely invalid. These would, I realize, have been "value judgments," but that was indeed one of my complaints about formal education. A professor need not *impose* his values on the students, but could he not at least offer the students objective standards to get them thinking for themselves? What makes a work of literature great? Merely the fact that certain (perhaps nameless) people have adjudged it so?

I remember one literature class, earlier at Haverford College, in which the professor asked us each to write a paper on our own criteria of literary greatness. That was at least closer to what I think a good education ought to offer, though I think he might have preceded his request with a lively discussion on the possible criteria involved. Since we'd been offered no criteria, however, I, in describing my own, wrote that I saw around the greatest works, like Homer's *Iliad*, a halo of white light; that, around lesser works, I saw some light, but in diminishing intensity, and darker in color. Around ordinary literary works, I said, I saw no light at all.

The professor, perhaps not surprisingly, gave a shrug of dismay and a flunking grade. Still, I think he might have helped the process along a bit beforehand with a little prior discussion.

I realize, too, that to convey wisdom one should also, in oneself, be wise. It is too much to expect every professor to have pretensions to wisdom. However, if wisdom were prized, many more of them would aspire to it, and perhaps most might achieve it to greater or lesser degrees.

The obstacle to wisdom is not the fact that few teachers are wise, but that wisdom itself is widely viewed as merely "relative," as subjective, and probably, scientifically speaking, as non-existent. This, I believe, is the supreme problem. It is why I have written two books, especially, on this very point: *Out of the Labyrinth*, and *Hope for a Better World!* I wrote these books to show that objective values *do* exist, and that there are standards by which they can be judged. I wrote those books also to show that, although values are, of course, relative in their application, that relativity is directional. Fundamental values are universally true, *in a directional sense*, in their relativity.

Education needs to take on the question from the very beginning. It needs to go into this question in ever greater depth, as one's studies move to higher and higher levels.

Has life any meaning? Is there something everyone is seeking, beneath the tangle of human desires and ambitions? Are religious teachings merely matters of *belief*? Can principles that are universally valid be abstracted, or condensed, from them regardless of one's beliefs? Is there anything in human existence that makes one particular kind of behavior more valid than another, because more justified in terms of what everyone is naturally seeking? What justification is there for knowledge itself, as opposed to learning *how to use that knowledge* effectively for greater worldly success?

Had college tried, even vaguely, to answer questions like these, I might be happily adding my own B.R.L. (Bachelor of Right Living) after my name. Or, perhaps, A.R.L. (Aspirant to Right Living).

God's Weaning Ways
(A Non-Essay)

Think what a thrilling drama is Life!
Typical of the spectacle—indeed, perhaps its greatest highlight—is that oldest of old stories: Two young people, a man and a woman, meet. Both are in radiant health, beautiful, happy, magnetic. They feel instantly attracted to each other as though, since time immemorial, they'd shared lives together. Perhaps indeed they have. Certainly the attraction is deeper than physical. Each senses in the other a quality that satisfies some deep need in himself. They reach out in yearning, as if to absorb a fulfillment long and ardently awaited.

Can their hopes ever be fulfilled? The attraction they feel is indefinable, elusive, evanescent. Its first inspiration may be a special, soft smile; a shining laugh of appreciation in the other's eyes; a ripple of warm feeling. They long to draw from each other something very special. But what is that something? a smile? a glimmer? a ripple? What can these be but moods only, the nature of which is as fleeting as a will-o'-the-wisp dancing on a breeze.

It is all a play of consciousness—ripples rising in expectation, cresting, then scattering in foam! thoughts and emotions that flicker in the sunlight on life's sea! wavelets that long to merge their separate identities in a larger wave. Waves themselves, however, are ephemeral. Moods pass. The starlight and the dancing, that gentle, sweet touch, those brief glimpses of beautiful, far-off scenes filled with love and happiness: All these change, and sooner or later disappear.

Is it all a mirage? The promise was believable, yet the contact and the merging are merely movements of two bodies, irrevocably separate from each other, their souls self-enclosed as if in suits of armor.

What purpose does it all serve? Is it only the Hegelian paradigm: thesis, antithesis, and synthesis? Is the union—to the extent that it even occurs—merely biological? Can it all, really, be so depressingly "Machiavellian"? Can God have so arranged human existence that it is based eternally on false hopes? The loving embrace, then its sequel: squalling children, each with its own interests and its self-created destiny! Has that ardent coming together had no other purpose than to perpetuate the species, of which we individuals count as scarcely more than statistics?

Sexual union brings fleeting pleasure at first, and exhilaration—followed by physical and emotional depletion, and, if over-indulged, by satiety and disgust. All this, to what purpose?

The expression in English is, "falling in love." Do other languages provide such a starkly realistic metaphor? The experience is indeed a fall from high expectations, a crash downward into brambles of disappointment, suffering, or—if the brambles are short and not too painful—of gray compromise.

Will it ever be possible to become fully absorbed in that sweet smile, that loving look, that radiance in the eyes? Never! Such is the tragedy of human love.

Love has, in fact, a reality far more spiritual than material. The physical body is only a container for its animating spirit, to which one's feelings truly belong. The less spiritual the feelings, however, the less also they qualify as love at all. They are selfish desires, ignoble passions. The Spanish language says it honestly: not, "I love you," but, "*Te quiero*— I *want* you."

Every human desire, ambition, and aspiration is destined for ultimate disappointment, unless it transcends its own humanity. Life is a drama—a dramatic dream, with numberless plots and subplots, all leading toward a wonderful ending. As Paramhansa Yogananda wrote in *The Rubaiyat of Omar Khayyam Explained,* "For a play to be successful, it must have suspense. It must beguile, puzzle, and bewilder. It must, above all, conclude with a glorious climax. The cosmic drama is complex, and so it needs to be—infinitely so, for its stage encompasses all time and space. It must above all come to a deeply satisfying conclusion, one that will bring some noble, lofty purpose to fulfillment."

Consider the basic structure within which the universe was manifested: *dwaita,* duality. The still, motionless consciousness of the Supreme Spirit had to set into motion a part of Itself: The dimensionless Ocean sent out a wind, as it were, over its surface creating waves, or vibrations. ("And the Spirit of God moved upon the face of the waters." Genesis 1:2) That one vast Consciousness thus moved, in a sense, in opposite directions from its state of rest at the center. Waves appeared on the surface of the great Ocean of Consciousness. With each wave there came a corresponding trough, or depression; the over-all ocean level could never change.

All this movement exists in thought only. Spirit alone is Absolute; vibrational movement is relative. Thus, "up" and "down" are not fixed positions, but directional and relative. There are degrees of height and depth which, for simplicity's sake, were divided in the scriptures of India into three stages, or *gunas* (qualities): *sattwa* (good, that which is closest to the middle position of Absolute Spirit); *rajas* (the active quality, which pushes energetically toward either exaltation or depression); and *tamas* (that quality which pulls as far away from, and thereby darkens, the reality of Spirit, whether in the false stimulation that is pleasure, or in the equally false depression that is sorrow and despair).

In the wave metaphor, *sattwa* represents that part of the wave which is closest to the ocean bosom, and to the mean level of that body of water; *rajas* represents that part in the middle of every rise or depression which moves toward the completion of its upward or downward movement; and *tamas* represents both the apex and the nadir of those two movements.

The gross, or violent, vibrations of *tamas* are those which most obscure the calm and subtle reality of the Supreme Spirit. They are seen in extreme. . . .

The Essay Aborted

Istopped writing this essay with those words, not even ending the last paragraph, for I found I simply wasn't satisfied with what I was doing. I might have simply dropped the essay from this book except for two things:

1. What I showed by aborting the essay was the importance of clarity. For I had worked hard to say what I meant, and in that attempt realized that the clarity I'd achieved undermined my very reason for writing the essay!

2. The metaphor of the wave I advanced here is slightly different from anything I've ever written before. It includes emphasis on the compensating depression for each rising wave. The point is interesting, though I now feel it is not necessary to elaborate further.

My reason for writing this essay was to show that the very delusions which keep us from God also help us, in the end, in our search for Him.

The ego, for example, albeit our chief obstacle to divine realization, is at the same time necessary to that end. For it isn't until self-consciousness gains clear definition in human awareness that one develops the incentive to broaden it. For example, it isn't until the vague reality of suffering is clearly identified as "*my* suffering" that one decides, "*I myself*, therefore, must do something to get out of this ego." The lower animals suffer, but don't have the same personal incentive and understanding to overcome suffering.

Again, the only true Friend we can ever have is God, but without human friendships we might never get a hint of His infinitely greater friendship for us, in our souls.

Moreover, although human love is, as Yogananda put it, "the greatest delusion," yet without it we might never feel inspired to seek its true and ultimate fulfillment: union with God.

Money, and the desire for possessions as well as for human fulfillment of all kinds, are among the great delusions, yet if we could never find enjoyment in their fulfillment we might never be able to discriminate and understand that the joy we derive from them isn't really from them at all, but comes rather from within ourselves, in our *reaction* to them.

The same, then, with that start of the essay as I carried it to the point I did. It is true that we can never find fulfillment anywhere except in the inner Self. Yet we *do* absorb qualities from one another by adopting those qualities, ourselves. And though we must shed every human trait, including the most *sattwic*, still, as long as we identify it as a quality possessed by the ego, even *sattwic* qualities suggest what I wanted to convey, namely, that in delusion itself lie the keys necessary for opening the door to enlightenment.

All this is true. My mistake was to begin my essay deliberately with a *sattwic* reality: human love in its most idealized form. I erred in saying we can't absorb anything from others, for we *can, and in fact do*. Ultimately, we absorb the Guru's consciousness into our own, thereby alone making it possible to escape egoic entanglements and self-justifications. Even in our egos, moreover, we do take on the ego-qualities of others. We are, as I have said elsewhere, an aggregate of qualities, none of which defines us as we really are in our Eternal, Infinite Self.

It may also be true, moreover, that perfection in Divine Love includes also the perfection of human love—not on a physical, sexual level, but on a soul level. For in God every human desire is satisfied.

The subject of soul mates is one Yogananda touched on, as far as I know, only once. It was in a magazine article in the 1930s, on the teachings of Jesus Christ. This subject is beyond my own understanding, but I see that it was a mistake to begin my essay at such a refined level, for it implies the impossibility of absorbing even states of consciousness from one another, and this, in fact, we can do, and in some ways do all the time.

The subject of God's "weaning" ways is endlessly fascinating, whether I finish this essay or not. Consider how, even from the beginning, evolution is explained much better in terms of a constant reaching out toward greater awareness than in the purely mechanical terms presented by Charles Darwin.

My main reason for even including in the present book what I wrote so far on this subject is, as I explained earlier, that it underscores the importance of working to achieve complete clarity in one's writing. Only in this way is it possible to see whether, and in what way, what one has attempted to say is valid or erroneous.

I am reminded of something Master said to me. After Boone had left the monastery, Master informed me that this disciple had taken to living a dissolute life. "I told him he should marry," was Master's comment.

"That would have been *infinitely* better!" I exclaimed.

"Well," Master concluded, "I consider everything evil that is out of God." His meaning here, of course, needed editing. More exactly, it was, "I consider everything evil that decreases one's attunement with God." In Boone's case, leaving his vocation was, for him, an evil, but marriage would have constituted at least a lesser evil. Master did not mean that marriage is evil in itself. He himself wrote a wedding ceremony, and performed it. Most of his highly advanced disciples, moreover, either were or had been married in the past.

We see, then, the relative aspect of our title, "God's Weaning Ways." At whatever stage one has reached spiritually, that which is below one's position on that ladder may be described as (relatively) evil, and whatever stage is above that position may be described as good.

The Bhagavad Gita states that even the worst of sinners, if he steadfastly meditates, quickly comes to God. The chances of this happening are slight, of course, for one who is steeped in sin rarely feels any incentive to meditate at all. Krishna's statement has practical value, however, for it gives hope to all that, wherever one is now standing on the ladder of spiritual evolution, nothing can prevent him from considering himself truly a son of God and potentially the equal to the greatest of saints. One should, in other words, never say to himself, "I am evil." Everyone should seek God with full confidence that the Lord loves him eternally, and sees him as forever His own.

My Guru said also, "Pray in this way: 'Divine Mother, naughty or good, I am Thy child. Thou *must* release me!'"

No action is wrong or evil *in itself*. It all depends on which direction it takes us: whether upward or downward; toward God, or away from Him.

Is it possible, then, to skip some of the rungs on that ladder? Krishna's statement seems to imply so. In most cases, however, the scientific statement holds true: "Nature never makes sudden leaps." Patience, it has been well said, is the fastest path to God. Nevertheless, I would not want to rule out the possibility for spiritual heroes to appear on the scene who are willing to brave the steepest mountain cliff in their eagerness to reach the heights.

For God loves boldness in all those who seek Him earnestly. Fear nothing, therefore! If you have deep faith that He will ever support you, why not leap even into the abyss? Remember that spiritual seeker, described in *Autobiography of a Yogi*, who, after being rejected by Babaji, leaped to his death, and was revived by Babaji himself, and then accepted into that select band of highly advanced disciples.

How to Develop Self-Confidence

"How," a young spiritual seeker once asked me, "can I develop self-confidence? Every book I've read on success stresses the importance of developing such confidence, *knowing* that one is good at whatever one does. Unfortunately, I simply haven't confidence. And I think these books must be right, for no matter how hard I try, I never seem to do things as well as I'd like to do them."

"I've glanced through some of those books," I replied. "What they try to do, it seems to me, is promote egotism. That is to say, pride, which my Guru called 'the death of wisdom.' Without wisdom, any success achieved will be fragile."

"Are you saying," my friend inquired, "that the kind of person those books describe as ideal is, himself, fragile? The self-confident people I've met certainly don't *seem* so! Many of them are rich, famous, or in some other way powerful. They impress me as having achieved everything they wanted."

"You are right, of course," I agreed. "Pride goes before a fall, but that fall doesn't necessarily come quickly. The fragility of those people lies like a seed, however, dormant in the very success they achieve. They think to find security in wealth, but they'll never be able to keep it forever. Fame, too, is short-lived. Worldly power soon passes on to someone else. My Guru remarked, 'Money and fame are like prostitutes: loyal to no man.'

"What I suggest, then," I continued, "is that you study various kinds of success, and of that self-confidence which led to success, and then consider which kind works best."

He: Are you saying that some kinds are less fragile, and more long-lasting, than others?

I: Of course. The success of a great artist is certainly more long-lasting than that of a mediocre one. In the case of a great spiritual master, like Jesus Christ, the influence he exerts on humanity is greater and more enduring than that of business tycoons or, let us say, of conquerors like Genghis Khan or Napoleon. And self-confidence that is rooted in calm self-knowledge, and is not boastful, is much more effective than that which suggests to the mind the sort of person who is a "crowing rooster."

He: Well, in any case I'm not interested in making great achievements! I just want to be able to do things well without dreading the possible consequences.

I: You've made me curious. I know you to be intelligent, eloquent, and nice looking. What do you think could have caused your problem?

He: Well, perhaps it was my father. I know it's a complex I have, but the fact is he made a practice of deprecating me. I guess he did it because I didn't seem destined to live up to his ambitions for me. In fact, I didn't at all share his interests in life.

I: I see. Well, however unfortunate that may have been in one sense—and this is, in fact, a common enough problem—it may be fortunate in another respect. As a specific cause of lacking self-confidence, parental disapproval can be major. No one likes to disappoint one's parents—perhaps especially not one's father. But the most important thing is that you've remained true to yourself.

As far as I know, most supposed "cures" for the inferiority complex you've developed are directed toward helping a person to build up his self-esteem. Affirmations can help in this respect. One might tell himself, for instance, "I have in me the power and the ability to rise victorious over every obstacle!" or one can affirm, "I am wise. I am strong. I am master of my destiny!" These thoughts are important aids. They have one major disadvantage, however: While they help in resuscitating a weak or ailing ego, they don't take into account the simple fact that *having an ego at all* is, in the highest sense, Self-damaging. Why so? Simply because it is self-limiting.

He: But what else can account for success—unless it be some wholly extraneous factor such as social influence, or good luck?

I: I grant you that. Worldly people haven't really much else to go on. You, however, are seeking Truth. This means you understand that the goal of life is to find God. In your search, the first thing you must overcome is the usual human focus on the egoic self. What attempts at creating self-esteem accomplish, generally, is that they replace an inferiority with a superiority complex. Both "complexes," my Guru told me, are obstacles to any true and long-lasting success.

He: Can you suggest ways that might help me to overcome this weakness?

I: Yes, certainly. A little book of mine, *Secrets of Success*, contains thirty-one such suggestions: one for every day of the month. All of them relate in one way or another to shifting one's focus *away from* self-preoccupation and to directing it toward the work one is doing. Once people become really good at anything, they usually do accept the simple fact of their competence and move on. The last two secrets in the book, however, focus on channeling a higher power into whatever one does.

For example, Secret Thirty says, "The secret of success is attuning your limited, human will to the infinite divine will." Secret Thirty-One states, "The secret of success is humility, realizing that pride is [as my Guru taught] the death of wisdom, and the paralysis of every worthwhile endeavor."

He: Are you speaking of success in spiritual undertakings? I can see the importance of praying for God's help when one is working for Him. My problem, however, relates to work I do to fulfill my more practical needs: work to support my family, perhaps, or even some quite trivial act such as defending a particular point of view.

I: It is a mistake to pray to, or to think of, God only when one is in church! The devotee should include Him in everything he does. Any work you do, then, can be done in attunement with Him.

He: But isn't it somehow wrong to ask Him to make me affluent, or to inspire me with ways of winning a discussion?

I: Of course it is! Speaking personally I too, in my desire to rise above the ego, have made it a practice not to pray even for my own real needs, such as a healing when I am ill, or even for a reduction of pain when I am suffering.

Many years ago, on Sunday morning when I was scheduled to give the service at our Ananda temple, I was suddenly smitten by a violent kidney stone attack. The pain was so great that I found my whole body trembling like a leaf in a high wind. A friend pleaded with me to let him drive me to a hospital. The mere thought, however, of swaying and bouncing down that long, winding, hilly road was more than I could face. Unable even to answer him, I simply shook my head to indicate that I simply couldn't do what he suggested.

So I lay there, trembling. The devotional service was scheduled for eleven o'clock: an hour and a half away. What was to be done? I couldn't speak; I couldn't even think clearly. So—I went on suffering in silence. This was the greatest pain I have ever endured.

At last I glanced at my watch. A quarter to eleven! I hadn't wanted to bother God with prayers for help, but now, realizing that in fifteen minutes I was expected to address a roomful of people, I at last prayed, "Divine Mother (that is how I usually think of God), if You want me to give this service, You will have to do something about it!"

Unbelievably, almost like breath fading from steel, the pain vanished completely to be replaced by a cool wave of intense joy! I gave the service. The joy that filled me was so overwhelming, however, that even now I couldn't speak normally. Words struggling to come out were impeded by waves of sheer happiness. Many people there that day imagined I was weeping for pain, but though tears fell, they were not tears of anguish, nor the kind of tears that come with relief. What I felt, in fact, was an exquisite, overwhelming sweetness: joy that burst the confines of verbal communication while singing, "Here I am! These halting words of mine cannot express what is filling my heart. Can't you yourselves feel this expanding joy? Can't you feel it filling your bodies?"

My prayer had been not for myself, but for my ability to serve those who had come to hear me, for I yearned to share God's bliss with all. How could self-confidence be an issue here, when my mere existence played such a subordinate theme in the dance of joy that flowed through me?

He: I think I understand you somewhat. And I hope I can learn to be able to work toward losing myself in a greater inspiration. Still, I think I'll always find myself worrying. Crises do, after all, arise in our lives. Well, I guess I'll just have to wait and see!

But now here's another point: I find my self-confidence waning when I find myself in situations where I'm expected to "produce." For example, if I am asked to speak in public, or perhaps only to express my ideas before people. Under such circumstances, I certainly do pray to God—perhaps even desperately! But I'm so worried about the impression I'm making on others that I'm afraid the thought of God gets rather pushed out of my mind.

I: I've been told that public speaking ranks among the supreme causes of nervousness. Strange to say, however, this is a fear I have never felt personally, even though I've given thousands of lectures.

Many years ago I mentioned this fact to a sister disciple. She responded with disdain; I could almost hear her exclaim mentally, "Why say anything to this clod? My God, what an EGO!" I remained silent. Perhaps it seemed to me I might find it spiritually helpful to accept her negative judgment of me silently, for it didn't seem to me such a bad thing for her to hold such a low opinion of me.

The truth of the matter is, however, that my lack of nervousness had nothing to do with self-esteem. My real problem was quite the opposite: I suffered from constant self-doubts. This failing deprived me, of course, of any self-esteem I might have had otherwise!

What I've always done when faced by any crisis in life is mentally form a "worst case scenario." If some project I've contemplated seems to contain the possibility of failure, I've tried to visualize and accept that possibility, asking myself, "Can I bear such failure with an even mind? Yes, I can! because my happiness doesn't depend on *anything* outside myself."

This practice has helped me also as a public speaker. I've simply asked myself, "What have I to fear? Is it that people might think me a fool? If they do, I don't mind accepting that maybe I *am* a fool! And if that's really what I am, why worry if this truth is discovered about me? Truth is all that matters. Whatever is, *is*. Whatever I am, I must accept it as the reality I have to work with. If I want to improve myself, I can only begin by working with present reality."

If in any other way I turn out to have bungled something, well, I certainly will try not to make the same mistake again, but in any case, having done my best, all I can do is leave the results in God's hands. I can't be responsible for being something I am not. My responsibility is only to try always to improve, letting matters turn out, then, as they will. "Nature," it has been said, "never makes sudden leaps."

What people think of me is their business, not mine. Sooner or later, if I do my best now, I will be sure to improve.

Suffering comes always because people wish things were different from what they are.

Many years ago I was assigned to work with my fellow monks on the construction of India Center, in Hollywood. I was, let us say, not the perfect fit for the job. As a carpenter, I was just about hopeless. I would strike nine times at a nail with my hammer before finally hitting it. And even then it was usually only a glancing blow, which bent the nail. After long minutes of frustration at my own incompetence, a sort of bleak despair would descend over me. I'd pause, breathe deeply a few times, then with clenched teeth affirm, "I can do it!" Always, though I kept on trying, the results were not encouraging.

I remember, when the job ended, that I said to our hired foreman, "I've sure learned a lot on this job, Andy!"

Andy gave me a long-suffering look, such as a wise parent might bestow on an idiot child. Then, opting for kindness, he remained silent. In fact, I did have some reason for feeling good—not only because the job was finished, but I had done my poor best. For me, this little best was a significant gain. No one could have asked more of me than that humble offering.

He: Thank you. I do recognize myself in that story, somewhat. Here, though, may be a thought for you to consider: Some of the books I've read tell people to visualize themselves doing a good job. Might it not have helped you to visualize yourself as a good carpenter?

I: We're being serious, right? Well, in that case let me admit it probably would have helped me a lot! I must confess, however, that carpentry has never been my shining ambition. Besides, the job didn't last long enough for me really to tune in to it on, let us say, a soul level. I do agree with you, however. If there is something one really wants to do well, he should make it a serious issue—something I admit I didn't do. Most of a person's ability to succeed at anything comes from attuning himself to a state of consciousness which resonates with success in that field.

Here is another story, one in which our Guru deliberately set himself to qualify in a new field.

Once, as the young director of a school he'd founded at Ranchi, India, he hired a well-known artist to paint a portrait of his param-guru (guru's guru), Lahiri Mahasaya. Yogananda's reaction, when the job had been completed, lacked a certain fervor no doubt expected by the artist. To Yogananda, although the painting displayed competence, it failed to capture the radiant spirit of its saintly subject.

"How long did it take you to master your craft?" he asked the artist.

"Twenty years," responded the older man.

"You mean it took you twenty years to convince yourself you could paint?" Yogananda was implying that self-persuasion was all the man had managed to accomplish; the man hadn't merged his self-consciousness in his art.

Well, as you can imagine, the artist was indignant. No doubt his thought was, "At least I've *earned* my reputation!" In reply he exclaimed, "I'd like to see you paint as well in *twice* that length of time!"

"Give me a week," came the unexpected, but calm, reply. To the artist this seemed a deliberate insult. He refused to say anything more, and left the room in a huff.

The young guru went to a local shop, bought a set of paints and brushes, and set to work creating his own painting. His first attempts were unsuccessful. Each time he failed, however, he tried again more carefully, attuning himself gradually to the skill required for the task. After a week, the new painting was finished. The Master hung it up and had the artist invited.

As the older man entered the room, the first thing he saw was this new work. "Who did that?" he cried in astonishment. "It's better than mine." The Master, who had been hiding behind a door, came out then and said, "You really want to know? I did it myself!" (One can see, here, that this man had at least the humility to admit that the new painting was better than his own. Yogananda, I suspect, had felt his sincerity, and therefore took the trouble to show him the importance of concentrating more on the deed than on oneself as the doer!)

So you see, you must bring God into your work. Don't pray merely, "Make me successful." Say, rather, "Guide me, that I understand how to do perfectly what I do."

I grant you, in my "carpentry days" those bent nails were some proof that I wasn't tuned in as I should have been. No doubt I should have tried harder. Actually, my thought was, "What am I even doing *here*?"

Whenever I've really wanted to do something well, however, I've found that, by asking God to guide my understanding rather than asking for the blessing to succeed, I've done many things for which no experience could have better prepared me. I've found, moreover, that when I tuned in to what was needed, the answers simply came to me almost effortlessly.

Strange as it may seem, I've never had much confidence in myself in anything. Writing, I suppose, might be considered an exception: I've always known I could write. At the age of nine I was already writing dramatic dialogue. When I was seven years old, my parents criticized something I'd written for school, commenting, "You've used the word 'and' too often." They were certainly right. What I find intriguing, however, is that my first thought (I didn't express it) was, "Who is anyone to tell *me* how to write?" It is probably safe to say that my self-confidence here, though far from justified, was a memory carried over from a previous incarnation. I should add, moreover, that this was the only exception I can remember to my usual lack of self-confidence.

On the one hand, I've always been certain I could do well anything to which I set my mind—not because I considered myself adept, but because I've accepted the higher truth, "Even if I don't see myself capable of doing that, God can do anything!"

Years ago, I was asked to write a book for Ananda's twentieth anniversary in 1988. My schedule was such that I had only one week in which to write it, after which my time was committed to other things. "I'm so sorry," I replied. "I know it would be a good thing, and I'd very much like to do it, but it just isn't possible for me." This person, who was in charge of our publications department, once more said, "It would be wonderful if you could."

Well, I knew she was right. Regretfully I repeated my statement, saying there just wasn't anything I could do about it.

Later, however, the thought suddenly came to me, "It's true that *I myself* couldn't possibly do it, but God can do *anything*! Why not open the flood-gates to Him and see what flows through me?" Banishing the thought of my own inability, I sat down at my computer and simply let flow through me what came. This process, I should add, was far from passive: it involved active *cooperation* on my part with whatever inspiration I received.

Ideas, and also the right words with which to clothe them, simply poured through my fingertips onto the computer keys. Satan must have taken an interest in the proceedings, for late in the second day someone came to work on the electrical system, and inadvertently threw a switch, costing me that entire day's output. This disaster so sapped my determination that I stopped working altogether, both the remainder of that day, and all the next day also. The third day, giving myself a stern lecture, I plunged in once again.

Despite the over-all time limitation, and even with these two whole days of lost work, I was able to get the book finished by the end of that week. Unbelievably (to me, at least), after I'd written the book I found it needed almost no editing. *Cities of Light* is its name. It has sold well over the years.

Here then, for the devotee, is an important solution to the problem of insufficient self-confidence. Even if you think, "I don't see how I can do it," remind yourself, "God can do anything!"

The matter also goes even deeper: It shows that lack of self-confidence can actually be an aid, not a hindrance, to successful accomplishment. Facing frankly, and accepting, the fact of one's own inability will dismiss from the mind the long, agonizing process: "Can I? *How* can I? What experience have I had to make this job possible? Couldn't others do it better? What's the use of even contemplating the job: I'd only make myself a laughingstock if I tried!"

Remember the formula: "*I* can't, but *God*, through me, can do *anything!*" How many times have I found the solution I sought in this simple thought! One consequence, in fact, has been that my own deep-seated self-doubts, brought over from past lives, along with their accompanying lack of self-confidence, have unlocked doors to what few, perhaps, would deny has been a successful incarnation. My lack of belief in myself, *directed outward and away from myself*, has resulted in my being able to complete many projects simply because in self-forgetfulness I could concentrate one-pointedly on whatever project presented itself.

Public speaking? I said earlier that I've never been nervous lecturing. The reason, again, is almost childishly simple. It is due to my complete absence of self-confidence.

My "initiation" into public speaking could not, as a matter of fact, have been more dramatic.

I was twenty-two years old at the time. Eight months beforehand (in the afternoon of September 12th, 1948), I'd been accepted by the great master, Paramhansa Yogananda, as a disciple. The following May, one sunny Saturday morning, I received a message from him via an older brother disciple: He wanted me to take his place conducting the Sunday morning service at our church in San Diego, California!

I happened to know that his appearance there that day had been widely announced, and was being eagerly anticipated by the parishioners. He had been speaking there on alternate Sundays, but for the past two months had not been able to be present. The congregation members had been told to check their newspapers on Saturday morning to see whether he would appear the next day. It was my job to send those announcements to the press, so I knew the announcement had been sent out.

With the news that Master wanted me to give the service the next day, I also learned that he wanted me to initiate a congregation member into Kriya Yoga, a ceremony I'd attended only once before, five months earlier.

Obediently I made the 100-mile journey south by bus from Los Angeles. I'll spare the reader most of this gruesome story. Suffice it to relate that, when the curtain opened that next morning to reveal this callow youth standing there, instead of the great Master everyone expected, I could sense an almost tangible shock pass through the whole audience. The church was full to overflowing; people were craning their heads to see in through the windows. If ever in my life there might be a time when I'd feel nervous, this was it.

Strange to say, I was calm. Slightly apprehensive, yes of course! But so keen was my sympathy for those poor people in their disappointment that I hadn't enough concern left over to feel sorry for myself.

The projection of sympathy I suggest contains another key to overcoming the lack of self-confidence. You won't have to worry about yourself if you can concentrate on the needs of your listeners. Don't make an issue of getting yourself out of the way. Simply focus on what needs to be done, and on the people you're serving.

I've found it very useful also to focus on that "worst case scenario." What images can I dream up as possibly the most fear-inspiring? Whatever they may be, I've visualized them clearly, in the context of a much broader reality, and have then asked myself, "Well, but is this *all*?" With an overall view of things, this eventuality doesn't seem so appalling after all. Most people manage somehow to survive things, and even to laugh about them, later.

Even death, when it comes, is not really the end of very much: It is only the end of a very brief phase of existence. If even death comes, then—should that be the outcome of that "worst case scenario"—it shouldn't be so very difficult to face. Tell yourself, "What of it? Death must come to me eventually, so why not keep myself in readiness for it?" This practice will spare you much suffering, and will also bring you much peace of mind. I've found, in holding that thought, that I am always peaceful, and am also able to relax before an audience, not feeling at all nervous while standing there, prepared to begin speaking.

I might add here that it does take a certain firmness of will to hold thoughts like these. A brother monk in the monastery where I lived was passing through a time of inner testing. He would enter my room and, sitting heavily on my bed as I worked at my desk, utter a deep sigh as if about to announce Doomsday. I sincerely wanted to encourage him. One day, however, insufficiently weighing the possible consequences,

I said to him, "Cheer up, old fellow. This can't last forever. Surely you'll be out of it at least in a few more years." My attempt to strengthen his will had unfortunate consequences: he went into a deeper slump that lasted weeks.

In my autobiography, *The Path*, I've told another story about a "worst case scenario." It was while I was a student at Haverford College. I was in my room late one evening, studying for an exam. Suddenly I heard footsteps approaching softly over the grass outside my window. Smiling to myself, I thought, "This is the hour the library closes. One of my friends must be coming back from there, and wants to give me a playful shock." To show him I was onto his game, I went to the window and looked out. The footsteps ran away hastily into the night. I smiled, sat down again, and waited for my friend to come in by the front door, upon which we'd have a good chuckle.

No one came.

Strange! Maybe—the thought appeared whimsically in my mind—someone had been planning to take a shot at me. The absurdity of the idea only broadened my smile, for of course it couldn't possibly be true.

Some fifteen minutes later, footsteps again came stealing over the grass—this time, if anything, even more cautiously. I thought, "None of my friends would be this persistent in a mere joke. Maybe someone *is* intending to shoot me!" Of course I didn't believe it, but the thought came, "How can I find out? I must let him carry out his intentions and not interrupt them."

A foot was placed cautiously on the ledge outside my window. A hand grasped the railing outside. I kept my gaze fixed on my book, smiling to myself as I pretended to notice nothing.

Suddenly: a loud shot! How could this be? The ringing in my ears died down, and I again heard the ticking of my clock on the mantelpiece. A car in the nearby parking lot started up, racing off into the distance. How perfectly absurd! I checked my body. Not a wound anywhere. I went over to the window and checked the screen: not even a hole. What on earth could have happened? I sat back in my chair and, believe it or not, laughed heartily! It seemed so ridiculous that my "fears" had actually been verified.

The following day it occurred to me that the evening before had been Halloween, when a certain latitude is given youngsters to play pranks. Some local boy, evidently, intending to frighten one of "those uppity college boys," had fired a blank pistol at me.

Well, I don't recommend such insouciance to people. Certainly it would be foolish actually to *court* death! At the same time, I do suggest that my carefree laughter was better than screams, tears, and wild heart palpitations, which others might have suffered. At least this much of a moral, then, might be drawn from that episode: If there is something you really can't help in your life, don't react emotionally: react *usefully.* This is the only way to save at least something from the wreckage.

What I suggest is that you see whether you can't bring yourself to accept *any possible* eventuality in your life. Be reasonably cautious, of course—I wasn't so, on that evening—but if things then turn out in a way that you'd rather they hadn't, why not condition your mind to accept an outcome that you can't help? Doing so will contribute greatly to your own ability to function efficiently and also appropriately.

It is sort of like—was it the red or the white queen in *Alice Through the Looking Glass,* where time itself moved backward? Anyway, that lady suddenly cried out in dismay, "Oh! Oh!"

"What's the matter." asked Alice anxiously.

"I'm going to prick myself with a needle!" cried the queen.

A moment later she was calm again. "Why are you now so relaxed?" Alice asked.

"Oh, I've pricked myself," came the nonchalant answer. It's happened. It's over. Why cry about it?

People tend to fear what *might* happen, but they become accepting once it has already occurred. Thus, again, the benefit of that "worst case scenario" as a visualization. Imagine the worst, gird yourself to accept it, and then simply move on. In this way you'll stop worrying about your own competence or lack of it.

As a little boy, I had a serious problem: A black panther used to crouch under my bed at night! I hardly dared to put my feet on the floor for fear of being seized in its jaws. Would my "worst case scenario" have worked in this case? Perhaps not. Well, this was one problem I never did have to settle. What occurred, I imagine, was that the fearsome beast became discouraged one day, and crept out of the house when I was at breakfast.

Basically, I think the reason I myself haven't had a problem with lack of self-confidence is not my lack of it, but rather that I've never had enough self-confidence to worry about not having it. By accepting things as they were, and telling myself, on the other hand, that God can do anything, I've always found I had nothing to worry about.

For instance, artificial hip replacements have made it quite impossible for me to run races or to go skiing (a sport I used to enjoy). Why fret about it? I might as well feel handicapped by my inability to fly. What would be the use of such a preoccupation? Human beings, unaided, simply can't fly; they haven't the needed equipment. So, let me direct my attention toward things I *can* do.

Psmith, a creation of the comic writer P.G. Wodehouse, in addressing Mike, a classmate he's meeting for the first time, asks him, "Are you the Bully, the Pride of the School, or the Boy who is Led Astray and takes to Drink in Chapter Sixteen?"

I'm afraid I'm no stock character. In fact, I don't really know who I am. I've no self-definition. For me, therefore, self-confidence simply isn't a problem. Whom is there that I'm supposed to have confidence in?

At this point you may ask me: "Did the young man who was interviewing you earlier have any more questions for you?" I don't know. Perhaps I just left him standing on a corner somewhere, as I went stumbling off down the street, mumbling these further ideas to myself.

Can Love Be Universalized?

A friend of mine in India once said to me, "My servant's son was recently murdered, over the debt of a mere few hundred rupees [hardly ten dollars]!

"I know," she continued, "that we are supposed to love everybody, but how is it possible to love someone who has committed such a vicious and pointless crime?"

Love, under such circumstances, may not be the first word that springs to mind! I told her, of course, that she can love God *impersonally* in all. Unfortunately even that, by itself, might have seemed too abstract to her, for I don't recall her as an especially ardent devotee.

That lack may have been even deeper in her, for if she was like many people, she had quite possibly asked herself, "How *lovable* can God be, anyway: He who allows injustice apparently so to thrive in this world?"

I didn't bother to remind her that it was surely that boy's karma to be slain—an explanation which, although valid, if given at such a time would have been tantamount to saying, "He deserved to be killed!" Yes, no doubt he did deserve what he got, for such is the Law of Karma. It would have been small comfort to tell her so, however, and even less comfort to the boy's poor mother. Perhaps in some former life the boy actually slew his present murderer. But how could I, at that moment, even hint at this possibility?

One thing I did say was this: "Why not reflect on the many lifetimes it takes the soul to reach perfection? This fact alone, surely, should help all of us to feel deeply for other human beings, fellow-sufferers with us on the same journey. We are all struggling—some of us more consciously than others—toward that common goal."

Paramhansa Yogananda stated, in his commentary on the *Rubaiyat* of Omar Khayyam, that the meaning of one quatrain (*rubai*) is that many of the souls that appeared as separate egos at the beginning of this Day of Brahma (which lasts for billions of years) will still be wandering in delusion at the end of that vast time period. God is manifested, however, in every human being. The one Divinity is asleep, as it were, in us all (asleep, that is to say, to our own awareness).

Eventually, the destiny of everyone on earth is to find the essence of his being in God alone. The forms we inhabit, and the qualities we acquire during our sojourns on earth, are often in themselves far from lovable. To hate any form or any quality, however, is to affirm it as a reality to ourselves. The changeless divine essence in us all is Bliss, which is infinitely lovable.

Both lovable and inspiring is the truth that the desire for bliss is the hidden motivation behind every action, both wise and ignorant. Look upon all beings, therefore, as struggling through trial and error toward their own deepest truth. This was what Jesus Christ meant when he said, "Love thy neighbor as thyself." In the final analysis, our true self *is* the Self of all!

We can see that murderer too, then, as only seeking, though mistakenly, his own bliss-nature. He will err again no doubt, perhaps millions of times. Love, however, will help him far more on his journey than hatred ever could. And although it is true that hatred and condemnation are necessary goads toward their eventual salvation, love can be their shortcut to that goal. In giving love to all, moreover, we greatly shorten our own pilgrimage to divine union. At the end of everyone's long road lies that common destiny: the realization of God as *Satchidananda*—ever-existing, ever-conscious, ever-new Bliss.

Through all the soul's bodily encasements, the ego faces innumerable choices. Whether or not to seek bliss, however, is the only real choice placed before us. Bliss is the right choice, and, next to that, whatever leads toward it. Bliss alone is, universally, the right answer, however late or soon we hit upon it.

That murderer's error in this life was simply that he thought he'd get what he wanted by giving vent to the disharmony he was feeling at the moment. He'll learn, in time, that such release is no solution at all; it merely affirms the emotion, thereby strengthening its hold. That man's inability to control his temper, like every white-flag surrender of one's self-control before the forces of evil, will give him nothing in the end but great pain and suffering. Surely we can compassionate even the vilest of evil-doers for the sorrows they are self-destined to experience.

Eventually, all souls must reach true understanding, which comes with wisdom. Wisdom, however, lies in a very different direction from that in which most people believe, and seek. It lies not outwardly, but in the Self.

There is another very practical reason for us to love everyone: In loving others, we ourselves find *happiness*! Our first reaction, especially when dear friends hurt us, may be to feel betrayed. This reaction, though natural, fails in not being *supernatural*. Resentment is an expression of the deluded ego, not of the soul. To feel hurt is a reaction that further involves one in *maya* (delusion). Those who desire to escape ego-bondage, however, offer every such pettiness up to the Infinite.

If anyone ever hurts you, or in other ways betrays you, ask yourself this simple question: "Is there any reason why I should suffer *twice*? I've been hurt, yes; my peace of mind has been shaken, true; but now let me be practical! Shouldn't my first responsibility be to my own peace of mind?" We can't control the behavior of others. They, on the other hand, can't take responsibility for our reactions to them. How *we* feel is our business and no one else's By refusing others the privilege of affecting our feelings about anything, we deprive them of any lingering power they may still have to hurt us.

Moreover, by denying them any control over us, we ourselves become inwardly stronger, and capable of helping many others.

Accept impersonally, therefore, whatever happens to you in life. If others criticize you, don't let them affect how you feel even toward them. Ask yourself this question: "*Is the criticism justified?*" If so, why not be grateful for it? In fact, why not thank them openly? (Doing so will take the sting out of anything further they may wish to say on the matter.) On the other hand, don't express gratitude too abjectly lest they throw your confession back at you someday in a moment of pique. It would be wiser, rather than admitting their rightness too humbly, to say only (after thanking them), "I appreciate the good will you've shown in correcting me, and will give the matter sincere and careful thought."

Refuse to be affected by other people's opinions of you, or of anything else. Reflect—not cynically, but kindly, and with thought also to your own fallibility—that people are wrong about most things! If they weren't, they'd probably be at a higher stage of evolution by now, and might even be inhabiting some more highly evolved planet! Even when they are right, remember, everyone makes mistakes, so don't be discouraged. We're all here together in the great school of Life, learning the lessons we need for graduation. In any case, opinions about truth don't really matter compared to the truth itself.

When people criticize you, when they betray you or in some other way hurt you, ask yourself another simple, very practical question: "Who is the captain of my ship?"

Be inwardly free! Even if people choose to define themselves as your enemies, why accept their definition as your definition of them? Be calmly settled in your inner Self.

With an attitude of true freedom it is possible to love others no matter how they behave toward you, or toward anyone else. Tell yourself, "My love is my own to give as I choose." Then ask yourself further, "Am I happier when I love others than when I hold harsh thoughts about them?" This simple act of discrimination will help you see that you are—that all of us are—much happier giving love than in withholding it. For your own sake then, if for no other reason, strive always to be kind, supportive, and helpful toward everyone. Next, if you are sufficiently non-attached, give them love.

If, on the other hand, what they themselves need is a good lesson, what better lesson could they receive than your kindly, or at least impersonal, reaction? If they actually wanted to make you suffer, it will drive them wild to see that their meanness hasn't touched you at all! Love them now, perhaps, more than ever, for they must need your compassion! The love you give them in return, then, will also be *their* shortcut to salvation.

Remember, compassion is enlightened self-interest: it springs from knowing yourself as the true Self of all.

In the last analysis, the best rationale for all moral behavior is the effect it has on you, the "behaver." Your own self, which is the Self of all, is what you must serve first of all.

Yogananda said that even Jesus Christ would not have willingly accepted persecution and crucifixion had he believed that, instead of pleasing God, he would suffer in hell for his sacrifice. It was the bliss he experienced in people's gain from those sacrifices that inspired him to his (egoically) completely selfless, heroic action.

There is a world of difference, my Guru explained, between enlightened self-interest and self-interest that is ego-centered. Selfishness and indifference to others is of the ego. Compassion is of the soul: the "self"-interest of enlightenment.

TOMORROW'S SUPERMEN?

A small group of us gathered in my home the other evening to watch a new electronic formatting (Blu-ray)
of the old movie, *2001: A Space Odyssey*. There was a general feeling of relief when "Intermission" flashed on the
screen and we were free to "jump ship" from that launch to
Jupiter.

Blessed respite! The movie penciled in for me once again
old, faded memories: the pale glow of drab expectations
held by millions; a gray, loveless future labeled, "Paradise,"
where laughter echoes mockingly down long, dark corridors
stripped of all joy, enthusiasm, and smiling hope.

In that two-dimensional "heaven," man will have out-
grown his emotions as "weaknesses." The human being will
be a strictly rational, unfeeling machine, with a heart like
a dry riverbed on which shining pebbles of logic lie where
they were placed, never to be washed away by any human
joy or sorrow.

What saddens me is to see in our times this excessive
trend toward intellectualization. People equate intelligence
with intellect, but not with awareness. Already centuries
ago, Thomas Aquinas (born 1225 A.D.) offered his famous
definition: "Man is a 'rational animal.'" Perhaps, then, we
should call this trend toward rationality a "Western" tendency. The trend has become ever stronger, however, since
the advent of science. What is particularly modern about
it is the lingering belief that man will someday be able to
develop mechanisms intelligent enough to out-think man
himself. Computers have made this expectation a reasonable possibility. An extraordinarily intuitive Indian lady
whom I saw years ago on television was able to beat a sophisticated computer in the speed with which she reached
computational conclusions. In one case she said (and was

later proved right) that the computer had erred (perhaps owing to a mistake in its programming). Nevertheless, this was only one exceptional human being. Shall we say, at least, that computers are already more intelligent than the rest of us bumbling human beings?

What I object to is equating intelligence with facility at reasoning. In that movie, the proof of man's inadequacy was that Hal, the supreme example of artificial intelligence, beat a brilliant human being at a game of chess. My own reaction is to ask myself, Do I consider myself *less* human for the fact that I am not necessarily brilliant at chess? My Guru once asked the whereabouts of a certain over-intellectual disciple named Bernard. On being told that the young man was playing chess, our Guru's only reaction was to exclaim, "What a waste of time!"

Do you, who read this, think it really matters one way or the other whether a person is clever enough to win at chess? or to see the pitfalls in a crossword puzzle and step gingerly around them?

I who write this am not a "lowbrow," anxious to deprecate what I cannot equal. In fact, I myself was Bernard's opponent in that deprecated chess game. (Much to his discomfiture, I beat him.) I once won a chess game against a reputed local champion by turning his own cleverness against him. He had a reputation for the clever use of his pawns. I therefore deliberately confused him by moving my pawns randomly, as if with deliberate purpose. He lost the first game, tied the next, then finally, rising in indignation, stalked away, conscious of having been merely fooled.

My own feelings about intellectual cleverness were, even then, more than equivocal. From early childhood, I simply distrusted it. There came a time, in college, when I realized that intellectuality was making me dry and unhappy. I remembered how happy I had been as a child and thought, Where have I gone wrong? Isn't happiness the true goal of life?

A classmate at Brown University said to me one day, "If ever I have met a genius, it is you." I was horrified by his seeming compliment. "What have I done," I asked myself, "to deserve that opinion? All I've done is talk cleverly!" I blushed with shame, and from then on withdrew from the coffee table discussions at which I had, I suppose, been a Voice.

A student in the women's section of the university kept hinting that she wanted me to take her out on a date. I liked her, and finally did ask her out. When I delivered her to her dorm, she exclaimed on the steps outside, "You are so *wonderful*!" My reaction was inner dismay, as I thought, "Anyone so lacking in discrimination had best be avoided." (I would rather she had said, "It is so wonderful to be with you!") I never took her out again. There was just something wrong with the whole scene I'd been building around myself. I was inwardly empty, and desperately needed to understand why.

At last I saw what I'd been lacking: God!

What, I thought, is human intellect? A puff of sand on the wind! *Happiness* is what I want. I will find that "pearl of great price" not by thinking my way to it, but only by getting my intellect out of the way and opening my heart to God.

Well, everyone who knows me knows also what happened then. I found *Autobiography of a Yogi*, and very soon thereafter became a direct disciple of the author, Paramhansa Yogananda. It was he who showed me the truth of the matter. People excuse themselves with the conveniently exculpatory statement, "Well, I'm only human." What Yogananda showed me was the higher truth: "I am trying, but I'm not yet fully human!"

To be a complete human being means to realize one's own full potential as a child of God. Until then, one is still only a sort of robot, functioning with varying degrees of efficiency, but unable, as yet, to go beyond merely functioning. I'll never forget a pithy comment by an old man I once knew regarding a younger man, known to us both, "Oh, B——! He's just barely conscious!"

The question is sometimes asked: "Will computers someday exceed human intelligence?" If it comes to specific problem-solving, why not? Computers are designed to spare man the effort of lengthy and tedious ratiocination. There are probably countless other reasoning functions for which computers would not be worth the trouble to program, but where they can serve us I for one have no objection. The intellect is only, in any case, what we might call an "electronic mechanism." It has nothing to do with actual awareness. Logic is not what lifts man above the animals. It is the much greater clarity of human awareness.

In that movie, someone said of Hal, "We've programmed him with some emotions, to make him seem more human." Oh, yeah? Impossible, I say! The most they could have programmed into that computer would have been the *semblance* of such reactions. As for the emotions, it would be out of the question. Feeling cannot be "programmed," for it is an essential aspect of consciousness itself.

People don't seem to understand that consciousness is a more basic reality than rational intelligence—more basic, and also more transcendent. Consciousness is our central reality. It cannot be defined: It can only be perceived. That perception, moreover, is *intuitive*, not rational. Descartes said, "I think, therefore I am." He was quite wrong! He should have said, "I *am*"—or perhaps better, "I am conscious of being"—"and therefore I am able to think."

An almost universal failing is the tendency to judge human excellence by personal standards. A banker may despise artists on the grounds that they lack down-to-earth practicality. Artists, again, may sneer at bankers as mere "money machines." Intellectuals may look down on ditch diggers as unrefined. Ditch diggers may return the compliment by scoffing at intellectuals as "highbrows." Men may object to women, as Professor Higgins did in *My Fair Lady*, lamenting, "Why can't a woman be more like a man?" And women, of course, may (and often do) retaliate. (Comments I have actually heard are: "Let's face it, women are more spiritual than men," and, "Let's face it [again], women are more intelligent than men.")

What I say is, Anyone who toots his own horn, especially at the expense of others, is already sounding a sour note.

The truth is that *clarity* of consciousness is the whole secret. This involves removing every obstacle to the achievement of that clarity. And the greatest obstacle of all is people's present-day skepticism regarding intuition itself. I don't mean the psychic's extra-sensory insight. Intuition begins with the simple awareness that we exist: a reality that can never be proved, for all of us are consciously *self*-existent, and *self*-aware. The self can indeed be analyzed, but it can never be *understood* through analysis, which at best can only rid us of false self-definitions. When all conceptual errors have been eliminated, there remains that indefinable, irreducible reality: our one Divine Self.

Swami Shankaracharya (often spoken of as *Adi*, the first of many who have taken the same name) wrote in a song: "Mind, nor intellect, nor ego, nor feelings am I: I am He! I am He! Blissful Spirit, I am He!" Ancient tradition divides human awareness into those four aspects: mind, intellect, ego, and feelings. I've put "feelings" in the plural here, because *feeling* (singular) includes also Bliss, which Shankara himself said is our essential nature. What is intellect, without feeling? What is consciousness itself, without feeling? And what is feeling, without *self*-consciousness?

It is in fact feeling which guides the intellect. That is why scientists do their best to exclude feeling from every reckoning: they fear it might prejudice their judgment. They are quite right, of course. The trouble is, no one can really exclude his feelings. All he can do is drive them underground, where, operating in darkness, they can trick the intellect with false justifications. What everyone needs is to calm his emotions, and thereby to develop intuitive feeling. Without feeling of any kind, the intellect can justify *any* conclusion, even the most monstrously evil. Without intuition, the intellect simply cannot be trusted. Only *uplifted* feeling shows the way to right understanding.

Those "supermen" of tomorrow, depicted in the movie we saw, were men without emotions, and also, therefore (according to the shallow understanding of those who perpetrated that movie), without feeling. They worked entirely by intellect: frozen-faced, solemn to the point of grimness, emotionally unresponsive: mere human abstractions. Hal, the so-named artificial intelligence in the movie, seemed more human than any of them. The only women I remember in the movie were two who came on only briefly, as stony-faced as the men. What a glorious future for mankind! Even in the present, when reflecting on the state of this poor planet, I find myself thinking, "What a bummer!"

The trouble is, it is equally a "bummer" to have an ego at all. So also is it to have emotions, rather than calm, intuitive feeling. Truly, being a human being is itself only a stop on the way to our true destiny: oneness with God.

Learn to See, Feel, and Think Differently

"**M**y thoughts are not your thoughts, neither are your ways my ways, saith the Lord." (Isa. 55:8)

To find God, it will help us to try to see, feel, and think of everything differently from what we are accustomed to doing. That is why, among devotees in India, much is made of the importance of *bhav*, right spiritual attitude. We must try constantly to rise above seeing everything in reference to our egos; we must stop thinking, "My home, my wife or husband, my children, my clothes, my job, my friends, my position in the world, my reputation, my talents, my strengths, my defects, my advantages, my disadvantages." You can see that the list might be continued indefinitely. Everything that most people see, even impersonally, they tend to relate back to the thought of their human selfhood. Even when they step out under the heavens at night and contemplate the infinite vastness, with its myriad stars and inconceivable reaches of space, their usual first thought is, "How small *I* feel, by comparison!"

An artist sees a beautiful sunset, and thinks, "I wonder if *I* could paint so beautifully?" Someone else contemplates a great deed performed by some other human being; his first thought is, "Could I ever do that deed? Well, if not, here's what I *can* do, and probably better than he." And so the drama plays on, every scene depicting the hero or heroine as one's little self, and the parts (s)he plays on the stage as being the most important: every actor the central character, even if that role is only the butler, gravely announcing a visitor.

One time, years ago, I made a recording of some chants: traditional Indian and others also by my Guru. A young Indian tabla drummer played the accompaniment. It was very evident, later, that he'd considered himself the whole show. Someone asked him, "How did the recording go?"

"Fine!" he replied. "I played such-and-such a *tala* (rhythm)."

If we want to find God, it is extremely important that we strive from the very beginning to look at everything differently from the way to which we've probably been—and most people quite certainly are—accustomed. New insight will of course come to us as we progress on the path, but it would help us from the start if we made an effort to adopt those attitudes which will come to us more naturally in time, and ever-more clearly as the veils of *maya* drop away, one by one, from before our gaze.

———

How does the enlightened soul view life? From the passage I quoted above in Isaiah, we see that there is much we may still have to learn, and much also to *unlearn*.

For one thing—indeed, for much more than that: for *everything*—we shall no longer think of things from a center of ego-consciousness. We shall no longer refer everything, or even anything, back to ourselves, unless the reference belongs to a completely impersonal view of reality.

To give an example: a good singer-saint may be aware that he has sung well, but he will never think, "It is *I* who have sung well." He will think, rather, "God sang His beauty through me." That is to say, he will be well aware—perhaps even more so than most people—of the beauty itself. But he will never think of himself as the producer of that beauty. He will understand that God alone, in everything, was and ever is the Doer.

For another thing, he will begin to look at everything from the inside, out: to view everything and everyone in terms of the divine consciousness residing *at the center* of all things.

These are not things I've read in a book, and perhaps I should make that fact clear lest someone wiser than I am tell me someday, "You've perceived (this or that point) incorrectly. What you've said is partly true, but here is another aspect of the matter you've overlooked." That may happen; I don't know. All I can say is that this is, so far, the understanding I've reached, and I think it worthwhile to share with others.

For when I think of that divine center in all things, and in all people, I find I see everything and everyone quite differently. When I relate to other people from my own center to their centers, instead of from my ego to theirs, I find myself feeling toward them in a different way altogether. I understand them better, and I also find that I evoke a new reaction in them. Even strangers are more likely to look upon me as their own, and somehow even to *know* me as their friend, in whom they can confide their troubles and depend upon to give them support and help in their difficulties. My perception of them is *from the inside*, not merely from their appearance. Perhaps that is why, as Asha noted in her book, though I am usually intensely conscious of colors, I never notice the color of people's eyes.[*]

I feel in some way related to them, even as though I recognized them, from before.

Best of all, perhaps, when I ponder the vast drama that is life, I see more clearly, and in such a way as to fill me with love and bliss, that it is God Himself who is directing the whole show. Through all the ups and downs of life—the joys and the sorrows, the victories and the defeats, the fulfillments and the disappointments—I feel as if life were a great symphony. Marvelous chords emerge. The dissonances resolve into exquisite harmonies. The melodies, whether expressing grief or an upward soaring in joy, all add to the

---

[*] *Swami Kriyananda As We Have Known Him,* by Asha Praver (Crystal Clarity Publishers, 2006).

overall marvel of the great epic of adventure and love. And I know that, for *everyone*, it will all end in ecstatic thrills of bliss and a sense of undying gratitude for everything that ever happened to one.

The countless stories, whether brief or long-lasting, of friendship, romance, tenderness, misunderstanding, enmity, revenge and reconciliation: all—*all* these work out their innumerable tangles and emerge at last into a beatifically divine simplicity and delight.

It all seems almost impossibly complex. And yet in fact it is so completely, so fundamentally simple as to make one shake his head in wonder. Having spent years struggling on the path, he asks himself, "How could I have been so blind as not to *understand*?" It all now seems so clear, so utterly obvious! *Of course* what we all want is eternally the same: never money; not power; not the Lethe of alcoholic forgetfulness; not wallowing in sex; not the prideful strut of self-importance; not the humble respect and deference of others. What all of us want is, simply, Bliss.

It was bliss alone we were seeking in all those lesser fulfillments. The reason everything has disappointed us, and has proved itself, at the end of every episode, to have been no fulfillment at all, is simply that those *denouements* were all dancing at our periphery: none of them arose from our own center; none resonated with *who we really were and forever are, inside*.

When disappointment or pain come to me, now, whatever the source, I remind myself that my center lies elsewhere—that indeed, since my true center is omnipresent, my reality comprises vastness itself, of which the center is the calmness in my own heart. Thus, I have undergone the sort of pains that make many people shudder—in the dentist's chair, or in the intensive care unit of a hospital after major surgery—and all I have felt is bliss. What happened to my body never happened to *me*: it was a mere incident in an infinite, timeless reality — like a fleeting ripple on the great sea of life. And though I cannot yet claim to be conscious of my actual oneness with that Divine Sea, yet the mere affirmation of it as my deepest reality has enabled me again and again to remain calm in the midst of turmoil around me.

I see all life, now, as a dream. Such, indeed, is its fundamental "reality." The entire cosmos is God's dream. Nothing is real except in His consciousness. Living in that thought, even without the final realization of its truth, helps me to perceive with conviction that this is all I am, and all life itself is.

I see someone fulfilling some ambition and think, "That is how it will be, when I find God! It will be a surcease, a release and relaxation from all striving — but it will be eternal, not lasting for the brief second that human fulfillment brings, always followed by boredom, disappointment, failure, or (sometimes) by great sorrow. In God, fulfillment itself is final, complete, and eternal!"

I see two human lovers united joyfully at last, perhaps after numerous trials, and I think, "Yes, *that* is what will happen, in God: divine unity in the very perfection, for all eternity, of every desire for love!"

I remember watching Walt Disney's movie cartoon, *Cinderella*. Indeed, I have watched it many times, and always my reaction has been the same: soaring devotion in the thought that all the trials, sorrows, betrayals, and disappointments of life must end, not in that ephemeral fleshy embrace of human love, but in the perfection of union with God — He who holds out his arms to us in our souls, and would unite us to Him in Bliss for eternity!

If I see people exulting in some worldly gain — whether it be success, or fame — I think joyfully, "Oh, how *wonderful* it is to contemplate that zenith of all longings, knowing that, in having Him, we'll have *everything*!"

And if I see people suffering, or weeping in the pain of bereavement or of some other disaster, or over some unexpected grief, I think, "How wonderful it will be for them at last, when they realize that all this was only a dream!" And I long to help them to see it as such, indeed—to show them not merely how to escape their present suffering, which in this world of *dwaita* (duality) is only temporary—but how to escape every possibility of ever suffering again.

For the more one learns to see things in an impersonal and divine way—and this *has* to be God's view; His consciousness is omnipresent and omniscient; for Him, time and space don't even exist, for past, present, and future, and also here, there, and everywhere are all but one reality—the more one realizes that the greatest service one can render anyone is the knowledge of one's own Divine, Inner Self. That alone, through eternity, has been, is, and ever shall be our sole reality.

Trying to see things with divine vision means to view everything, even if only in imagination, as an ever-changing play of light, shadow, and color on the cosmic screen of duality.

It means contemplating the vastness of the universe and telling oneself, "At my own deepest center I am in touch with it all. *I am that!* Whatever happens in the most distant galaxy happens, in some way, also to *me!*"

It means to see the inconveniences of life—the bothersome insects, excessive heat and cold, the physical discomforts, the change and disintegration of everything we love and appreciate in this world—and to think, "I am grateful! These things help me to keep constantly in mind that my home is in Him alone."

It means to see life's countless joys and sorrows, and to think, "How wonderful is this drama, that after all the suspense, uncertainty, and tragedy man endures, it will all end in a way so supremely and utterly satisfying! There is no other story even imaginably comparable to the one which God has written for every one of us!"

Life's bubble-existence makes us experience either a constant renewal of disappointment, suffering, and pain, or else ever-new joy in the discovery that it has always been Him alone we ever wanted and loved. He alone can—and *will*, eventually—grant us all that we ever wished for in life.

And so we should view birth, life, death, merry comings together and tearful partings, laughter of joy and sighs of sadness, and through all of them let our hearts soar upward in song, knowing that all of it has been for a supremely good end. There is a *wonderful* purpose to life! Everything we do, therefore, should be a song of unceasing gratitude and bliss.

Laughter as an Expression of Spirit

There are many kinds of laughter, from heartfelt to cynical to divinely inspiring. I never knew anyone who laughed so delightfully from inner, spiritual consciousness as did my Guru, Paramhansa Yogananda. A passage from my book, *Conversations with Yogananda*, expresses this wonderful quality in him in such a way as to show that *all* laughter can be uplifting.

"I used," my Guru once said to us, "to laugh a lot when I was a boy, because of my inner joy in God. The saints I met, most of whom were outwardly grave, welcomed my laughter as coming from God.

"Bhadhuri Mahasaya (the 'levitating saint,' as I've described him in my *Autobiography*) enjoyed my laughter for the same reason. It upset a few of his disciples, however, to see me laugh in the presence of their ever-serious Master. One time he said to me, 'I understand, and appreciate why you like to laugh, but as it disturbs some of those here, do you think, perhaps, you should be more serious for their sake?'

"'I understand what you mean,' I replied, 'but can they not see that it springs from my joy in God's inner presence, and in your company?'

"He relented. 'All right, laugh if you feel to. I will try to explain to them that it is from God.'"

Laughter is an expression, usually, of happiness. We should see to it, however, that it comes from within, and is not born of a merely outward sense of hilarity. Joy that fills us with emotion can disturb our inner peace. Whenever we feel joyful and inclined to laugh for any reason, we can nourish the soul-joy within us by seeing that joy as a reminder of our own bliss-nature, within.

Turn inward every joy you feel in life. That is why most saints are grave, outwardly. Live more within yourself. See nothing outward as a cause for happiness. The more you have of inner joy, the more delight you will find in everything. God's nature is bliss. So also, the more you have of Him, will yours be. Live always, therefore, at your own center, and you will live ever-increasingly in bliss.

Part Three

Thoughts of a Disciple

The following essays are more particularly directed to those of my own religious persuasion. I have included them here because I hope they will also have universal relevance. Everything I write expresses my own sincere beliefs and convictions. It is difficult for me, therefore, to separate sincere expressions intended for the "uninitiated" from those intended for people who share my spiritual outlook more personally. Indeed, I believe that all will be able to benefit from what I write for the latter group, and in that belief (or at least hope) I include the following section in this book.

"Is Yogananda My Guru? Is Krishna? Is Jesus Christ?"

The Dilemma

A *guru* is a teacher In general parlance he can be a school teacher, someone high up in the financial world, or somebody looked up to as an authority in virtually any sphere of activity. The original meaning of the word, however, derives from the Sanskrit, *gur:* "to raise or uplift." In ancient spiritual tradition, guru means more even than a wise teacher. In the highest sense, it refers to the *satguru:* one who has reached oneness with God, is empowered by God to bring people to Him, and is specifically commissioned to bring *you* to Him. A true understanding of what it means to be this kind of guru is exemplified in Paramhansa Yogananda's *Autobiography of a Yogi.*

Yogananda announced, toward the end of his life, that he was the last in his line of gurus. There was plenty of precedent for this statement. When an *avatar** comes on earth, he plays a special role, and will continue to do so, for ages to come, in the lives of his spiritual descendants. Krishna, for example, is still viewed by many Hindus as their Supreme Guru. Buddha stands above all the saints in Buddhism who have appeared since he lived. And Jesus Christ is accepted even now, after 2,000 years, as the Supreme Savior of all Christians. Thus, Yogananda's announcement that the line of gurus he represented would end with him was neither startling nor unprecedented.

The Bible says, "Jesus himself baptized not, but his disciples." (John 4:2) Master's disciples often initiated people into Kriya Yoga on his behalf, and at his request. I myself

---

* The descent to earth of a fully liberated master, who has been sent with a special dispensation for the salvation of many. An *avatar* comes, usually, to bring a new direction in religion.

did so on several occasions. And, during the last two years of his life, it was I who accepted most of the male applicants into the ashram.

Thus, that Paramhansa Yogananda should be the last of our line of gurus is fully consonant with ancient tradition. All the masters in his line were *avatars*.

Other statements Master made to me personally must be taken into account also, however, if we would understand fully what he meant by that statement. The official claim his organization, Self-Realization Fellowship/Yogoda Satsanga Society (SRF/YSS), makes is that, among all his spiritual descendants, there will never be another guru. I am completely certain this was not at all his intention.

Statements he made to me personally, and also in my presence to several disciples, contradict that claim. Yet it has evolved over the years since his passing into a firm dogma, a fact which poses a dilemma that, if it is left unresolved, can only worsen as the years go by. I *know* he uttered the statements to which I am referring. Between them, and what has already become accepted as a dogma, there is a yawning chasm. If this chasm isn't bridged, the consequences for the Master's work will be far-reaching and drastic.

Master said to me one day when we were alone together at his desert retreat, "There has to be, *in the present life*, at least one physical contact with the guru." I have italicized that one phrase as crucial to this statement.

He told me also, "One must free at least six others before becoming finally liberated, oneself." This statement obviously needs clarification, for if "freeing" six others means giving them final liberation it can only signify, further, that those six won't be finally liberated until they, too, . . . Well, surely you get the point. What Master meant was, "free them from earth karma," at least, and perhaps also, "bestow on them *nirbikalpa samadhi*": the state from which one will never fall again.

Again, after Sister Gyanamata passed away Master told a group of us monks. "I saw her sink into that watchful state [final freedom, and complete soul-union with God]." Sister, as he called her, had suffered enough, he said. Never again would she return to this realm of manifested existence.* As I heard him utter those words, the thought crossed my mind, "But what about those six others she must have freed, first?" Master caught my thought and answered: "She *had* disciples."

History tells us that certain Christian saints, too, had disciples "in Christ." I was told that Master had said (I never personally heard him say this) that those saints themselves also had gurus. All Christians, of course, including both those saints and their disciples, have always considered themselves disciples above all of Jesus Christ. Many Hindus, similarly, consider themselves disciples of Krishna.

On the other hand, I have known gurus in India (Swami Muktananda, for example) who claimed that once a guru leaves his body, he can no longer guide his disciples. This statement, at least where great masters are concerned, is simply not true. A *true* guru constantly helps his disciples, even long after he leaves his body. Many a master has materialized to his disciples, as Jesus did, after death. Paramhansa Yogananda himself has appeared in physical form to several of his disciples. And I can attest that I myself have received help from him many times, including important guidance when I needed it. Without his help I could never have accomplished much of what I have done in this life.

Once, at his retreat in Twenty-Nine Palms, I asked him, "Will you be as close to us after you are gone as you are now?" His answer came unhesitatingly, "To those who *think* me near, I will be near."

---

* Indeed, it is rare for souls, once they achieve final liberation, to return to the realm of *maya* to help others. They are too fully satisfied, having attained at last the blissful state of oneness with God.

The solution to the dilemma I've presented is perfectly clear. Paramhansa Yogananda was an *avatar*, a state much higher than that of "ordinary" sainthood. The other gurus of our line also, including Jesus Christ (who first requested Babaji to send this teaching to the West), were all *avatars*. It is quite appropriate even for future saints on this path to accept disciples themselves *in the name of* our line of gurus.

To insist, instead, that after Yogananda (as the last of our line) there will never be another guru *in* this work, demonstrates a serious misunderstanding of his intentions. Sooner or later, were this dogma to continue to be declared officially, the doubt must inevitably arise in people's minds that these teachings are not spiritually valid. It is a fact, after all, that teachings are truly spiritual *only to the extent* that they can take people to God.

Let us consider again the evidence I've presented:

First: Master told me personally that direct contact with a living guru is necessary for one who would find God.

Second: to have a guru means that the disciple must have at least one direct, physical contact with him in this life.

Third: No one can attain final liberation until he, himself, has freed at least six others.

Fourth, and finally: If Master's most advanced woman disciple, Sister Gyanamata, had disciples of her own, that fact alone negates the claim that there can be no future gurus *in*, rather than *of*, our line. Were the present dogma valid, there could never be on this path, in all futurity, an enlightened saint. No one, after Yogananda, would achieve even the state of *jivan mukta*,* what to speak of becoming a *param mukta* (one who has attained final liberation, as "Sister" in fact did), for there would be no living guru to raise him to that state.

---

* One who, in *nirbikalpa samadhi*, has achieved freedom from ego-consciousness, but still has past karma to work out.

Were Yogananda really the last of the gurus in our line, it would mean that devotees of this teaching would be able to seek spiritual guidance now, only or primarily, by studying printed lessons, and perhaps also from letters (which, usually, come only after a delay of several months) from the headquarters of SRF/YSS, written by disciples of uncertain authority themselves since many of them are neophytes on the path. If any saint should appear on this path, now or in the future, he would not be officially permitted to have even the minimum six disciples required for advancement toward final liberation.

Actually, the divine law must prevail, despite any and every "institutional convenience." Any saints, therefore, who appeared in the work would no doubt attract disciples anyway, though (just as probably) they'd be officially branded as heretics. Such, for example, was the fate of that great Christian saint and mystic, Meister Eckhart, in Germany, whom the Catholic Church excommunicated (fortunately, for his sake, after his death).

At the first Kriya Yoga initiation I attended (in 1948), Master announced, "Of those here today, there will be a few *siddhas* (fully liberated souls), and quite a few *jivan muktas.*" The conclusion is inescapable: *Based on his own statements,* there will simply *have to be* true gurus, whether officially recognized as such or not, among the large numbers of his spiritual descendants. There can be no other resolution to the dilemma I've posed.

To summarize, then: Those who are highly advanced on this path will *of necessity* have to free others themselves. They will inevitably, in that case, be gurus also. This is not to say they will merit placement on the official altars of our line of gurus. They will be gurus, rather, to their own groups of disciples. In other words, they will be gurus *in,* but not *of,* Master's work.

Spiritual truths transcend every mere organizational convenience. It may be *convenient* for organizations to claim that, since they were founded by a true master, they have become themselves, now, the "living guru." Alternatively, it may be *convenient* to say that his writings (if he left any) have, since his earthly passing, become the guru. Convenient, maybe, but for all that, untrue. In no way does it resolve the dilemma I've posed.

By no anguished stretch of the imagination can any organizational structure be justified in assuming the role of guru. In no religion on earth is there any tradition that endorses such a claim. The role of the disciples at an institution's headquarters is, of course, defined by the organization itself, which expects them to serve above all the organization itself. Such disciples cannot themselves act as guru-substitutes, even if the organization they serve is supposed to act in that capacity. Those who work at answering letters in the main office may, as I've said, be newcomers on the path; it is by no means unheard-of for them even to forsake their spiritual calling, in time. The ancient claim in Christianity—and a major reason, I suspect, why Master coined the word, "Churchianity"—is that the Church is the "body of Christ." (Protestant Christians speak of the worldwide congregation of worshipers as his "body." This is in a sense a more valid claim, though it is really little more than a poetic figure of speech.)

There can, besides, be no validity to the claim that Master stated, whether actually or in effect, "The lessons will be the guru." This claim has been, and is, made officially by SRF/YSS. *Master* said to me personally, however, "No scripture can be the guru. If you question a scripture, it cannot answer you. If you quote passages from scripture in support of some wrong direction you may be contemplating, scripture will not correct you. Only an enlightened, living guru can guide you rightly, answer your questions, and warn you if you are about to make a mistake." (He didn't add something I already knew very well, that only a guru, whether in the body or not, can change his disciples' consciousness *from within*.)

What did Master mean by saying one must have a *living* guru? Putting together his several utterances on this subject, the conclusion is obvious: *He will continue to be the guru, through his living disciples.*

Even in India, there are people who insist that their scriptures are the guru. Can any mere written document really be so? In the deepest sense, never. A scripture may rightly *be revered*, of course. Direct instruction, however, can come only from a living teacher. Indeed, many, even among those in India who claim scripture as their guru, actually have human gurus of their own.

Daya Mata, during the time we spent together in India in 1958–59, was promulgating the doctrine that Master was the last guru for this path. She also insisted that Master had said, "The lessons will be the guru." He may actually have said that (or something similar), but certainly he did not mean it in the sense she wanted to be accepted. It was not, so to speak, an eternal truth carved in stone. What he can only have meant was, "My words are there. They will state the teachings authoritatively." In India, Daya Mata heard about those Indians who hold a comparable belief, and seized on this fact as the justification she'd been seeking, since it reinforced her resolution to officially declare the lessons themselves, now, the guru.

After a great master passes away, claims often get made that require careful and *objective* scrutiny. That scrutiny ought to include the following questions: Might a claim have been made with an ulterior motive—institutional *convenience*, perhaps? Did the guru really, himself, make *every* statement that is now being circulated by his followers? Might he have said something different, and even contradictory, to those statements? To what extent is he being quoted *correct-ly*? And, finally, might something he said to one person have been applied by others in ways that he never intended?

I recall an episode when his meaning became immediately, and obviously, distorted. Master had said something to Oliver Rogers, one of the monks, in the presence of several of us. "Rogers," he announced, "you will have clear sailing!"

Some of those present wondered, quite naturally, "What about *me*?" Master caught their thought, and, not wanting to leave them "hanging," added (but with rather less conviction), "And you will all have clear sailing, if you remain loyal to the end."

Afterward, several of the monks exulted together, "Did you hear *that*? Master said *we'll all have clear sailing*!"

Need I point out the obvious? Their enthusiasm was a structure raised on the quicksand of wishful thinking! Indeed, not all of them, as it turned out, remained "loyal to the end." Oliver Rogers (Brother Devananda) did.

Another point needs to be taken into consideration also: A master's words may sometimes need editing. Our own Guru made no bones about it where his own writings were concerned. He *wanted* his meanings to be presented as clearly and exactly as possible—suitably, of course, to his own style of expression, and not clumsily or pedantically. He himself went primarily by intuition. It was something of an "obstacle course" for him to enter into the clumsy process of careful reasoning, necessary to the process of conscientious editing. I've compared the job of editing, elsewhere, to plumbing: a process primarily of shifting words and phrases about to improve their flow, and painstakingly seeking just the right words for exact meaning, clarity, rhythm, and harmonious resonance.

Master once, for example, said to me, "The dreamer is not conscious of his dream." That sentence obviously needed editing, since if the dreamer is not conscious of his dream, he can't be dreaming at all!

The editor of his first published book of sayings, *The Master Said*, tried to clarify that statement by making it read, "The dreamer is not cognizant of the hallucinatory fabric of his dream." (Does anyone *ever* speak like that?) In a book of his sayings that I myself edited years later, I changed that sentence to read: "The dreamer is not conscious of the fact that he is dreaming." Surely my version is simpler, clearer, and closer to what he actually said. I offer this example to show that a guru's statements may not only need editing sometimes, but that this fact introduces the danger that they may also get changed in the process as to their actual meaning—a possibility Master himself was particularly concerned about. It is important, therefore, that a guru's writings be edited only by his close disciples, those who are at least more likely to understand his subtle nuances of thinking, and that the editing not be done by people merely whose English is good, but who are not familiar with these nuances. (Indeed, some of the Master's early editors actually intruded into his writings philosophical concepts of their own!)

This is especially true of statements he may have made—as everyone does when speaking casually—without taking into account any possible misconstruction of his meaning, and that might become *mis*quoted, or quoted in the wrong context. Indeed, Master stated, of the four Gospels of the Bible, that a master's disciples are not likely to be infallible in quoting him, even if they are completely conscientious. A person can express only those thoughts which accord with his own *level of understanding*. There is also the danger of *mis*quoting when some special—usually institutional—agenda exists.

In those statements of Master's I quoted above, I've repeated his words exactly—without editing, and without the slightest "hidden agenda." I cannot say the same of every statement I've heard quoted.

There is a claim that has been made by some of Yogananda's disciples that he prophesied all future presidents of his organization would be Self-realized. Can he possibly, really, have made such a statement? It goes against all logical probability. This is another example of quotations that need to be carefully weighed and scrutinized, for common sense rejects it out of hand. If nothing else, there is no precedent for it. This claim has all the earmarks, in fact, of "Churchianity." That is to say, it sounds suspiciously like a boost for the institution.

For anyone to be promoted to the top position in an institution, he or she, clearly, must be qualified for that job, which, apart from any other consideration, is administrative in nature. The skills demanded of a president are quite separate and distinct from the qualifications a devotee needs for spiritual development. Managerial skills may, of course, exist side by side in the same person. Reason tells us, however, that this is likely to be so only very rarely.

I myself, moreover, for ten years after Yogananda left his body, held several high positions in that organization. I became, toward the end, the first vice president and a member of the Board of Directors. I was an insider, in other words, as fully "in the know" as it was possible to be. I make the following statement, in other words, from first-hand knowledge:

I am perfectly certain Master *never* said anything of this nature. I certainly never heard him so quoted with anything like authoritative support. He never made such a statement about all future SRF presidents. He did say that Rajarshi Janakananda was already Self-realized, but that was not a prediction: It was a statement of Rajarshi's actual present state. The fact that this supposed prophecy never surfaced during the ten years I was on the scene after Master's passing means that any claim that has surfaced since then must be treated as fiction.

I do remember Tara once making a statement at a Christmas banquet which might have become distorted, over time. I was present on that occasion. What she said was, "Master predicted that no future SRF president would ever fail to live up to his ideals." Even this statement had, to my mind, a certain ring of "institutional convenience." Indeed, I remember Tara as someone who was not always averse to altering Master's words, when a change in them might serve an institutional end. One such change, indeed, dates back to my own years in the organization. I remember it particularly—to my subsequent embarrassment—for she made it *in consequence of a suggestion I myself had made!*

At the Christmas banquet to which I've referred, the statement she quoted (which I couldn't help questioning, anyway) was the *only* one I can imagine that *might conceivably* have evolved over time, and with frequent repetition, into the belief that *all* future SRF presidents would be Self-realized.

High position in a spiritual organization is no guarantee of profound spirituality. Abundant proof of this fact may be seen in the history of the Catholic popes, not all of whom were even worthy of that title. In my book, *Revelations of Christ, Proclaimed by Paramhansa Yogananda*, I made this point. What I said there was that spirituality depends primarily on a person's purity of heart, whereas high position in an institution depends primarily on one's secular abilities. To be the president of an institution, one must be above all a good administrator. Many of those "lowest on the totem pole" may, in fact, be the true saints. Sainthood cannot reasonably, in other words, be even considered a necessary qualification for the presidency, or for any institutional position. True saints, indeed, may not even find themselves on that "totem pole" at all.

There is another thought in need of clarification:

A member of SRF, a woman who lived near Encinitas, kept a photograph of Dr. Lewis* on her altar. One of the nuns saw that altar, and told the woman she shouldn't keep anything there but the pictures of our gurus. This occurred while Master was still alive. The woman, since she was particularly devoted to Dr. Lewis, made it a point to ask Master for a direct ruling in this matter. He told her, "On your own private altar it is fine to keep other pictures. It is our church altars that should be confined to the pictures of our gurus."

Master's "ruling" on this point raises an important issue: We are sometimes asked at Ananda, "Why have you removed the picture of Krishna from your altars?" Our reply is, "We *didn't remove* it! SRF *added* it to *their* altars, *since* Master's passing."

This inclusion of Krishna is another thing Daya Mata herself did after her 1958 visit to India. One assumes she did so out of concern lest Hindus in India complain—as they understandably might—at Jesus Christ, without Krishna, being central on our altars. Evidently she thought, "Well, since Master said Babaji is an incarnation of Krishna, and since he actually led us in prayers to 'Babaji-Krishna,' it seems all right to place Krishna centrally there also."

A problem results from this decision, however. Even though the teachings of Krishna were certainly an important part of Master's message to the West and to the world, Krishna, *as Krishna*, was not responsible for *launching* this message. Jesus Christ, on the other hand, *as* himself requested Babaji to have this message sent to the West. By placing Krishna on the altar, the message conveyed is that Jesus was only a great master whose teachings we revere, along with those of Krishna. This message neglects the central role played by Jesus himself in our Gurus' lineage. Krishna did

---

* Yogananda's first Kriya Yoga disciple in America.

inspire Master's teachings. Jesus, however, was responsible for actively *sending* them. The fact that Babaji is an incarnation of Krishna, as Babaji has himself said, must be balanced against the fact that Master, who understood every aspect of this issue, never placed him *as Krishna* on our altars.

For this reason, I have kept Master's original design, with only the five gurus there, and with Jesus at the center. In India, as a concession to Hindus, I've had an artist paint a picture with Krishna positioned behind Jesus Christ as if blessing him. This painting emphasizes Christ's central role, without in any way denigrating Krishna. Krishna lived centuries before Jesus Christ, moreover, and is certainly a fundamental inspiration behind our teachings. It was, as I implied, Krishna's later incarnation as Babaji that, in concert with Christ, launched this message for the New Age.

This may seem to some people a trivial point. In any case, it underscores something that I consider important: I have always tried to be completely orthodox to my Guru's stated wishes.

Finally, the question may arise: Why have I written these thoughts? I've done so for two reasons. First, I can think of no one else who could write them even if he wanted to. Second, it is important for these thoughts to be expressed, lest in future the dogma of Master's being the last of our gurus becomes so firmly established in people's minds that any teacher to whom people looked as a representative of this path would soon come under a cloud of official suspicion and might even, perhaps, find himself excommunicated.

For years while I was in SRF I thought—indeed, I was conditioned to think—of my job of teaching and lecturing, which Master had assigned me, as serving only the purpose of bringing people *to him.* Once students were on the path, it was, I thought, my duty to turn them over to him, my officially sanctioned idea being that any guidance they needed from then on was the concern of letter writers in the head office at Mt. Washington. It was easy for me to renounce further responsibility in the matter, for my first thought has always been to please my Guru. If this was what he wanted, as I'd been assured it was, I was satisfied to let my efforts stop there.

I came gradually, however, even while I was still in SRF, to realize that people need *ongoing, direct guidance* from someone *they know personally*, rather than from shadowy figures "off-stage," so to speak, residing at headquarters. I realized, moreover, that it wasn't fair to tell students they could get their more important guidance only from Master, in meditation. Observing people over the years, I came to realize that those who insisted on going straight to him, without the help they might have received in person from disciples of long standing, never went very deeply into the teachings. Often, in fact, I noted that they wandered off sooner or later to other teachings altogether.

Were the dogma to be fully established that Master is not only the last of our line of gurus, but also the last one who could guide or inspire anyone spiritually, it would mean that no one on this path could or should ever take special pains to offer spiritual help to people. Such a prohibition would raise doubts as to the very authenticity of these teachings. Sincere spiritual seekers would wonder if they might not do better to seek elsewhere, from teachers who offered more sympathetic counsel.

This suggestion is not fanciful. Such a situation actually occurred, years ago, in the case of Yogacharya Oliver Black. I personally heard Master say, of this disciple, that he was highly advanced spiritually. During a visit to Mt. Washington, Yogacharya Oliver made a reference to certain persons he was guiding personally. This "heretical" statement drew stern criticism from the nuns there. Daya Mata herself, in conversation with me, referred critically to that statement. It is clear to me, even from this single example, that were the prevalent dogma extended into future generations, any personal guidance people received from teachers on this path would be looked at askance by higher officials, and would even be officially repudiated.

Such is the reality. It cannot but leave many students of this path feeling like beached whales. The truth Master left us, however, is very different. It is therefore vitally important for all disciples of Master to understand that their *responsibility* is to share not only his teachings, but his spiritual grace, his inspiration, even his blessings with others to the fullest extent they are able. It is wrong for them to remove themselves altogether from the scene of service.

Daya Mata tells people, "I don't presume to bless anyone." Her practice, in consequence, is to stand quietly before people and, perhaps not even touching them, ask Master to bless them. That she should do so is understandable. After all, she spent many years in Master's company, and remembers vividly the many times he blessed her personally. Not surprisingly, she finds it difficult to see herself acting similarly in his place. Her memory, however, is particular and very personal. Considering the matter impersonally, it must appear to everyone she approaches in this way that, even while she prays to him for his blessings, she is already blessing others, personally. Moreover, though she asks Master to bless them, they themselves cannot help seeing her as Master's instrument. They accept what she does as a blessing from him, through her.

It would be well, in fact, for *all* Master's disciples—both those who knew him and those who have become his disciples since he left his body—to see themselves as not merely praying for others, but as blessing them *in his name*.

A Further Dilemma

What I have written so far calls for serious consideration. Our real duty, *as* Master's disciples, is to try to act as *channels* for his blessings.

My own way, when writing or teaching, has always been to try to bring the discussion down from abstractions to the individual reader or listener and ask, "What does this mean *for you*?" Again, my practice is to ask, more generally, "What does it mean *for all of us*?" In the present essay, I've so far kept the discussion on an impersonal level. Now, I must bring it down to the personal.

What does everything I've written mean, then, *for you*? You may have wondered already, "What can I do about these important issues?" You may have wondered also: "Now that we no longer have Master with us in the body, and because there may be, after all, other gurus on this path in future, who is a guru *now*? Is Daya Mata herself a guru? Are you, Kriyananda? Is anyone else? If no one on this path is entitled to serve in that capacity, what hope is there for the rest of us who never even met Master?"

The first and most urgent question is quite personal. As I said, What about *you*? Master's divine mission wasn't only to bring a *teaching*. When he told me, "To those who think me near, I will be near," he was promising to be near to those disciples not only who lived near him physically, but those also who lived at a distance, those who had never met him, and those who would continue to come to him in the future.

I said earlier that, in my experience, those who never met Master, but who believe they can develop attunement with him on their own, without the association of other disciples who may have been on the path for many years—that such persons have seemed to lack something. They've shown a different quality in their eyes—a kind of "in this world, and also of it" consciousness. Can this difference be attributed to anything outward? Does it exist because long-term disciples make Master, by the example they set, in some way more real? Is it because they somehow reflect his personality, his mannerisms? Surely, if there is a difference it must be rather because sincere disciples transmit some of Master's actual consciousness, energy, and blessings. Even those who never knew him physically, provided they are in tune with him inwardly, serve to a greater or lesser degree (depending on their own development) as *channels* for the divine grace which flows from him, through them, to others.

The second explanation is the obviously correct one. I myself *do* frequently feel Master's grace flowing through me, and I can't really say to what extent, if at all, my mannerisms reflect his personality. True, I am kinder, more supportive of others, more loving than I used to be. (When young, I could sometimes be rather caustic.) These are not *mannerisms*, however, though they reflect a different manner of behavior. I am a very different person from what I was in my youth. The change has come, however, from an *inward* change of outlook and consciousness, consequent on my inner attunement.

It is normal for me to try to project to others the love and joy I feel from Master in my heart. How can I not do so? I *feel* his presence like a divine aura, within and around me. Kriyananda seems to me hardly more than a shell. My *inner* life is what is being defined more and more by my awareness of his presence within me.

There is one important difference, however: Master asked me to give him my obedience, and I gave it to him unconditionally. I for my part, on the other hand, have never requested obedience of anyone. The reason is simple: I am not spiritually ready to do so. I consider myself everyone's spiritual brother, and nobody's teacher.

Master's statement that he was the last of our line of gurus meant, in a more personal sense, that he would continue to work through all those who dedicate themselves to deepening their attunement with him. Teachers in Master's work who sincerely try to develop spiritually, whether or not they have achieved Self-realization, *can* be channels for our line of masters. Our Guru works through all—though of course, as I said, to varying degrees—who are open to him. The requirement is that they follow him and his teachings humbly and sincerely. He can work best, also, through those who sincerely want to help others in his name.

And, of course, he can help best through those who are in tune with him. People may ask, "How can I attune myself to Master?" The answer he himself gave was, first, to gaze deeply into his photograph, especially concentrating on the eyes. Then visualize those eyes, as you meditate, and call to him mentally, "Reveal thyself! Reveal thyself!" Try, next, to feel his response in your heart. The answer, when it comes, will bring a distinct awareness of his presence and vibrations.

Everyone who, in this spirit, shares Master's teachings with others has a duty to take personal *interest* in helping others. More even than serving them, he should *love* them and *want* the best for them. The love he expresses for others should never be personal. He should never think, "It is *my* love I am giving to *you*." Such an ego-constrictive thought will raise within oneself those supreme barriers to spiritual development: outward attraction, and attachment. Love God and Guru in all, then, as children of God.

One thing I have found helpful is to ask Master to expand my aura that it fill any auditorium in which I am speaking, or to encompass any group I address, whether small or large. Indeed, I *feel* this expansion. When I meditate with a group, also, I try to feel him expanding my aura that it touch all present. People tell me that this, more even than whatever words I utter, is what reaches them. I've made this suggestion, too, to our choirs and singing groups. It is, I think, deeply important.

My own particular way of loving is to see Master in my audiences when I lecture, and in the individuals I try to help. A fellow disciple once, after reading this statement in a diary I'd been keeping, protested, "How can you see yourself as teaching your own *guru*!?" She had missed the point. Trying to see Master in everyone is like trying to see God in all. For Master is not only a guru: he is one with God's infinite love and bliss.

I used for a time to pray to him, "Help me to love you as you love me." He subtly corrected me one day. Glancing at me, he asked rhetorically, "How can the little cup hold the whole ocean?"

Once he addressed me even more clearly on this point. I had questioned him about an experience I'd had the previous night. Master surprised me by requesting details. What occasioned my surprise was that he himself had been an important part of that experience. "Sir," I asked him, "didn't you *know*?"

His reply seemed almost impatient. (My question had shown superficial understanding.) "When you are one with God," he remarked dismissively, "you *are* God!"

What I mean, then, in saying that I see Master in the people I serve when teaching or counseling, isn't that I look upon them as my teachers! I am of course happy to learn from anyone, for I consider all whom I meet as potential sources of understanding for myself. God can teach us, moreover, even through "the mouths of babes." What I try to do, then, is see God Himself manifested in all whom I try to serve. The point is to see others not in terms of their egos, but of their souls—of the divine Self residing at the center of everyone and everything.

I have been hinting at a further and very important point. As, in a relay race, the baton gets passed on from runner to runner, so Master's power is especially passed from one disciple to another. This, then, is another point that needs clarification for students on this path. They should also, in addition to receiving printed lessons, try to get these teachings from one who has himself received them *directly*. They should try to see Master as especially present in those who teach in his name, and in attunement with him.

Yogananda *can and does* work through his loyal disciples. Who, then, are such disciples? They are all those who have received the "touch" from some other, true disciple, and who deeply accept Master in their hearts as their guru. By no means everyone who attends lectures and classes on these teachings has achieved the level of inner acceptance. And by no means everyone who gives lectures and classes on these teachings is, for that reason alone, able to pass on the "baton" to others. When a teacher thinks of Master as residing in those he teaches, however, he invites Master to bless those people *inwardly*. This thought increases the likelihood of his recognizing the divine presence within himself. And when those who listen to him see him as a channel for the Guru, they will receive more from Master than they could if they thought of Master more remotely, as if in the third person.

Can those who *are* ready for a guru be brought to God *through* those disciples of our Guru who, in their hearts, are deeply attuned to him? Will anyone find God *through* those disciples? The real question is, Will Master be able to bring them to God through his disciples? The answer is, Yes. Of course, and obviously, it depends also on how deeply in tune with him they themselves, and also those disciples, are.

There is another important point to be considered here: Certain realities change—or perhaps I should say, expand— in the case of masters who come to earth with divine dispensations: the *avatars*. They come with the divine power to lift many souls—even limitless numbers of them. Though a few saints say that a guru cannot continue to guide people after he leaves his physical body, they evidently have not experienced the power that flows, even after he leaves this world, through an *avatar*. Avatars have far more power than any lesser saint to bless, uplift, and even bestow salvation on countless disciples long after they leave their bodies. Their usual way of functioning, however, is *through* disciples who are in tune with them.

Finding one's personal guru is a matter between the devotee and God. What Master was saying when he spoke of himself as the last of our gurus was, first of all, that he would continue always to work through disciples who are in tune, and who teach humbly in his name. Thus, if anyone feels drawn to this path, he can be guided by our line of masters, and especially by Paramhansa Yogananda (as the one who brought these teachings to the modern world), *through a successive line of disciples.*

Are there any enlightened souls presently in Master's work? I don't know, though I'm sure there must be. It is vitally important, however, for students on this path not to get into an "enlightened teachers sweepstakes": "This one is more enlightened than that one." "Oh, you don't know *anything*! Can't you see, this other one is *leagues* ahead of *that* fool!"— and so on. If Paramhansa Yogananda is still the guru (and he, especially, is whom we ourselves, his followers, look to), then it is his power, primarily, that every faithful disciple transmits. The "official" statement is that Daya Mata—as the SRF president, and as the present example of Master's supposed (but never uttered) promise regarding all future presidents—is acting in Master's place as at least a sort of "substitute guru" for everyone on this path. She herself makes it clear, however, that she doesn't see herself as a guru. Indeed, several years ago, when speaking with me, she forcefully repudiated this notion. She also states (as I said earlier), "I don't presume to bless."

If what I have expressed so far is the truth—namely, that Master blesses people *through* his sincere disciples—then the sort of competition I've seen already among students of this path may be dismissed as mere sibling rivalry: petty, and not worthy of serious attention.

Unfortunately, human nature generally insists on making distinctions. Rivalry exists between the followers of the various great religions. It exists *within* every one of those religions. Rivalry in Master's work has raised its dragon head among Master's own direct disciples. I would not be writing this essay were it not for the fact that I perceive a great need to correct certain serious errors in the statements made by my fellow disciples. And although I would greatly prefer simply to leave the reader with what I have stated so far, I have in fact been obliged for many years to defend myself against charges of being, myself, beyond the pale—a traitor to the very Guru whom I worship as God Himself. That story is not one I'll go into here. Those who have read others of my writings—particularly my book, *A Place Called Ananda*—will understand to what I refer. If I seem here to be treating lightly a very sad episode in my life, it is because what happened, with God's grace, actually released me to do the work my Guru had given me to do. It was no light ordeal for me at the time, however. These things, as I say, simply happen. I don't suppose anything can be done about them.

Is Daya Mata, herself, Self-realized? If the answer to that question is perceived as pertinent to any discussion of this matter, then it demands an answer. On this point, however, I can only give my opinion. I haven't seen in her any sign of that omniscience which comes with Self-realization. I won't take the subject further, for I believe she is in any case not only capable of serving as a channel for Master, but is *more* capable of doing so than the great majority even of Master's direct disciples.* Let us do our best, then, to avoid unflattering comparisons. They are, as we've all heard, "odious."

---

* My book of letters, *In Divine Friendship*, goes into this matter in greater depth.

On, then, to another question, one that is perhaps more pressing: To what extent is it important even to know whether a disciple is Self-realized? Master is our guru. His disciples can serve as his channels to others. This is how things are, and will continue throughout futurity. All who consider themselves Master's disciples should do their best to perpetuate not only his teachings, but also his special ray of Divine Grace.

The ray, itself, is what matters, and is even more important than the teachings. I once read the statement in a newspaper in India to the effect (I am paraphrasing): "There is no need for gurus nowadays, since education has become nearly universal, and most people can read timeless truths in books that are available at every bookstore." The writer of that article had overlooked—indeed, evidently was ignorant of—the fact that many true gurus are *"maunis"* observing a vow of perpetual silence.

A certain disciple, many years ago, decided to leave Master and follow another teacher as his guru. Master accepted the man's decision without demur, stating simply, "Very well then. I withdraw my ray." And so it happened. Virtually overnight, the disciple seemed to become almost a different, and much lesser, person.

I have seen the same thing happen in other cases, when disciples forsook this path. Usually the results were deleterious. Even had they not been so, however—that is to say, if the student chose as his guru a different but *good* teacher—it would no longer have been Master's ray, but a different one, that infused the disciple.

In *Autobiography of a Yogi*, Yogananda states, "Thoughts are universally and not individually rooted." All of us express whatever ray of universal consciousness we accept into our lives. Delusions, too, have a cosmic origin. This deep truth, which I've described in *Revelations of Christ, Proclaimed by*

Paramhansa Yogananda, underscores also the Bible's teachings on Satan.

The divine ray, then, when it is experienced inwardly, is even more essential for the truth seeker than any intellectual teaching. If a seeker is a follower of Paramhansa Yogananda, it is the Master's blessing he must try to experience, especially as it *flows through* his disciples. All sincere seekers who accept this truth, and who try to act in attunement with it, will themselves be able, in time, to transmit Master's ray to others. Any disciple, by contrast, who announces, "*I* am your guru," can only be speaking from ego-consciousness. Such a person is not a true disciple. Master declared many times, of himself, "I am not the guru: *God* is the guru." He too, you see, was simply transmitting a special divine ray into this world, as God willed. The difference is only this: Yogananda was *fully conscious* of serving the particular ray of Divine Grace he represented.

I asked Master one evening at his Twenty-Nine Palms retreat, "Sir, will I find God in this life?" He answered, "Yes, but don't think about it." He added that, meanwhile, I had much work to do. "Your life," he told me, "will be one of intense activity, and meditation." Later he predicted to me, "God won't come to you until the end of life. Death itself is the final sacrifice you'll have to make." I might add that all these statements were made when we were alone together. Indeed, I can sincerely say that I *do* feel Master's blissful presence with me, almost always. And the more wholeheartedly I embrace the "intense activity" he ordained for me, the more joyful I become inwardly. I have not yet experienced *samadhi*, but I can't help thinking that, were I in that state, I would not feel anything like the strong urge I feel to help others.

I recently saw a movie on DVD, *What Dreams May Come.* Much of the action took place in an astral heaven after death, though some of it occurred also in a hellish region to which, it was said, suicides go. The movie was interesting. To my surprise, however, I also found myself identifying more with the spiritual needs of those poor suicides than with the happiness other souls were enjoying in heaven.

I do believe I have spent time in the past in heavenly regions. Indeed, in a sense I have always felt more at home there than here. The souls depicted in heaven by that movie, however, seemed to me to be enjoying their astral heaven only passively. They weren't sharing their happiness with others. Nor did they seem to have any desire to help anyone. They weren't even doing anything to further their own spiritual progress. It was as if they were all drifting in a sort of hallucinogenic daze. Indeed, it is said that people in the astral heavens—the lower heavens, not those high spheres to which saints go—are so satisfied with their lot that they feel no incentive to make any further progress. They are simply enjoying, temporarily, the fruits of whatever good karma won them their heavenly respite. Those poor suicides, on the other hand, were in desperate need of help. Seeing them, I couldn't help wanting, with almost equal desperation, to reach out to them with hope, and to share with them a clearer understanding of the truth.

Anyone who, now and in the future, teaches in Master's name *will* certainly be helped and guided in his sincere, humble, and loving efforts to be of service to others. Master once said to a close disciple of his, "Those who 'fall by the wayside,' my devotees will pick up."

I have tried my best in these pages to express an important truth. If in any way I have failed, I believe I will have at least opened up important questions for further discussion. What I hope to have accomplished is bury forever two mistaken beliefs that are now prevalent: first, that Master is the last guru *on* this path, rather than only *of* this path; and second, that everyone who now teaches in Master's name has no further responsibility for the student's ongoing welfare after whatever lectures or classes he has given; that, having brought devotees to the Guru, he must leave everything to Master now, and cease to occupy himself with their future progress.

Indeed, the existing problem seems, from all reports, to be even graver than I have stated it. Reports come to me concerning certain self-styled disciples who don't seem even to feel a need to make an effort to share Master's teachings. I'm told they behave discourteously even toward those who come with an interest in these teachings. The rationale behind this wholly unacceptable behavior is that Master is doing everything necessary anyway, and that their duty is to focus on their own spiritual practices.

Daya Mata once asked our Guru, "What can possibly replace you, Master, once you've gone?" He answered with a loving smile, "Only love can take my place." To her, his words meant (as she has since expressed it), "Be so in love with God that He becomes your only reality." Is this *all* that Master meant by those words? Certainly, God should come first in our lives. I cannot help feeling, however, that if our love for God doesn't extend to loving others also *in God*, Master's work will be in danger of becoming a wasteland of indifference to anyone else's spiritual needs.

I do not say that Daya Mata sanctions this attitude. Indeed, she herself once quoted him to me as saying, "Don't think you can win God's love, if you can't win the love of your fellowman." Nevertheless, this attitude is distressingly widespread among his disciples.

These wrong, and completely unspiritual, ideas need to be corrected. As I have said, the divine ray Master represents can function *only* through living instruments. God Himself functions on earth—indeed, in the very universe—*through* instruments. His vast Creation was accomplished through certain highly advanced beings. Master gave that as the reason for the Holy Bible's statement, "Let *us* make man in our image." (Genesis 1:26) In such a way, God sends *avatars* to earth: to teach and uplift souls into the Supreme Truth.

WHY I LOVE MY GURU, PARAMHANSA YOGANANDA

Friendship, Yogananda used to say, is the most reward-ing human experience because it is a free gift, without any compulsion. Even in mother's love a certain compul-sion exists: the compulsion of nature in the thought that her children are *her own*. Were some child of hers to die and be reborn next door, would she feel the same love for it? Not possessive love, certainly.

Noble an "institution" as friendship is, however, it was not until I met my Guru that I came to understand its high-er octaves. As a divine friend he was perfection itself. For friendship should be uplifting, and that is something it is not, always. So long as a relationship is between two egos, it may only reinforce ego-consciousness.

Much can be said, all the same, in favor of ordi-nary human friendship, even when it only affects the ego. Experiments have been done on plants showing that when a plant is given love it flourishes, whereas if love is denied it, its growth becomes stunted by comparison. Moreover, if hate and rejection are directed at it, it often withers and dies. Friendship is like that. Even if it offers only ego-balm, a healthy ego is much more to be desired than a crippled, sickly one, forever unsure of itself, inwardly wilting, and cringing before everything and everybody.

Though much, then, might be said of the possible nega-tive influences of ordinary human friendship, basically it is something all human beings need.

I have in this life been fortunate in many respects, but perhaps in none of them so much as in two inborn quali-ties: first, never to be influenced in my opinions of others by what they thought of me; and second, never to feel even tempted to justify myself (not to myself either) when I knew

I was in the wrong. These qualities have been my strength. True friendship must spring not from need, but from inner strength; only in this way can it be purely giving.

One danger of friendship lies in the fact that friends *want* you to agree with them. Bad friends, consequently, want you to agree with and support them in error. As my Guru put it, "If you try to talk to them of higher things, they reply jovially, 'Oh, get off it! Come have a drink!'" This is *friendship*?

Too often, in other words, a person's apparent friends are actually enemies to his highest interests. As the Bhagavad Gita puts it, "When the self is the friend of the Self, it is its greatest friend. But when the self is the enemy of the Self, it is its greatest enemy."

A true friend is one who helps you to befriend that higher Self. He supports everything that is best and truest for your highest welfare. He sympathizes with you, and tries to understand your point of view. He will not condemn you hastily for any disagreement, nor separate himself from you in his sympathy owing to any divergence of opinion. There are both dignity and mutual respect in such a relationship, and, yes, a shared sense of fun also. For an ability to laugh kindly together is one way of sharing trust, confidence, and mutual support.

I hadn't the advantage in my childhood and youth of many close friendships, for I was never in one place long enough to form them. I did live till I was nine in Teleajen (Romania), but childhood friendships are not often deep, and many of my friends lived there just as temporarily as we did, until their fathers were shifted further by their company. I spent a year and a half in Switzerland, where I was ill most of the time. Six months followed in Bucharest, and then two years at school in England. We moved to America in 1939, where I spent a year at Hackley School near Tarrytown, New York; two years at Kent School in Connecticut; a year at Scarsdale High; two years at Haverford College; a year and a half at Brown University; a year in Charleston, South Carolina; and then—Master and SRF (fourteen years with the latter; sixty years, so far, with the former).

Rod, my best friend in college, had a twofold influence on me: one for the good, the other for the not so good. He helped me to regain my self-confidence when I needed it. Unfortunately, though brilliant, he had the fault of intellectual pride, by which he infected me. My intellect being perhaps my strong point, it also became my weak link.

Through all the years that followed, my one truest and best of all possible friends was always my Guru, Paramhansa Yogananda. He was true in *every* respect: the human quite as much as the divine. It's true that I couldn't joke with him in the familiar way friends enjoy with one another. Though I couldn't altogether repress my sense of humor with him, I was too young not to be always in deep awe of him. For me, being with him was like being in the presence of God Himself. Yet I asked him endless questions—more, perhaps, than anyone else. And he answered me, for he *wanted* me to understand. Again, if *he* joked with *me*, I, with my lively sense of humor, would joke back. Yet I couldn't help holding him at a certain distance, never quite sure of myself in his presence.

That much said, he was with me *not at all* the kind of stern disciplinarian he has sometimes been described as being. He was kind, forgiving, endlessly and deeply understanding, supportive of all my (indeed, of everyone's) human feelings and failings—not, indeed of the failings themselves, but of *us*, as people. I found him to be ever anxious to help us in our efforts to mature and to grow out of our every delusion.

Once he scolded me for my involvement in a confrontation where I had felt righteously indignant. It took me a little while to adjust mentally to this *volte-face* of being scolded for (as I saw it) doing right, but I said to him the next day, "Please, Master, scold me more often." Looking at me deeply, with heartfelt understanding, he answered, "I understand, but that isn't what you need. You need more devotion."

He also encouraged me in every little gain; often, no one else even noticed him doing so. One day he said to me lovingly, "Keep on with your devotion, Walter. Just see how dry your life is, when you depend on intellect."

And one time, feeling intensely my separation from him, I went to Encinitas, where he had gone for a visit, on purpose to see him. As soon as we met, he responded kindly, "I have missed you, Walter." That evening, David Smith (a brother disciple) involved us in worldly chatter, and my devotion slipped. When I saw Master the next day, he tugged at a lock of my hair lightly, and reminded me with the same loving smile (though with a hint of reproof), "I have missed you."

It pains me when I hear people say coldly, "*Master* wouldn't have approved of that! *Master* wouldn't tolerate disorder! *Master* was always a strict taskmaster!" These things have been said to justify the disciple's own lack of kindness, sympathy, and simple human charity. But I remember one time (I've quoted it elsewhere in these essays) when he came into the monks' dining room and found it in utter, embarrassing chaos. His only comment then was, "Well, it might be worse!"

In his treatment of the other disciples, I never saw him speak to them harshly. In fact, I wonder whether their impression of harshness didn't come from their own rebellious egos. The few times he scolded me, I saw only regret in his eyes for having to speak strongly to me. He did so for my benefit, purely.

There was a period in Daya's discipleship, she told me, when he scolded her almost daily. She resented it, especially because his manner was then so different from what he had shown her when she first came. One evening she prayed, "From now on, Divine Mother, I will direct my love first to You." When she went indoors for his blessing, he tapped her lightly on the top of her head and murmured approvingly, "Very good." The scoldings stopped. He had wanted to break her of an excessively human attachment to him.

With those who were not disciples he was affability itself: kindly, warm, entirely accepting, and forgiving of any insult or calumny. I remember one time (I mentioned this occasion in my book, *The Path*) at a public function, a man from India was a bit tipsy and treated Master with a familiarity no one else would have ever dreamed of: putting his arms around Master, laughing jovially, and talking familiarly. Debi, a Bengali disciple, ridiculed the man to Master in Bengali (a language unknown to this Indian) for his inebriation. "Don't!" Master scolded him quietly, so that the man himself wouldn't notice. Master saw this man in the full dignity of a human being, not as someone who, in his drunkenness, had lost that dignity.

Another time the Master, as he was entering a hotel, was approached by a drunken stranger who embraced him and cried, "Hello, Jeshush Chrisht!"

"Hello," Master responded affably, then shared with him a touch of the inner bliss he himself was experiencing. "Shay! What're *you* drinkin'?" demanded the man.

"I can tell you, it has a lot of kick in it!" the Master replied. He then touched this man on the forehead, leaving him sober though perhaps somewhat bewildered.

These are stories I have shared before elsewhere. Here is another one. A member of the Indian community came to Mt. Washington with Ambassador Binay R. Sen just days before Master left his body. This Indian lived in Los Angeles and had devoted years to persecuting the Master by spreading untruths against him. At a certain moment that afternoon the two of them were briefly alone together. Master said to the man, "Remember, I will always love you." Herbert Freed, a brother disciple, overheard the Master's words. A photograph of Master taken at that moment shows the visitor's expression; it reveals a mixture of emotions: wonder, shame, perhaps dismay at his own pettiness. For those who understand the inwardness of that moment, it is a dramatic photograph. (It was this episode, incidentally, that gave me the inspiration for my one-act play, *The Jewel in the Lotus*.)

The Master simply accepted people as they were, with never a breath of criticism, but always with love. It often surprised me to see the completeness of his acceptance. People whom I myself might have turned away from with distaste, Master treated kindly and with a gentle, though always dignified, smile.

Not everyone understood him, by any means. I'll never forget a neighbor of the Master's at Twenty-Nine Palms, when that man gave one of my brother disciples his view. Master used to share fruits with him, an act of generosity that, to this man, seemed beyond comprehension. One day he said, speaking of Master, "You know, he's a little [making a circular movement to indicate someone a little 'tetched' in the head], but," he added admiringly, "he's got a heart of gold!"

The Master was a true friend to everybody, seeing all as his very own. That is why, wherever he went, he always found people friendly and eager to help him.

Yet, when someone came to him and asked to be accepted as a disciple, he saw his responsibility *as a divine friend* to be the highest type of friend he could be to that person. In this sense he might be compared to a divine fisherman: never letting the line get too tight, but if it slackened, testing it to see how forcefully he could reel it in without letting it break.

He was infinitely kind to us, forgiving, supportive, gentle, humorous, one with us in friendship, and ever completely loving. Yet he was also careful, always, to turn our minds and aspirations toward our own highest potential in God. Never did I see him come down from that high purpose. And always in his calm gaze I saw a complete absence of ego-motive, including the slightest impulse either to act or react personally. People—men perhaps especially—who lack personal motivation are often misunderstood by others, bound as almost all people are by personal desires. Master had many self-styled enemies who fancied they saw in him someone dark, someone scheming for subtle, hidden ends which he was not frank enough to admit openly, and which must therefore (so they imagined) have been all the more sinister. I think it was his very strength they feared. Their fears, however, were nothing but projections of a darkness in their own natures. Perhaps it was his strength, also, that made some of the disciples think of him as harsh. Otherwise, I can't imagine how anyone saw him as anything but a strong bulwark, supportive always of our true needs. No, I think those disciples, too, simply hadn't the humility or the sensitivity to see in him the truest divine friend they would or could ever have.

Only consider his poem, "God's Boatman." In that poem he promised to come back, "if need be a trillion times, as long as one stray brother sits weeping by the wayside." Think of it! There was no personal necessity for him to return to this material plane. He came here out of a purely selfless desire to bring others out of delusion, and lead them back to God's kingdom. How many times, I have often wondered, has he returned to earth already in perfect freedom? I have good reason to believe he has been coming back for many thousands of years, and always with the same purpose, and with the same universal love. He himself often told us, "I killed Yogananda long ago. Only God lives in this temple now." And I heard him declare also, "I was freed many lifetimes ago." Think of it!

The vast majority of souls who achieve oneness with God are satisfied never to emerge from that blissful state again. Divine Bliss is too perfectly satisfying to them, and they suffered enough before attaining it. All they want, now, is eternal, complete rest in the Lord. What did our Guru want from us? Nothing! Nothing, that is, but *our* highest good. Could any friend be more perfect, more dear, more wonderful than that?

When I met him, he said to me, "I give you my unconditional love." No treasure could be greater, surely, than that sacred promise! He has fulfilled it in countless ways. More and more through the years, I have found him mentally guiding me, leading me toward final, inner freedom, filling me with inner bliss.

He hasn't made the way easy—unless, indeed, I consider (as I do) that every hardship has become, in the end, a supernal blessing. No, I can think of no experience in my life that has not ended in sweetness, in an expansion of love, and in deep gratefulness. Forgiveness for wrongs, hurts, betrayals, tests? All I can say is, *what tests? what* betrayals? *what* hurts? *what* wrongs? They were never wrongs, personally, *to me.*

In all my dealings with Master in the body, I always knew he was on my side: not *against* anyone or anything else, but supportive of me in all my struggles toward perfection. He responded supportively to my least thought. If I was wrong, he said so in such a way that only I (if others were present) could know what he was talking about. He never blurted out anything. All his words were carefully measured so as to be as understandable and acceptable to me as possible. There was, as I said, a dignity about him that was completely innate and natural. He was, indeed, a king among men, and I think most people felt it instinctively. And everything I ever saw him do or heard him say was completely *appropriate* to the occasion.

Tara (a sister disciple) once remarked to me about him, "Every time I think I've understood him, I find he's much more than that." I didn't say so to her, but I was astonished that anyone could even *think* of understanding him! To me it seemed like trying to "understand" the ocean. His friendship for each of us was deeply personal, yet he was, for each of us, like a window onto infinity, inviting us to "come outside" and merge in that vastness.

I love my Guru, as he himself wrote about his own guru Swami Sri Yukteswar, "as the spoken voice of silent God." He was ever, and is now more than ever, my nearest, dearest companion. If I am right, I feel his inner smile. If I am wrong, I feel his inner encouragement to do better.

He is *on my side* in every struggle against delusion. Could anyone be a better, truer friend than that?

Addendum

This will be brief.

Yesterday, someone who had just read my essay on my love for my Guru suggested to me, "It would be wonderful if you would write further articles on each of Master's outstanding qualities."

I disagreed, for as I pointed out, "Master was *beyond* all qualities: *triguna rahitam*, beyond all the three *gunas*, or qualities, especially as they are expressed in human nature." To describe even his friendship for us as a *quality* is, in the highest sense of the term, a misnomer. His friendship for us is God's love, channeled through that human vehicle. Our love for Master himself must be not only for him personally, but above all for *God through him.*

One time Norman, a brother disciple, wrote Master a note that said, "When I see you, I see only Divine Mother in you." Master, who was humility itself, might have disclaimed his own unworthiness of such a comparison. Instead, he quietly replied, "Then behave accordingly."

For this reason I asked that my letter be withdrawn from *In Divine Friendship* (a book of my letters) concerning a quality of Master's: his enormous will power. I had described that as the foremost of his qualities in which, it seems to me, all of his disciples share. I withdrew that letter because I realized, later, that it wasn't adequate. What *true* disciples share is something much deeper, and perhaps not even something that can be put into words: a subtle attunement with his special *ray* of the Divine Consciousness.

Several people have told me, or have written to say, that, as I feel toward Master, so they feel toward me. I had a dream last night which may help to clarify that thought. I won't relate the dream itself, as it was personal, but I took it as a warning from Master to pass on to all of you.

The essential difference between attunement with Master and attunement with me is that Master lives eternally in cosmic consciousness, whereas I am still struggling to reach that state. What he channels to us is the Infinite Lord Himself. What I am able to channel to you is whatever I have succeeded so far in experiencing within myself of Master's consciousness. That I feel his bliss is a cause of deep gratitude for myself. But I feel it is very important for everyone to realize that whatever I have to give anyone is *not, and must never become, personal.* To the extent that anyone takes it as such it can be binding not only for that person, but also, potentially, for me.

Therefore I plead with you—for my own sake quite as much as for yours: "See me *only* as a channel for our Guru." I try my best to serve you in that capacity, and am grateful if, to any extent, I succeed in that effort. If, however, I seem to be for some of you—if only by default!—the best instrument you've found during your search, please always remember for what, and for whom, this instrument lives. I have no other desire than to bring you closer to God by bringing you into deeper spiritual attunement with my Guru.

He is our actual, ever-living channel to God.

Please never forget this important distinction. And please always remember it in your own dealings with others who come to Master through you, if they seek you out for inspiration and guidance.

INSPIRATION VS. INSTRUCTION
(GOING TO SAINTS)

We who follow the teachings of Self-realization pray to the "saints of all religions." We acknowledge their greatness, and aspire to that greatness in ourselves. It is natural that, for inspiration and upliftment, we should seek out their company. It is normal for us anyway, after all, as human beings, to seek out the company of others. Why not, then, seek *satsang* (*good* company) of the highest type? It is indeed *right* for us, when the opportunity presents itself, to go to saints and spend time with them.

However—and there *is*, here, a **HOWEVER**—as there is more than one true religion, so also is there more than one path within every religion that leads up the mountain of divine attainment. And although many of them lead all the way to the summit, by no means all of them do. Most of them go up also by different routes, and up many sides of the mountain depending on people's diverse temperaments and points of departure.

Krishna describes some of those ways in the Bhagavad Gita. For a person whose feet are already (or, perhaps, finally) planted firmly on his own path, the differences become superficial; one understands at last the underlying purpose of each path, and sees why the good advice of this teacher may differ in some respects from the equally good advice of that one. One who is firmly on his own path also understands what makes that way right, *for him.*

Newcomers to the path, however, may not perceive the unifying rationale behind those differences, and may therefore be confused by them

Apart from the beginner's lack of philosophical sophistication, however, there are other problems connected with going to saints, which can make the practice of going to them a kind of two-edged sword. The first problem is a common one: fickleness in one's loyalties. People in whom the active quality of *rajo guna* has not been transcended tend to think "the grass may be greener" on the other side of the fence. Not having yet found satisfaction within, they tend to seek it constantly in new directions outside themselves.

This tendency is symptomatic especially of our modern, very *rajasic* times. As people struggle to adjust to the rays of a higher age of energy, their tendency toward fickleness increases. Great benefits come to us also, of course, from this new age, one of them being a deeper understanding of the universality of truth. There are also, unfortunately, certain disadvantages. For one thing, *Dwapara Yuga*, being an age of energy, also increases the tendency to "fizz." People, in their resulting fickleness, change wives, husbands, jobs, and philosophies—the last, at the sight of a book or the arrival of news of some new teacher, just come to town. One consequence—in the business world, for example—is that a very high percentage of new ventures fold within a year. It is important to stick firmly to one's commitments. Many people, to their own detriment, are like the common quip about New Year's resolutions: making their resolutions on January First only to break them on January Second.

When it comes to making a serious spiritual commitment, moreover, it is important to understand what such a commitment involves. For it is *much more* important than any other commitment one can make.

If a person wants to be a mountain climber, he will do well to find a guide—in fact, he'd be foolish not to—who can teach him that skill, for even a little slip might send him crashing to his death at the bottom of a cliff. Physical death is almost insignificant, however, compared to spiritual death. Death of the body means only "crashing out" for one lifetime. A spiritual fall, on the other hand, may bring a subtler form of death that can last for many incarnations.

I am not saying that leaving one path for another necessarily implies, in itself, even crashing at all. A change may be beneficial, and a consequence of newer, truer insight. If the change is due merely to fickleness, however, it may increase in oneself his *rajasic* tendency; may result in a diminution of calm, discriminating *sattwa guna*; and may therefore conclude with a lessening of the *upward*, spiritual tendency in one's own nature.

I particularly recall a young male disciple of Yogananda's, a monk who lived at Mt. Washington while I was there. This young man experienced many high spiritual experiences, so much so that all of us often marveled, for he himself didn't seem correspondingly deep. His interests were at the same time very eclectic, and led him into many spiritual doubts which awakened in him, gradually, many worldly tendencies.

That young man's karma, our Guru told him, was very complex. He had good spiritual karma, which gave him his deep experiences, but those experiences were, as the Master hinted, the result of the disciple's soul desperately trying to pull him back from the brink.

Master once said to him, "If you leave the spiritual path this time, you will wander for another 200 incarnations before you return to the point you have reached already in your spiritual evolution."

Alas, the young man did leave the path. Later, he came back to the Master on a visit, and wept "so bitterly" that, Master told us, "I wept with him." There was nothing our Guru could do about it, however. No Master will prevent anyone by force from erring, if this is what that person is determined to do. To prevent him against his will would be to interfere with his inalienable right of free will. Master did say to him, when he paid that visit, "If you try hard now, you may reduce the number of those incarnations to seven." Alas, the boy's directional flow of energy was already too strong toward worldliness. From all I've heard about him since then, he has simply resigned himself. Instead of saying, "I haven't yet succeeded," he has accepted, sadly, that in this life he has fallen completely. He wouldn't have had to accept this conclusion, had he summoned sufficient will power. The subconscious mind—unfortunately (and yet, fortunately in other cases)—can exert a very strong hold on one's conscious will.

To another disciple Master once remarked, "I lost touch with you for a few incarnations. Now that you've come back, I'll never lose touch with you again." That man—a wonderful person—would sometimes remind Master, "Remember your promise to me, Master!" And Master always replied, "I remember. I won't lose touch with you again."

Let us consider briefly, once more, the alternatives I've proposed. A man falls to his death off a mountain cliff. He may spend some time in the astral world before being reborn. He may return to earth in his next life with a fear of heights. Is that so bad, however? There are, after all, many other things he can do to keep himself busy in this world to his own satisfaction. Let us next consider the other alternative: A man, after achieving a measure of inner peace and happiness through his meditation practices, allows himself to get involved yet *once more* in the coils of *maya*. He loses that inner peace. Alas, *nothing* in this world can replace it. Having rejected peace itself, he cannot but suffer intensely, now, in his heart. The deeper the peace he once knew, the deeper his contrasting misery.

Yes indeed, he, too, will spend time in the astral world— perhaps a *long* time, owing to his good (and especially to his meditative) karma. That subconscious memory of astral enjoyment, too, will act on his conscience as a goad which impels him to seek God again when he is reborn on earth. His loss of peace, however, will continue to disturb him inwardly, and will also constitute a barrier to his spiritual success.

This is the meaning of "blasphemy against the Holy Ghost," of which Jesus Christ spoke. Jesus said this sin can be forgiven only by the transgressor himself. The soul must return of *his own free will* to that inner peace. Here is what Jesus is reported actually to have said: "Wherefore I say unto you, All manner of sin and blasphemy shall be forgiven unto men: but the blasphemy against the Holy Ghost shall not be forgiven unto men." (Matt. 12:31) And this was how Yogananda explained that sin.

It isn't that straying off to other paths results necessarily in a spiritual fall. What it does do, however—as I have said, and as I want to make very clear—is to send one skating across the surface of outer reality, never really diving deep, and also, therefore, never finding inner satisfaction. The disappointment or disillusionment which too often ensues from a willingness to keep on seeking out other paths sends many "seekers" eventually back to the world, where they will have to repeat over and over again the necessary lesson of loyalty and one-pointed dedication.

Actually it is right and good, generally speaking, at the beginning of your spiritual search to test different ways before deciding which one is most suitable for you. After you've settled firmly on one way, however, and have made a commitment to it, then it is that the particular dangers arise. For the very thought, "Oh, all paths are the same," has just enough truth in it to constitute also a pitfall. Understood superficially, that thought does open up broader vistas of understanding, and may keep one from developing intolerance or fanaticism. Yet there is something Jesus said also that remains eternally true: "Enter ye in at the strait [narrow] gate: for wide is the gate, and broad is the way, that lead-eth to destruction, and many there be which go in thereat." (Matt. 7:13)

Until a person has risen above his conscious mind, which may fairly be described as "feeding on" doubts, and until he has learned to live more by superconscious guid-ance, the differences between one teaching and another may easily lead into a bog of confusion.

For it must be understood that differences do, in fact, exist. Many true saints, even, though they certainly preach deep spiritual truths, may for all that cause puzzlement in the spiritual novice, who is still trying to "figure things out" intellectually for himself. The beginner may protest, "But I feel such deep inspiration in the company of that saint!" Well and good. Rather, *very* well, and *very* good! It is one thing, however, to go to saints for *inspiration*, and quite another to go to them for *instruction*. And it isn't always easy to separate these two. Master was strong in himself, and could therefore, as he wrote in his autobiography, de-rive inspiration from various saints' company without being confused by their divergent spiritual instructions. He was even so gracious, in reporting his discussions with Mahatma Gandhi, as to leave Gandhi with the last word on the impor-tant subject of non-violence.

Shop around first, then, if you feel the need. Do not expect, however, to be able to "figure it all out" for yourself intellectually. Spiritual truths soar high above the gifts avail-able to the vagrant intellect. (Look at materialistic science, which has never yet, and never will, settle on any one basic explanation for everything.)

I myself had what I now realize was the extremely good fortune to *know*, utterly and completely, after reading my Guru's *Autobiography of a Yogi*, that he was my own, and that his way was my way. In the sixty years since then as his disciple, I have never for a moment doubted these two basic truths: that his way, and that he himself, were my own.

Yet I have been astonished to find how many true saints have suggested to me practices which, I could see, were subtly different from what my Guru had taught me. I have remained firmly loyal to him, and have remained simply deaf to other spiritual seekers who scoffed at me for what they called my "narrow-mindedness." Their criticism hasn't touched me, for I've always known where I was going, and whom I was following.

My own role as a disciple has turned out to be a somewhat special one. It has been, as Master wanted me to do, to explain to others as clearly as I could what my Guru's path really is, and how important it is to all mankind in this new Dwapara Yuga. I've had to explain the ways in which it is not only basically the same truth as all others and fully in keeping with the highest teachings of the ages, but also special and different from all other ways. Yet the paths to God *are* many, when you get down to the fine points, and can also be surprisingly *diverse*.

As Master put it, suppose you set out to cross America from Los Angeles in a Ford motor car. Then, on reaching Phoenix, you decide you'd have been more comfortable in a Chevrolet. So you return to your car dealer in Los Angeles, sell your Ford, and purchase a Chevrolet, then set out on your journey once again. This time you may get as far as Albuquerque before realizing you might have done better, considering the length of the journey, to have bought a Cadillac. So—back you go again to that dealer in Los Angeles, sell him your Chevrolet, and buy a Cadillac. This time you may get even farther before having second thoughts about your purchase.

How many times you return to Los Angeles and set out yet once more in a new car may depend finally on the number of automobile makes available! Meanwhile, some one else, perhaps in more humble circumstances, had set out from Los Angeles on a bicycle. By the time you are making your last choice, he may actually have reached New York!

Certainly there are good, better, and best ways of seeking God. Nevertheless, *for you yourself* it will be much the better course, after having "walked the counter" and after finding the way that seems to suit you best, to choose that *one way*. Far better this than following one path after another, even if all those ways should be capable of taking one to the same final destination.

Once you've made your selection, it is important that you make it wholly your own. Think of it as simply the way to which God has led *you*. It is important for you to be firmly loyal to your way, and to accept simply that it is not possible to follow more than one teaching at a time—any more than one can go by more than one route at a time.

As with the several trails up a mountainside, there may be sunny trails and shady trails; trails that are roughly strewn with many rocks; trails that are grassy and smooth; grassy slopes that are, however, very steep in places, where the grass is slippery and dangerous; and rock trails where you may stumble as you walk. Two things are important: first, to select a good guide, one who knows his trail and knows *from experience* whether it will lead all the way to the mountaintop; and second, once you have found a good guide, to follow him to that end faithfully *and implicitly*.

It is better, indeed, to follow a second-best trail to the top than keep looking about for easier, shorter, or more direct trails. If you are sincere in your seeking, God Himself will take charge of the matter for you.

After all, let's face it: the way is in any case *not easy*. You will encounter many tests and many difficulties. The chances of your passing all your tests must be weighed against the undeniable certainty that you have missed the path already many times in the past. Is it a case, then, of "Here I am, still stumbling about in the foothills!"?

I remember someone who once tried to convert me to his path. I tried to explain to him why I was perfectly satisfied with my own way, and was simply not interested in following any other. He went on insisting, however, belaboring his theme by telling me that if I didn't go his way I would go to hell. Finally I decided I'd had enough. I said, "Listen, your way may be positively the *best* of all possible ways— a thousand times better, if you like, than my way. I'm willing to grant you anything you like, just to bring this foolish discussion to an end. I only insist on one thing: *My* way, whether second-best, third-best, or anything else you want to call it, is simply *my way*."

There may—I might have added—be many women in the world who might have made better mothers to me than my own mother. Mine, however, is *my own*; why should I seek another? I think we must all reach the point, similarly, where our path, our guide, and our teachings are, to us, simply *our own*, regardless of anything anyone else says to us on the matter.

The plain truth is, it is God we're seeking, not an infinity of different paths, even if all of them lead—the truth is, many of them do not—to the same destination: God-consciousness. Many paths may be just as good as others (though there are, of course, as I've suggested, false trails also which so-called "guides" offer who merely "suppose" this way or that one to be good). Even so, why "sniff about" for other trails? You can follow only one trail at a time.

I completely agree, and in fact *I know*, that many roads lead up the same mountain, and that many vehicles are capable of taking us to the top. I also believe, and have myself *experienced*, the blessings that flow from true saints, who have inspired me greatly on my own path, and have given me many insights into aspects of my own Guru's teachings. However, I feel I must add here the same very serious caution: Until you *deeply accept, from your very depths,* your own guru's teachings as your own, you may end up deeply confused. It is my duty to warn you, though I hope you'll notice that I don't insist.

One saint, a Swami Shantananda—a good man, though nothing compared to my own Guru—introduced me at a lecture I was to give in New Delhi many years ago. After hearing my discourse he was so well impressed that he actually declared afterward in public, "I have found my Vivekananda!" Well, I did feel inspiration in his presence. Moreover, not wanting to accept that he could possibly have meant what his words had seemed to imply, I went on visiting him for a time. When I found, however, that he actually did hope to make me his disciple, I gave him such a good scolding that—poor fellow!—he was horrified. I think I was right to do so, moreover, though it pained me to offend him.

Other saints have tried to get me into their camp. Some have tried to tell me that my Guru was, in one way or another, simply wrong. Others have said, "Well, your guru's dead now, so why not follow me?" Some of them, I suspect, may even have considered me a "good catch." Fortunately, I've never felt even tempted to follow them.

There was something I perhaps didn't tell clearly enough about Swami Muktananda in my book, *Visits to Saints of India*, though I hinted at it. He actually tried to take me away from my Guru (and thereby, to my mind, proved his own complete lack of worthiness). I mentioned in that book that he took issue with me on the correct practice of watching the breath while mentally repeating the mantra, "Hong Sau." He insisted, as I recounted, that the correct mantra was "So Ham." I tried to smooth the waters with a reasonable explanation for the difference, but he would have none of it. In other ways too, moreover—ways I didn't mention in that book—he tried to get me to forsake my path and follow his. It took me very little time to decide that I'd had enough. I left his ashram with considerable displeasure on my side.

Later on, two other true scriptural authorities told me "Hong Sau" is the *more correct* mantra. I hadn't doubted its rightness, but for the sake of those people whom I have to teach I was glad to be able to offer scriptural corroboration for Master's way. For I am, unfortunately, at a disadvantage when it comes to Sanskrit, in which I am not schooled. I like, however, when possible, to present reasoned arguments, and I greatly prefer not to have to say, "Accept what I say, even if I don't know why you should do so except that Master taught it." Some students may not have as much faith in Master as I have. Therefore to be able to give them good reasons is helpful.

So why did Muktananda presume to try to correct my Guru? I can only attribute it to the possibility that he had not yet climbed out of the pit of ego-identity. Such, evidently, was the case also with Swami Shantananda. Very few, even among saints, have dissolved their egos completely in God. The all-too-human tendency to say, "I alone know," is not yet dead in many of them, and is particularly pernicious because, in a sense, they *do* know!

Sri Rama Yogi (a great master, as my own Guru told me), said to me when I visited him, "Always ask yourself, 'Who am I?'" I replied, "My Guru didn't teach us that." But he answered me quite rightly, "If all the disciples of the great masters understood everything their gurus taught them, there wouldn't be the fighting one sees all over the world in religion." He was, as I say, perfectly right. With a smile, I acknowledged his correctness. Moreover, my Guru *did* teach us to go beyond the ego. As he often said, "When this I shall die, then shall I know who am I."

However—and there *is*, here, a "however"—the issue is not *how* we get out of the ego, but *that we get out of it* somehow. Master didn't specifically teach that mode of self-inquiry as his means to that end (a method Krishna mentions also in the Bhagavad Gita). And the important thing, of course, is to get *out* of the ego! Master's way was to concentrate on the positive side: to visualize vastness and infinity; to offer the fruits of all one's actions, as Krishna taught, to God; to feel in everything we do that God is acting *through* us. In countless ways, Master taught us the importance of rising above the ego, and how to do so. All these ways work, and people have found God through them. I might add with considerable justification, however, that Master's experience in teaching people spiritually was much greater than that of either Sri Rama Yogi or Ramana Maharshi, his guru.

I've mentioned elsewhere my meeting with another saint in Puri, in 1958. This man was 132 years old, a fact which speaks well, I think, for his sainthood. His advice to me was never to find enjoyment in anything. This is a valid path, certainly, and one which many saints of both East and West have followed to the end. *However* (once again), it wasn't Master's path, and I myself consider Master's way immeasurably better for the simple reason that it works more naturally for everyone.

Master taught us to discriminate between two kinds of enjoyment: outward, and inward. We should, he said, view all things with an attitude of inner detachment, *enjoying them with the joy of God*. His way was life affirming, not life rejecting or negating. What it offered was a way to affirm God at every moment of our lives, instead of dividing our attention between denying this thing on the one hand, and affirming that one on the other. His way makes it possible, moreover, to live with an attitude of devotion, which Sri Yukteswar himself—a great *gyana yogi*—described as the first need on the spiritual path. Indeed, Sri Yukteswar wrote that without devotion one cannot even set one foot in front of the other.

The way taught by that Puri yogi is very dry. He too was (in my opinion) very dry. His was a *gyanic* way—*gyana yoga* being the path of discrimination and wisdom. This path seems to exert an appeal especially for intellectuals whose tendency is, in any case, toward a kind of mental aloofness. I myself used to be far too intellectual. I can therefore understand the appeal of that way. Mental aloofness, however, can lead to an *increase* of ego-consciousness, and therefore of pride. I have met many self-styled *gyanis* who walked that road. I myself, before coming to Master, had reached the point at last of realizing that that way hadn't made me happy. I compared my mental state, then to the time when I was a child, and I quickly reached the conclusion that childlike devotion was *in every way* what appealed to me most. As Jesus Christ said, "Suffer little children to come unto me, and forbid them not: for of such is the kingdom of God." (Luke 18:16)

Many intellectuals, in their mental aloofness, justify what in the end is evidently only pride. They believe they've attained true non-attachment when, in fact, all they've done is either suppress or deaden their feeling quality. How much sweeter and, indeed, wiser is Master's way, and how much more effective in helping us to accomplish the one thing necessary: to climb out of this deep pit of ego-consciousness into the fresh air of universal, divine love!

There was another saint—this one in the same line of descent as our Guru's from Lahiri Mahasaya. He told me I wasn't doing Kriya Yoga correctly. A friend of mine persuaded me that it was all in Lahiri's line anyway, and that it wasn't wrong, therefore, to learn what I could from this man. After all, he emphasized, it really comes from Lahiri Mahasaya anyway; how, then, could it in any sense mean disloyalty to my Guru? I wanted to correct any misunderstandings I might have had. So, armed therefore with this reasoning, I allowed myself to accept this similar, but divergent, teaching.

From then on, to my dismay, I felt a subtle inner barrier between myself and Master. It wasn't until, from my heart, I'd repudiated that saint's teaching that I felt Master's loving presence with me once more.

I should mention, finally, that even Anandamayee Ma, whom I loved as my spiritual mother, gave me different counsel in certain respects from that which I'd received from my own Guru. In some ways, I should add, she also clarified for me certain of his other teachings. Still, she for her part had no interest in spiritual organizations, and even used to tell her followers, "It is *your* organization, not mine!"

She would have liked for me to live the life of a hermit. It is a good path, and I myself, as I'd told Master, had always felt drawn to that way of life. (He replied, "That's because you've done it before.") It was disconcerting, in fact, to have Master tell me, "Your path is one of *intense* activity, and meditation." (He actually placed meditation *second* in this sequence.)

I will go further: I'll say that Anandamayee Ma actually said to me one day, "What would you say if I were to ask you to stay here with me?" She didn't want me to leave Master in my heart. I think she had foreseen the trouble I would soon suffer from my fellow disciples in Master's organization, which ended in their dismissing me altogether. I think what she wanted was to offer me protection. I replied, however, "I know you would never really make that request, and you know I wouldn't accept it. I am wholly my Guru's disciple."

Hers would have been a good way, certainly. It could never have been *my* way, however, for I was too deeply committed to doing the many things Master himself had told me I *must* do. As things happened, my Guru made it impossible for me, anyway, to live with her, for I was denied a visa for India until Ananda Village had become well grounded and functioning.

I have come to understand, since then, the basic reason for the difference between her thought that I should spend all my time meditating, and Master's, who wanted me to lecture and to be (as he'd put it to me), "intensely active." Her advice was, spiritually speaking, perfectly correct as a general counsel. Master, however, had been my guru for many lifetimes, and knew what I myself, particularly, needed to work out in light of my own previous mistakes. What Ma said was valid *in principle*, but—as one consideration—she was not yet fully liberated, and hadn't the all-round understanding of my nature that Master had. She had, moreover, not been my guide for countless incarnations, and wasn't addressing any particular karmic tangle in my own *samskaras* (tendencies). Master had (as he himself told me) known me for many incarnations. For my particular nature, he was responding to certain things in my nature that I needed for my own development.

Moreover, I believe I have helped him before, in his missions as an *avatar* (divine incarnation). *Therein*, I know, lies my salvation: in serving him, and in doing his will. As he once wrote of his own guru (I'm paraphrasing), "Even if all the gods are displeased, but you [my guru] are pleased, I am protected within the bulwarks of your grace."

I remember another great saint to whom I once went. When he heard I was Master's disciple, he remarked, of Yogananda, "*Bade yogi the*—he was a great yogi." Yet the way of this saint was not to spread the truth by lecturing, but only to seek God in meditation. He didn't favor my lecturing. As a matter of fact, his own chief disciple confided to a friend of mine, "When he leaves us, I will be able to spread his teachings as I feel inspired to do."

Master gave me the job of teaching. Once, when I pleaded with him to spare me that public work, he replied, "You'd better learn to like it! That is what you will have to do." It is, in fact (as I've said) the path I've needed for my own salvation. I can see, now, how important for my own spiritual development the job of teaching others has been. In past lives, Master told me, I suffered from many doubts. I no longer have doubts, but by helping other people to resolve *their* doubts I've greatly strengthened my own faith. I really don't believe that anything, now, could shake that faith.

People have, over the years, "stepped up to bat" with many attempts to prove to me that Master was wrong, and that they alone were right. In Muktananda's case, I simply compared him with Master and saw that the comparison was like the difference between night and day! Of all the saints I have met, Master stands supreme. Far, indeed, from considering him "second best"—as I was willing to do for the sake of that foolish "missionary" who once threatened me with hellfire if I didn't go his way—I am profoundly certain that Yogananda is the greatest master I have ever met. So confident am I that, really, I didn't at all mind giving that man the freedom to think as he liked. To me, comparisons of good, better, and best have simply never mattered.

It *does* matter to me, however, when I find people straying away from a good thing in the hope of finding something better. Almost never has anyone I've known made a good choice in going a different path. *Has* anyone, then, made what seemed to me a good choice? Yes, perhaps so, but only in very rare cases.

Jesus Christ himself warned his disciples that many would come pretending to be Jesus himself, reincarnated. This sort of thing simply happens. People were bound to do the same thing with our own Guru. People have been bound also to come up with claims that they've replaced him in our line of gurus. Satan, I have to say, has many arrows in his quiver. And one of his best arrows consists of that wood out of which such claims as these are made

Suppose Master did come back. Wouldn't he at least look up his old disciples? Again, if he came back, would he go to countries where the chances of a new spiritual renaissance are slight compared to the state of consciousness that prevails in other lands? Would he teach something *less* central, spiritually, than Kriya Yoga—traditional mantras, for example? Master himself, finally, said that he would not come again for another 200 years. He also described how and where that lifetime would be spent.

What about the several teachers who claim to represent Babaji and who insist, therefore, that their teaching supersedes anything that Master taught? For heaven's sake! Master was an *avatar*, sent by Babaji himself. Does anyone seriously believe Babaji would send anyone to *correct* Master? I remember Master saying something to me, when discussing Babaji, after mentioning that he himself had been Arjuna, and that Babaji had been Krishna. What he said was, "That's why I am so close to Babaji."

Some people may say they don't like, or perhaps don't approve of, this or that Ananda teacher. They may add that they've found someone else who, in their eyes, is more pleasing or more effective. If their change of loyalties means, however, their leaving a true line of descent from our gurus, that divine ray will no longer be there to guide them. I say, Suit yourselves. However, I do urge everyone to remember the price of leaving this ray of our masters, for it is not a small one.

I myself am not in the game of "winning disciples" for Master. I'm happy simply to inspire people to seek God. In fact, I often tell my audiences, "The only thing I want to convert you to is *your own higher Self*." If people decide to move on to other paths and other teachings, I won't try to talk them out of it. Everyone must be allowed the free will in such matters to make his own decisions.

I do grieve, however, when I see people starting off on yet another circle. For, all too often, that is all that it turns out to be. When people leave, then after a time come back to us, they may well by that time have established a certain habit pattern in their lives that will take them off yet again, after some time, in new directions. I'm happy to help them as long as they want my help, but in this essay I have wanted to help people to understand the pros and cons of loyalty vs. fleeting enthusiasms.

I urge you: Be wise in your seeking. The emotional affirmation and excitement of finding new ways must always be balanced against something our own Master often said, "Loyalty is the first law of God." Be wary, I say—and I speak with the support of a great deal of experience, born of many lifetimes: Beware the innumerable wiles Satan places before the *un*wary.

Finally, please understand, I am not at all saying that Satan infuses those teachers to whom people go *instead of* Master. My meaning is that the Satanic element is what infuses people's restless desire to seek ever-new satisfaction from mere novelty.

EDITING

Editing is a very different process from writing. Certain of my brother disciples, members of the Self-Realization Fellowship Board of Directors and followers of Paramhansa Yogananda, had the temerity to tell me recently that I didn't so much edit our Guru's writings in the books I have put out in his name as write my own books, and attach his name to them for the sake of wider circulation. I found their allegation so deeply offensive that I've decided to publish an analysis I made many years ago of my own editing, versus Self-Realization Fellowship's, of a single quatrain from Yogananda's explanation of *The Rubaiyat of Omar Khayyam*: three versions of the first *rubai*, or quatrain, with critical commentary.

The purpose of editing is to clarify, simplify, and make more fluid and easy to understand what has been written. When editing, one should never add ideas of his own. As a direct disciple of Paramhansa Yogananda, commissioned *by him personally* to teach, write, and edit *in his name*, I have both a *right* and a *duty* to present his teachings as clearly and correctly as I can.

I do not claim to be the only disciple to whom he gave this duty. I do claim, however, that there were very few whom he commissioned to do this work. I am also in a position to judge whether, and to what extent, the editing done by others has been faithful to his meaning and to the deep subtlety of his spirit.

I became deeply concerned when Laurie Pratt (Tara Mata), his chief editor, announced to me once, many years ago, after Yogananda's passing, "People don't need more books! They already have everything they need, to find God." I suspected that she was offering this reasoning as an excuse for avoiding the work our Guru had given her: that of editing as many of his books as possible Instead, she focused on administration, a responsibility he had left to others, and involved herself constantly in "people problems." (In fact, Master had said to Daya Mata years earlier, "Keep her from getting involved with people." For this sphere of activity she had no talent at all, being more inclined—like Shiva—to destroy than—like Vishnu—to preserve.) She was at last removed from the scene altogether by God, with her death in 1971.

The disciple who took on the editing work after Tara's demise was Mrinalini Mata, who claims that our Guru told her she would have to finish any work Tara had left undone. I am unable to endorse Mrinalini's claim, but I can state unequivocally that the work I know he asked her to do—namely, the editing of his correspondence course lessons—has yet to be finished and, for all I know, has not even been started.

During the years I was with them, I stated repeatedly and forcefully at our committee meetings, "Until the lessons are finished, we'll never be able to get this 'show on the road.'" My own work was to bring Master's teachings to the public. It made me painfully aware of what a hole existed in consequence of this unfinished labor.*

I have not been happy with the books Self-Realization Fellowship has put out in our Guru's name. Their editing seems to me adolescent, short on literary merit, and (in some cases) either inexact or untrue to our Guru's teachings. What that representative of their Board of Directors said to me recently about the book, *God Is for Everyone*, was essentially that I had lied in attributing it to Yogananda. Evidently they are not themselves familiar with the genesis of that book. Let me explain its genesis here:

---

* In India, where I lived from 1958–1962, I spent over a year organizing the lessons into a more logical sequence, better designed for the aspiring student. In 1962, with my unwilling separation from that organization, it was decided that my labor should be discarded. It had been contingent in any case on Mrinalini's completion of the new course.

In the mid 1950s, SRF's editor-in-chief, Laurie Pratt (Tara Mata), told me she was thinking of dropping that book from SRF's publications. I protested, for, as I insisted, "It contains the very core of Master's teachings. Why on earth would you think of dropping it?"

"Master never wrote it," she proceeded to inform me. "It was written by Swami Dhirananda [a monk who later betrayed him and nearly destroyed his work in America]. Dhirananda was a pompous intellectual who prided himself on his pedantry, but he never really 'got' the true spirit of Master's teachings. The book itself is heavy with muddy logic, and doesn't breathe with Master's spirit. The only reason Master has kept it in print is that it does, for all that, present basic concepts of his teachings."

Tara had come to our Guru in the early 1920s, and could speak on these matters from her own experience. Daya Mata herself came later, in 1931.

When I was in India from 1958–1962 I had an opportunity to speak also with Swami Satyananda, a boyhood friend and disciple of Paramhansa Yogananda (as Dhirananda also had been). Satyananda told me, "During Paramhansaji's visit to Japan [in about 1915], he was inspired with insight into the best way to present his message to the modern world. For Japan itself he felt less attraction, finding the general consciousness to be too sensual. His message, however, which he brought to a focus during his visit there, was timeless, profound, and utterly practical.

"He wrote out this central message," Satyananda continued, "in the form of a simple but basic outline. Not confident of his own mastery of the English language, he asked our mutual friend and scholar, Swami Dhirananda, to expand on those central concepts and make them into a book for publication in English. This book, *The Science of Religion*, was accordingly printed in 1920, and proved very helpful later that year in launching Yogananda's mission to America."

Tara Mata had wanted to drop the book's publication because it so much breathed the spirit of one who, as she knew from her own memories, had betrayed our Guru. Yet I, whose job it was to present these teachings to the public, dissuaded her from this intention because I knew from experience how very central this book's message was for bringing people to our Guru's teachings.

Many years later, I resolved to resuscitate this book and to restate its contents in such a way as to express the Master's teachings in all their simplicity and clarity, remaining of course as faithful as possible to his spirit. My intention was to keep the same name, *The Science of Religion*, for I felt that what I'd written said at last what Master had originally intended, and was in fact truly representative of his wishes.

When I stated my intentions publicly, the announcement aroused a storm of protest from SRF. Daya Mata, SRF's president, expostulated to me on the phone, "But Master *loved* that book!" Tara had told me the inside story, but she had evidently not shared it with Daya. Daya herself is not a trained writer or editor. I was confident of my facts, but to keep peace I agreed to give the new edition a different name: *God Is for Everyone*. I clarified my part in the writing by stating on the cover at the bottom: "As taught to, and understood by, his disciple (myself)."

I explained all these things in the preface to the book. Quite lately, however, when that SRF Board member accused me of lying in designating Yogananda as the author of this book, I was righteously indignant. As our Guru's direct disciple, commissioned by him personally to edit his works, I felt my position would have been falsified if I'd presented his teachings as my own.

There are many differences, however, between my view of our Guru's teachings and writings and the views held by some of my fellow disciples. My distress goes beyond any perception of their literary incompetence. I am also dismayed by their determination to "polish" his public image to reflect the prim, rather "old-maidish" image which they themselves seem to hold of him. One consequence of this attempt of theirs seems to be to eliminate any suggestion of his perfectly marvelous sense of humor. Evidently they don't realize, or else are unable to appreciate, how wonderfully human he was, though always divinely so.

Autobiography of a Yogi, in the chapter titled "Years in My Master's Hermitage," mentions, "It was simplicity itself to discover when Master [Sri Yukteswar] had awakened: abrupt halt of stupendous snores." A footnote followed: "Snoring, according to physiologists, is an indication of perfect relaxation." In the book's first edition the author added, "(to the oblivious practitioner, solely)." This harmless parenthetical quip was removed from later editions. Evidently the editors felt that it lacked dignity.

Again, at the Master's last birthday party his disciple, Dr. Lewis, teased him saying, "Do you think you can blow out all those candles?"

"Oh, I think I have enough breath left in me," replied the Master. He added jocularly, "I must just be careful I don't blow the cake away!" This second sentence was later removed from the recording by editors who evidently worried lest listeners consider it boastful.

More than a decade ago, when I was working on my Guru's deeply spiritual explanation of the *Rubaiyat of Omar Khayyam*, I took the time to analyze the first stanza of the poem from several points of view: his own; SRF's version, which later appeared under the name, *Wine of the Mystic*, and my version, which appeared under the title: *The Rubaiyat of Omar Khayyam Explained by Paramhansa Yogananda*—edited by myself

Let me present that paper here, for it shows all three versions, with appropriate analytical commentaries, and demonstrates clearly not only the process of good editing, but also how much work I myself have put into the process of editing his works.

━━◆━━

I

Original Version by Paramhansa Yogananda, from *Inner Culture Magazine*, **August, 1937**

Stanza One
Awake! for Morning in the Bowl of Night
Has flung the Stone that puts the Stars to Flight:
> **And Lo! the Hunter of the East has caught**
The Sultan's Turret in a Noose of Light.

Spiritual Interpretation:
The inner Silence silently sang: "Awake, forsake the sleep of ignorance, for the dawn of wisdom has thrown the stone of discipline to break the bowl of nocturnal unknowing, and put the starlike, pale, mock-lustred material desires to flight.

"Behold, the hunter of Eastern wisdom has cast a noose of light to catch the kingly minaret of pride of the soul and dispel its darkness."

Moral:
Forsake melancholia, bask in the Light of Peace which destroys all false pride and inner gloom.

Glossary:
1. **Morning**—Dawn of awakening from delusive earthly existence.
2. **Bowl of Night**—Nocturnal ignorance.

3. **Stone**—Stone of discipline.

4. **Stars**—The pseudo-attractive desires.

5. **Hunter of the East**—The Eastern wisdom which hunts and destroys all delusion.

6. **Sultan's Turret**—The kingly minaret of pride of the soul.

7. **Noose of Light**—Light of wisdom which traps inner darkness and destroys it.

II

My own edited version of this Stanza, from *The Rubaiyat of Omar Khayyam Explained by Paramhansa Yogananda*

Awake! for Morning in the Bowl of Night
Has flung the Stone that puts the Stars to Flight:
     And Lo! the Hunter of the East has caught
The Sultan's Turret in a Noose of Light.

Paraphrase
    Thus sang the inner Silence:
    "Forsake your sleep of ignorance: Awake!
    "For the dawn of wisdom has flung into the dark bowl of your unknowing the stone of spiritual discipline—that weapon of divine power that can break the bowl and put to flight the paling stars of earthly desire.
    "Behold, Wisdom—'the Hunter of the East'—has cast a noose of light to encircle the kingly minaret of your egoic pride: wisdom to free you at last from the long night of spiritual ignorance!"

Expanded Meaning
    Forsake delusion! Absorb into your innermost Self the calm light of Wisdom.

Listen! your soul calls you to embrace a new adventure. As the sun travels from east to west across the sky, so does the light of civilization and of knowledge move across the earth. From the east comes Wisdom's call: Awake! all you who sleep in ignorance.

What has pride brought you but melancholia and pain?—dark products of soul-ignorance. Dispel gloom forever: Abide from today onward in the light of inner peace.

Keys to Meaning

Morning—The dawn of awakening from delusive material existence.

Bowl of Night—The dark night of soul-ignorance.

Stone—Delusion-shattering acts of spiritual self-discipline.

Stars—Falsely attractive material desires.

Hunter of the East—Eastern wisdom, hunter and destroyer of delusion.

Sultan's Turret—The kingly minaret of pride.

Noose of Light—The light of wisdom, which, like a lasso, haloes the darkness of ego to ensnare it, transforming it forever into kindred light.

Editorial Comment (also contained in my book)

It has long been a tradition in the East to face eastward during prayer and meditation. The reason, Paramhansa Yogananda explained, is that subtle rays of wisdom radiate westward over the earth.

It is a tenet in other traditions also that enlightenment comes from the east. American Indian tribes, for example, believe that a dwelling place should be built with its entrance eastward—"from whence," claim the Sioux Indians, "all good things come."

"*Kedem*" (meaning, "that which lies before, or in front") is the Hebrew word for "east," and implies the direction to be faced during prayer.

In mystical tradition, "east" also represents the forehead, specifically the point midway between the eyebrows. Modern medicine would identify this point with the region just behind it, in the frontal lobe of the brain. This area is, anatomically speaking, the most advanced part of the brain. The devotee, by concentrating deeply here, finds the "sun" of inner, spiritual vision dawning upon his consciousness.

III

My Editing Explained

Preliminary Commentary on the Headings:

My Guru used different headings at various times throughout the book, which, being serialized, took about a decade to appear in its entirety. Sometimes he would say, "Spiritual Interpretation" and "Moral." Other times he would say, "Applied to Daily Life," or, "Practical Application." I forget all the variations, but generally they added up to nothing more shocking than a lack of consistency, which it seemed to me was required in order to give the book coherence. Many times Master would begin his commentary with a paraphrase of the quatrain. Sometimes the paraphrase came later in the text. Sometimes there was no actual paraphrase. The ideal format, it seemed to me, was what he did here, and in many other stanzas. Accordingly, I decided to label the first section, following every quatrain (or *rubai*), "Paraphrase."

His heading, "Interpretation," covered more than the concept implied in a paraphrase. I ended up not using it at all, because the word "interpretation" implied a more *tentative* meaning, whereas what Master really did was *explain* the meaning from a deep, intuitive level. The word "interpretation" lacks, besides, the weight of divine authority. There can be many "interpretations" of a scripture, each one conveying a suggestion of intellectual opinion as opposed to intuited certainty. I therefore changed the heading of the second section, in every case, to read, "Expanded Meaning." Master's heading, "Moral," which he used in this stanza, worked sometimes in other stanzas, but in other cases was not applicable and was not used by him.

It seemed unnecessary to me to include more than two headings. The entire subject matter could be conveniently fitted under these headings: "Paraphrase," and "Expanded Meaning." Occasionally, when the explanation under "Expanded Meaning" passed from the strictly spiritual to a more outward meaning, I included a subheading or two. Usually, however, I was able to indicate the new direction in the text itself.

"Glossary" seemed to me too scholarly a term, and less fitting for Master's spiritual explanations than the heading I finally decided on: "Keys to Meaning."

The Paraphrase:

The Master wrote, **"The inner Silence silently sang."** "Silently" is redundant. Of the two thoughts ("inner Silence" and "sang"), "inner Silence" is the more important. I put it at the end to give it emphasis. The whole sentence, I felt, needed power, especially as it is the opening shot, announcing the whole book. I therefore made it a separate paragraph, and announced its importance by the word, "thus." Hence: "Thus sang the inner Silence:".

Master then followed, first, with the word, **"Awake"** (as Omar—or Fitzgerald, rather—did in the poem): **"Awake, forsake the sleep of ignorance."** These words, however, serve not only to explain the words in the poem. They are a paraphrase, and need first to explain what the reader is being told to awake *from* — not, in other words, from normal sleep, but from the sleep of ignorance. To make that point first and *then* cry, "Awake!" gives the reader a clearer sense of direction. So much power, indeed, do the first words of this sentence have that I gave them the full authority of a separate paragraph of their own. They present a thought to be dwelt on, not hurried past. (Incidentally, I changed "the sleep" to "your sleep," in order to give the phrase greater immediacy.) As for the rest of the paragraph, it needs the separate emphasis I gave it, so that every concept, every image, be relished in its full richness.

"... for the dawn of wisdom has thrown the stone of discipline to break the bowl." I changed this to read, "For the dawn of wisdom has flung into the dark bowl of your unknowing the stone of spiritual discipline." The mind puzzles for a moment, on reading the first version, to ask why wisdom should be throwing stones. *After* the succeeding explanation the point comes clear, but it would be well to spare the reader this brief moment of uncertainty, even of skepticism. This is a minor point, but the sentence reads better anyway if "bowl" is put first to suggest an *object* for reason's otherwise seemingly unreasonable act (though it be only fleetingly so). "Thrown the stone," by the way, rhymes in such a way as to seem faintly comical. I changed it back, therefore, to Fitzgerald's "flung ... the stone."

"... to break the bowl of Nocturnal unknowing." "Nocturnal," in Yogananda's version, is unclear. Although it is meant to suggest the darkness of spiritual unknowing, this darkness is not yet obvious and might leave the reader confused between the possibility of darkness as a symbol and the suggestion (stronger to the literal mind) that one's unknowing happens only at night. Or perhaps (so the reader might wonder) there may be some other kind of unknowing that is *diurnal*—that is to say, which happens only in daylight. The point needs clarifying not because the intelligent reader can't figure out what is meant, but because the less the mind is left to play with these alternatives the straighter its arrow of concentration can fly to its real target of meaning. In my version, I left out "nocturnal" for its possible confusion with the earthly night, and made it instead, "the *dark* bowl." For clarity, it is in any case "bowl" which needs modifying here, since bowl is the image that Omar has presented to describe "unknowing." To say "bowl," and then offer "nocturnal" as another description of "unknowing," is weakening to the thought—if not confusing to it.

Again, to make it clear that this was a direct, not an abstract, teaching, I made it, "the dark bowl of *your* unknowing." After all, the whole stanza is a direct exhortation, made more so by Master's "paraphrase." It is not an abstract philosophical statement.

The next part was difficult. The bowl can easily be understood as the "inverted bowl" of the sky, and the whole thing offered as a symbol of the sky of our own consciousness. I had a hard time, however, with the concept of *breaking* the bowl so as to put one's desires to flight. It seemed to me—especially for the purposes of a poetic paraphrase—too elaborate to explain that old mental concepts have to be shattered before new, spiritual understanding can shine in. Moreover, while I tried to clarify Master's concepts, it was not my job to add concepts of my own. If he chose not to elaborate this somewhat difficult point, I didn't feel it my place to do so. I therefore decided to leave this concept pretty much as it was, just as Master did. Indeed, it seems to me one can kill the spirit of a poem with too much explanation.

Master had an engaging tendency (one that I've kept wherever possible, out of sheer delight in the exuberance of his writing!) to string adjectives together, thus: "**and put the starlike, pale, mock-lustred material desires to flight.**" In this case, however, as in several others, the abundance of adjectives weakened the teaching instead of strengthening it. What I wanted to convey above all was the sense of authority in Master's inspiration.

I'm not wholly satisfied with my solution here, but it is the best I could come up with to preserve all of the meaning, adding none of my own, and at the same time to make the sentence as clear and spiritually authoritative as possible.

"Mock-lustred" I changed to "paling" because "mock-lustred" makes the mind stumble: The stars are *not* "mock"-lustred; they shine with their own brilliancy. Granted, desires *are* mock-lustred, since their light is only a reflection of the inner life. It was not for their falsity, however, that they were compared to stars. The comparison was based only on the fact that their luster is faint and tiny compared with that of the sun of wisdom. There is, on the other hand, nothing *false* about the stars' luster. "Paling" seemed to me more fitting in this context, as well as being, poetically, a lovely word.

"**Flight**" ("**and put the ... desires to flight**"). I put "flight" first—"put to flight the paling stars of earthly desire"—because the sentence ends more powerfully with the noun. It was stronger, too, to bring the verbal phrase (or whatever the word is) all together, thus: "and put to flight the paling stars" (rather than say, "and put the ... desires to flight").

I changed "material desires" to "earthly desires" simply to enhance the rhythm of the sentence. Many writers are unaware of how much the power of a sentence depends on rhythm alone. I have tried always to preserve Master's rhythms, which is one way of saying his *vibrations*, and the vibrations and power he intuited in the poetry of Omar Khayyam. His attunement with Omar had to be more with Omar's consciousness than with the words of his poetry, which were in any case a translation from the original. The rhythm seemed to me, in this case, to justify the slight change.

Second paragraph: **"Behold, the hunter of Eastern wisdom has cast. . . ."** Here again, the word-placement is confusing. Is Eastern wisdom (one asks) the hunter, or the hunted? Moreover, what is the difference between Eastern and Western wisdom? Why select the one as if in deprecation of the other? If "Eastern" wisdom refers simply to the fact that Omar Khayyam lived in the East, it seems pointless to explain that his wisdom was *Eastern*. Wisdom is simply wisdom. Besides that, wisdom, to the readers for whom Omar was presumably writing, came to them outwardly from the city of Mecca, which lies *westward* of where he lived.

Better, I thought, to clarify this point of "Eastern" wisdom immediately, so as not to tire the reader, who has enough work as it is to understand what Omar, and Yogananda, are really trying to say. Thus, I put "wisdom" first, without qualifying it. Wisdom—to repeat—is a universal quality. I then qualified it as much as I dared, and included in a separate "Editorial Comment" a fuller explanation, already touched on in the "Glossary," of why Omar would qualify "wisdom" as "eastern." (The "light of civilization" flows westward around the world.)

Thus, I wrote: **"Behold, Wisdom—'the Hunter of the East'—has cast. . . ."**

I changed one word in the next clause. Instead of **". . . has cast a noose of light to *catch* the kingly minaret . . ."** I wrote, **"has cast a noose of light to *encircle* the kingly minaret."** When you *catch* something in a noose you usually pull on it, probably to pull it down, the way a cowboy does when lassoing a cow. The stressful image of pulling wasn't intended here. "Encircle" gives, rather, the intended image of *enlightening*.

Master continued: ". . . **the kingly minaret of pride of
the soul.**" From his teachings, however, it is clear that he
didn't mean to say that the soul is proud. Pride is of the ego.
I therefore changed this to read, ". . . **the kingly minaret of
your egoic pride.**" I included "your," again, to fit the mood of
the stanza, and of Master's paraphrase of it. I felt that Master
would want to make the phrase more strongly admonitory.

He ended this paragraph thus: ". . . **and dispel its
darkness.**" The soul is not dark, of course. "Soul darkness"
is an acceptable expression if one is referring to the darkness
of our unawareness. But what makes human consciousness
dark, anyway? The reader needs to have this point explained
to him, since he hasn't yet been made to understand that
spiritual ignorance is the darkness being described. Thus, I
developed the thought, changing ". . . **and dispel its darkness**"
to read, "**Wisdom to free you at last from the long night
of spiritual ignorance.**" My reason for adding the word
"long" was primarily for the sake of rhythm, but also to add
poignancy to man's need to banish this darkness at last.

The Expanded Meaning:

Master's "Moral" at the end is so brief ("**Forsake melancholia, bask in the Light of Peace which destroys all false
pride and inner gloom**") that I felt it necessary to expand
on it, particularly since its concepts are so condensed and so
rich with meaning.

They also need clarification. Master wrote, "**Forsake
melancholia.**" Why "melancholia"? Should we seek divine awakening only after we've reached the point of being
melancholic over our condition of delusion? Wouldn't it be
better to seek awakening sooner? And is melancholy *always*
the accompaniment of delusion? Far from it! There are often
feelings of pleasure and delight. (If there weren't, people
would have no difficulty in giving up delusion.) Melancholy,
moreover, is not the only darkness suggested by the image

of spiritual ignorance. Ignorance (with or without its resultant melancholia), as Master has made clear earlier, is the real darkness being described here.

What I did was lead up to this concept of melancholia as being only one consequence of delusion. To do so, it was necessary to extend the thoughts, restating in more literal terms the concepts Master had already expressed in his "Paraphrase." Thus, I used the "Expanded Meaning" to clarify, not to express new ideas. To make it clear that melancholia is a *result* of soul-ignorance, not an alternate expression for ignorance itself, I began with the clarion call: "Forsake delusion!"

Master wrote, "**Bask in the Light of Peace.**" "Bask" is a passive word. One "basks" when sunbathing. One "basks" in the "light" of flattery. "Bask" doesn't imply *active* participation. I substituted for it two expressions, to bring out Master's obvious intention of active involvement. First, I said, "**Absorb into your innermost Self the calm light of Wisdom.**" Next, at the end of this section I put, "*Abide from today onward* **in the light of inner peace.**"

Because *Eastern* wisdom was so central a thought to the thesis of Master's paraphrase, I felt it necessary, even though I went into the subject in greater detail in the "Editorial Comment," to touch on it briefly in the "Expanded Meaning." In the "Expanded Meaning," I made a brief explanation of this concept in the central paragraph, though I kept it brief, wanting to heighten the explanation without laboring the concept lest I detract from the "mood" of Master's beautiful commentary.

Keys to Meaning:

Master called this section, "Glossary." I've changed it to avoid the common association of this word with intellectual scholarship. What ensues is the text of Master's "Glossary," followed by my changes:

1. **Morning** — (Master's version:) "**Dawn of awakening from delusive earthly existence**." I changed "earthly" to "material," here, to emphasize that it isn't our existence on earth that makes for our delusion, but, rather, our *materialistic* existence. After all, saints live on earth also. I used "material" rather than "materialistic" because the description of this existence was covered by the word "delusive." I used it also for purposes of rhythm, because, of the two considerations, rhythm, at this point, seemed the more important.

2. **Bowl of Night** — (Master's:) "**Nocturnal ignorance.**" I wrote, "**The dark night of soul-ignorance,**" for reasons explained above, and also for rhythm.

3. **Stone** — (Master's:) "**Stone of discipline.**" I wrote, "**Delusion-shattering acts of spiritual self-discipline,**" to make clearer what kind of discipline was intended, and that the discipline being referred to was *self*-discipline, not discipline from without.

4. **Stars** — (Master's:) "**The pseudo-attractive desires.**" Not all desires are harmful. The desire for God, for example, is important if one would attain enlightenment. Noble, selfless desires uplift the consciousness. The reader needs to know why the attraction of some desires is pseudo, and, if not all are such, why the attraction of others is not pseudo. This point is too involved to be explained clearly in the single paragraph of a glossary. Moreover, Master explains it fully and beautifully in later stanzas. I therefore satisfied myself with merely hinting at the truth by adding the word, "material," thus: "**Falsely attractive material desires.**" "Falsely attractive" seemed to me more poetic, and less reminiscent of intellectual scholarship than "pseudo-attractive."

5. **Hunter of the East** — (Master's:) "**The Eastern wisdom which hunts and destroys all delusion.**" To make the main thought in this phrase look like a supportive clause,

through the use of "which," seemed to me a weaker way of putting it. I changed the phrase also for the purposes of poetic rhythm, thus: **"Eastern wisdom, hunter and destroyer of delusion."**

6. **Sultan's Turret**—(Master's:) **"The kingly minaret of pride of the soul."** Pride is not a soul-attribute. It is possible to interpret this word here not as egoic pride, but rather as the noble dignity of a Self-realized soul. Master, however, has already committed himself to another meaning for "pride": He has allied it to the concept of spiritual darkness. To bring in a new meaning at this point by making "pride" refer to another state of consciousness altogether—especially when the "Glossary" is meant to explain the earlier commentary—is to place a greater burden on this single stanza than the stanza itself can bear. I therefore changed this statement to read, **"The kingly minaret of pride."**

7. **Noose of Light**—(Master's:) **"Light of wisdom which traps inner darkness and destroys it."** One doesn't think of a noose as *trapping* anything. A trap is something that encloses what it catches, shutting it in. *Ensnaring* the inner darkness is better. My version expands on Master's meaning, clarifying it and making it more magnetic: **"The light of wisdom, which, like a lasso, haloes the darkness of ego and ensnares it, transforming it forever into kindred light."**

Editorial Comment:

I added this section to several of the stanzas (fewer than a third) to bring out thoughts that I felt would enhance the text, but that I didn't want to present as Master's commentary. In this case, I showed how the tradition of wisdom coming from the East is not Master's invention, merely, but a tradition encountered in many parts of the world. Thus, I gave weight to Master's explanation of a thought that will be new to most

readers—that of the light of civilization moving *westward*—
and will benefit them by its further development.

IV
SRF'S EDITION, *Wine of the Mystic*

Awake, for Morning in the Bowl of Night
Has flung the Stone that puts the Stars to Flight:
> **And Lo! the Hunter of the East has caught**
The Sultan's Turret in a Noose of Light.

Spiritual Interpretation:

The inner Silence sings:

"Awake! Forsake the sleep of ignorance, for the dawn of wisdom has come. Hurl the hard stone of spiritual discipline that breaks the bowl of dark unknowing, putting to flight the pale stars of mock-lustered material desires.

"Behold, the Eastern Wisdom, the Hunter and Destroyer of delusion, has caught the proud minaret of the kingly soul in a noose of Light, dispelling darkness."

I have been inspired further to interpret this introductory quatrain as Omar's personal clarion call to the spiritually sleeping:

"O inhabitants of the City of Delusion, sleep no more! The sunlight of my awakening message of mystic wisdom has arrived. Learn how to use the hard stone of spiritual discipline to break the bowl of your dark ignorance, dashing from its hold the desire for momentarily attractive material pleasures.

"Behold with envy how the Hunter of Wisdom has been searching out and gathering the lofty, kingly, spiritually advanced devotees of Truth, encompassing their souls with a halo of the everlasting Light of Freedom."

Practical Application:

Most people, though apparently awake, are really asleep in delusion. Pursued by the compelling commands of their hounding habits, they have not yet been awakened by wisdom to walk its pleasant pathways. Where life is in danger for lack of watchfulness, it is not safe to sleep. So it is unwise to slumber in the dark doorways of evil habits, which invite the danger of possible death to wisdom and true happiness.

The ordinary man earns a living, eats three times a day, amuses himself with trivial entertainments, remaining engrossed in the mechanical performance of material duties without ever awakening to the importance of understanding the purpose of life: attaining true happiness and sharing it with others. The wise man gives up false pride in self-perfection, the thought that "I am all right as I am." Using the net of introspection, he catches delusion and destroys it. Forsake the slumber of ignorant habits and awaken wisdom by performing those good habits which alone can free life from danger and crown it with lasting happiness.

To be drunk with the daily round of haunting useless habits, to be negatively the same every day for years, is a wasted existence. Destroy false pride. Awaken the soul and remain ever wakeful, striving each day to be different and better in all ways. Your soul was not meant to be a prisoner of passion, sleeping behind bars of ignorance. Jerk yourself from the stupor of sloth; race forward with progressive activities, and catch success in the net of soul creativity.

Forsake spiritual lethargy and melancholia. Bask in the light of meditative peace and Self-realization, which destroys false pride of material existence and banishes inner soul gloom.

V

MY COMMENTS ON SRF'S *Wine of the Mystic*

I shall not go into an analysis of each and every change, as to do so would be burdensome both to write and to read.

One comment, first: The "Glossary" is missing from SRF's version of the first stanza. I don't know why. Elsewhere it is included. The editors changed Master's placement, which was at the end of his commentary, placing it instead at the beginning. Their reason for doing so is clear: They wanted to explain and justify immediately the explanations Master wrote for each stanza. There is more concerned here, however, than a simple matter of taste. To put the glossary first almost demands that the commentary be changed from the poetic, intuitive emphasis Master gave to it an intellectual analysis. In fact, SRF's version of the whole book demonstrates this difference.

Spiritual Interpretation:

SRF's edition, *Wine of the Mystic*, strengthens the first sentence, as my edition did, by giving it a paragraph of its own. The alliterative repetition, "**The inner Silence sings**" is weakening, however, not strengthening to the flow. Master's redundancy—"**The inner Silence *silently* sang**"—is removed, but alliteration, though a recognized poetic device, needs careful attention lest it defeat its poetic purpose. One reason I put "sang" earlier in my version was to break what is, in fact, an awkward alliteration. To refresh the reader's memory, the way I put it was: "**Thus sang the inner Silence.**" (My more important reason for changing the word sequence was, as I stated earlier, to give greater power to the expression, "inner silence.")

SRF's edition ('*Wine*') changes the tense from past to present: Instead of Master's "... silently sang," and my "Thus sang," SRF wrote, "The inner Silence *sings*." The reason for the change is understandable, but I admit to a preference for Master's use of the past tense. With "sang," the sentence announces a dramatic event in a person's life. "Sings" turns it into a suggestion of something that happens repeatedly during the soul's evolution. Again—to reiterate my earlier comment—this sentence is the opening salvo of the entire book. It *needs* dramatic emphasis. I've already explained why I changed "*the* sleep of ignorance" to "*your* sleep of ignorance." "Your" is more immediate, more admonitory. This is a minor point. SRF either didn't consider it, or didn't think it important enough to introduce.

SRF also didn't consider, or didn't think it important, to give this clause the strength I've given it by putting it in a paragraph by itself. Rather, *Wine* diminishes the impact of the clause by pairing it with another: "**Forsake the sleep of ignorance,** *for the dawn of wisdom has come.*" In this sentence, two important thoughts are weakened by pairing them. The placement of "has come" at the end of the sentence puts it in the position of greatest power. They are not strong words, here, in themselves—not nearly so strong as the concepts preceding them. Coming as they do, however, at the end of the sentence, it seems as if the editors wanted deliberately to give them power. Lacking natural power of their own, their placement makes them seem peremptory. Indeed, the flow suggests movement toward a brick wall. In another context this device might work, but in the present one it doesn't, for the sentence is not a final statement. It serves, rather, to introduce another thought—several others, in fact: "Hurl the hard stone of spiritual discipline that breaks the bowl of dark unknowing . . ." etc. The rhythm is wrong: Where the ending of the sentence ("The dawn of wisdom has come") should suggest an open window to further ideas, the rhythm—*especially* its rhythm—conveys the feeling, rather, of a slamming door.

In the poem, and in Master's paraphrase of it, it is the dawn itself that flings the stone of discipline. *Wine* tells the reader, instead: "Hurl the hard stone of spiritual discipline. . . ." This change is not really alarming, for it is in fact the devotee himself who must do the hurling. Nevertheless, the SRF editors tuned in to Master's thought without tuning into *Master's own attunement* with Omar Khayyam. Throughout this poem, Master remained true to Omar's thoughts, even when his explanation took those thoughts to deeper-than-apparent levels of meaning. In this case, although SRF is (quite reasonably) telling the devotee to do the hurling, both Omar and Yogananda present the act as something broader, even cosmic, that has been accomplished *through* the devotee.

"Hurl," incidentally, is a less happy choice than either "flung" [Fitzgerald's and mine] or "thrown" [Master's]. "Hurl" conveys a suggestion of something thrown in violence, perhaps even in anger. Such, indeed, is its dictionary definition.

I think something valuable is lost in SRF's transferring to the devotee the job of "hurling." This loss might not be apparent to many readers. Still, I believe it is important to respect as much as possible *all* the nuances of the Master's meanings. The serious student and seeker should be invited to penetrate deeply into the teachings. It is not enough only for the editor to be satisfied in his own mind that the thought has been expressed. Master's explanations of this poem are, in my opinion, a great Scripture. They must be presented with the fullest possible respect for their hidden meanings.

Another point, albeit a small one: Why say, "the *hard* stone"? Are not all stones hard? To use an adjective to emphasize the obvious is not only indicative of lack of imagination (like, "the wet water"), but uses up that precious store of available space for adjectives which the conscientious writer must hoard, if his writing is to convey the sense of economy that is essential to literary clarity.

"**Hurl the hard stone of spiritual discipline** *that breaks the bowl of dark unknowing*." *Wine* caught the problem existing in Master's expression, mentioned by me earlier: "*nocturnal* unknowing." "Bowl" is the image here, however, offered as the poet's description of our "unknowing." It is "*bowl*," therefore, that needs qualifying. Otherwise, the assumption must be that all bowls are dark, leaving only our "unknowing" to be brought into the image by calling it "dark." When an image is clear enough, further qualification of the thing being described is unnecessary.

The expression, "the bowl of dark unknowing," weakens the image, for it makes two images do the work of one: a bowl, and "dark" *unknowing* (as opposed to other kinds of unknowing). My version reads better: "**For the dawn of wisdom has flung into the dark bowl of your unknowing . . . ,**" etc.

Wine caught the weakening effect of Master's string of adjectives ("**the starlike, pale, mock-lustred material desires**"). It also caught the advantage of uniting the "verbal phrase," "putting to flight," over Master's, "**putting the starlike . . . material desires to flight**." SRF kept Master's expression, "mock-lustred." As I pointed out earlier, whereas desires *are* "mock-lustred," stars are not. The comparison of desires to stars occurs in the poem to show how weak both starlight and desires are compared to the blazing "sun" of wisdom.

"**. . . the Eastern Wisdom, the Hunter and Destroyer of delusion**." Here the editor caught the problem, mentioned earlier, that the reader must be made to understand who is the hunter and who the hunted. One further (though admittedly minor) comment: It is clumsy to repeat "the" in this sentence so soon. It is perfectly easy, and reads better, to say, simply, "Eastern Wisdom, the Hunter . . ." etc.

"... has caught the proud minaret. ..." Master wrote, "has cast a noose of light to catch." *Wine's* editor evidently wanted to be more concise, which is something one needs to be when writing poetry, but not when *explaining* a poem. I've explained earlier my reason for changing "catch" to "encircle" *Wine*, though more "no nonsense" and to the point, is less poetic than Master's version. His expression, "has cast," suggests graceful movement. "Has caught," although this is the term Fitzgerald used in his translation, appears in the stanza out of poetic necessity. In the subsequent paraphrase there is no need to count one's syllables so carefully. Thus, in the paraphrase (not in the stanza), "caught" suggests a more aggressive image — perhaps of a "noose of light" seizing its prey (which the mind imagines cowering fearfully in a corner).

"... has caught the proud minaret of the kingly soul." This clause, though different from Master's expression ("the kingly minaret of pride of the soul"), doesn't essentially improve on it. The real problem here is that pride is not a soul-attribute. For this reason, my version — "the kingly minaret of your egoic pride" — works better.

Another weakness in *Wine* is that the mind is asked to visualize two concepts, both of which will be new to the reader: "proud minaret," and "kingly soul." Master's image is easier to grasp in such a brief sequence of words, since he gives us only "kingly minaret." Poetically, his is better than the version in *Wine*. Moreover, while one may think of minarets as kingly, only the reader who is familiar with Master's Bhagavad Gita interpretations finds himself on familiar ground with the expression, "kingly souL"

There is another problem with *Wine's* version of this sentence. *Wine* states, "Eastern wisdom ... has caught the proud minaret of the kingly soul in a noose of Light, dispelling darkness." How is this "capture" of the minaret of the soul going to translate in the reader's mind to "dispelling its darkness"? Light dispels darkness, true; "catching," however, is not a word that lends itself to dispelling anything.

These two paragraphs of the original were extended, following an introductory remark which I suspect was not written by Master. In fact, this entire extension does not feel to me like Master's writing. One thing that makes me suspicious is the plethora of images. Master simply wrote better than that. It is preferable to offer fewer images, carefully developed, than dozens of them. The reason for using images is to clarify one's concepts, not to complicate them. This extension was, I suspect, put there by *Wine's* editors in order to explain some of the philosophy behind the concept of spiritual awakening, and behind the need for inner discipline. I don't really feel the extension adds anything that is not said much better, and in good enough time, in Master's later commentaries.

The extension begins: "**I have been inspired further to interpret this introductory quatrain as Omar's personal clarion call to the spiritually sleeping:**" We have *already had* Omar's "personal clarion call," both in the stanza itself and in Master's paraphrase. What need is there to introduce this further material as a clarion call? What need is there to emphasize that it is "personal"? And what need is there to say, "I have been inspired further," as though the first inspiration had been insufficient?

"**O inhabitants of the City of Delusion, sleep no more!**" The image of a city of delusion is confusing. First, it implies that the whole city is in delusion, whereas the very purpose of Omar's poem, and of Master's explanation of it, is to challenge people individually to awake from their delusion. What are they expected to do after they awake? Emigrate?

The image is not only confusing: It is self-defeating. A city of delusion raises images in the mind of shadows, darknesses, perhaps of hungry cats prowling in dark alleys. Omar's image, however, is one of light, of the darkness being dispersed. It is not an image of mists waiting for the dawn to dispel them.

"O inhabitants of the City of Delusion, *sleep no more!*" It has already been made clear that the sleep described is the sleep of ignorance. To awaken, however, *while still living in* the city of delusion suggests that the city's inhabitants are equally in delusion whether they are awake or asleep. For one assumes that they *must* be awake at least half the time, in order to pursue their daily round of delusive activities. The reader is given no clear idea of what it means to be either awake or asleep in the City of Delusion.

"The sunlight of my *awakening message* [emphasis mine] of mystic wisdom has arrived." We were given a clearer image by Omar and Master, earlier, when it was the sunlight of wisdom itself that did the awakening. Now, that image has been weakened by the fact of being presented as a mere *message* of wisdom. This is the unfortunate consequence of the decision to tell the reader to do the "hurling," rather than making it wisdom itself which throws the stone.

"Learn how to use the hard stone of discipline." Again, the original image is weakened. The first command—it is at least implied in Master's version, and is stated openly in SRF's—was, "*Use*" the stone. Now we are told, "Learn *how to use* it." A course of study is implied here: perhaps classes, lessons, detailed instructions. The immediacy of the original inspiration, which describes action occurring on an intuitive level, is still further distanced by this new call to make an intellectual effort to "learn how."

Incidentally, the expression, "hard stone," is employed again here. In editing, two minuses do not make a plus.

"... **the hard stone of spiritual discipline to break the bowl of your dark ignorance,** *dashing from its hold.* ..." I've already gone into the reasons for making "dark" modify "bowl" rather than "ignorance." Another problem now presents itself: To what does "*its* hold" refer? To the bowl? To the hand (implied, though not mentioned) which holds the bowl? Or does it apply to "your dark ignorance," which one visualizes only with difficulty as actually "holding" anything? The image is muddy.

"**Behold** *with envy* [emphasis mine] **how the Hunter of Wisdom has been searching out and gathering ...,**" etc. Envy is a spiritual flaw. I can't imagine Master counseling anyone to look on others, even on saints, with envy. What is intended here, of course, is that one should *emulate* the saints. It should be so stated.

"**Behold with envy how the Hunter of Wisdom has been searching out and gathering the lofty, kingly, spiritually advanced devotees of Truth, encompassing their souls with a halo of the everlasting Light of Freedom.**" In addition to the mistaken use of "envy," and to the fact that we are left wondering whether Wisdom is the hunter or the hunted, the whole sentence is burdensome. It adds no new thought to the discussion, and only bewilders the mind. For we had, earlier, the word "kingly" applied to egoic pride— or, anyway, to pride. Now, suddenly, we find it applied to "spiritually advanced devotees of Truth"—to people, in other words, who don't *need* awakening since (one assumes) they are either already awake, or at least well on the way toward awakening. The image of a lofty minaret was applied first to a spiritual flaw, pride. Now, suddenly, we find it applied to high spiritual advancement. The reader no longer knows what to think. The editors would have done better, surely, especially in consideration of the brevity of Master's commentary, to hold to a single image, and not to offer two that conflict actively with each other.

Practical Application:

I will touch on only a few points here. To analyze the material too deeply would be counterproductive. My main point is that this entire extension serves no particularly useful purpose, especially since the points are brought out better, and in better contexts, later on.

"**Pursued by the compelling commands of their hounding habits.**" "Compelling commands" works well enough as alliteration "Hounding habits," however, suggests the image of pursuing hounds. What "compelling commands" would a pack of pursuing hounds utter? The only one I can imagine is, "Halt and be eaten!"

"Hounding habits" is alliterative, but it is not poetically so. Those two "aitches" deepen no mood, reinforce no "compelling command." The only thing they do is suggest to the mind the need to pronounce them gaspingly.

Pursued by these commands, "**most people . . . have not yet been awakened by wisdom to walk its pleasant pathways.**" If you're running for your life (as must be assumed from the fact that you're being pursued by hounds), it is difficult to imagine how you can be asleep. Yet at this point "most people" are described as "not yet awakened." The image of awakening, moreover, and immediately afterward of walking wisdom's "pleasant pathways" is too much of a mental stretch. First, I'm running for my life; next, I'm being somehow awakened by wisdom; and finally, after managing to swallow that metaphor, I'm suddenly walking pleasant pathways. It is just too much weight to accept without proper preparation.

"**Where life is in danger for lack of watchfulness.**" Danger from what? From "hounding habits," one assumes, but somehow those hounds have gone out of focus in the welter of intervening metaphors. Anyway, granting the reality of the hounds, what else am I supposed to watch out for, to protect my life? Surely I am well enough aware of the hounds at my heels to need no advice to "watch out" for them.

Oh, one can of course figure it all out. In the end, however, the effort costs the reader too much commitment to what he is reading.

"**Where life is in danger from lack of watchfulness,** *it is not safe to sleep.*" If the danger to one's life makes it unsafe to sleep, the question of lack of watchfulness is quite secondary. The first safeguard, surely, is to be *awake*. Only when wakefulness has been accomplished does the possibility for watchfulness become even an issue.

"**So it is unwise to slumber in the dark doorways of evil habits, which invite the danger of possible death to wisdom and true happiness.**" Again, there I am, sleeping it all off—despite the fury of the chase. Assuming the presence of other death-dealing enemies besides those pursuing hounds (who of course know of my existence, and probably know my actual whereabouts), I should have thought that the darker the doorway, the greater my chances of remaining undetected.

Moreover, if I'm sleeping in "dark doorways of evil habits," what "wisdom and true happiness" can I be hoarding that might be endangered? I should think my supposed "wisdom and true happiness" were pretty well dead already.

"**The ordinary man earns a living, eats three times a day, amuses himself with trivial entertainments,** *remaining engrossed* [emphasis mine] **in the mechanical performance of material duties. . . .**" That gerund, "remaining" (engrossed), modifies each of the three clauses before it. In other words, what is being said is, "The ordinary man earns a living *remaining engrossed in the mechanical performance of material duties* [redundant]";

"the ordinary man eats three times a day *remaining engrossed in the mechanical performance of material duties* [difficult to imagine how he accomplishes both tasks at once]"; "the ordinary man amuses himself with trivial entertainments *remaining engrossed in the mechanical performance of material duties* [an utter contradiction in terms]."

"The wise man gives up false pride in self-perfection." First consider the expression, "false pride." Is there such a thing as *"true* pride"? Maybe, but it will have to be explained if the reader is not to be left mystified. Master uses this expression in his "Moral," above, but the way he uses it is not really confusing. The mind even accepts, at least as a point on which to meditate, that the "Light of Peace" (Master's term) may well destroy false pride.

In the present context, however, confusion intervenes—though only momentarily, I grant you. Pride is a spiritual flaw. The goal in life is self-perfection. How is it—the mind wonders—that pride is being equated with self-perfection? The point is clarified a moment later by the explanation, "the thought that 'I am all right as I am,'" but by then the damage has already been done. The reader stops at his point of initial confusion and tries to work it all out before proceeding any further.

The thought, moreover, "I am all right as I am," is *not* a definition of self-perfection on any level, not even in something so ordinary as learning to play tennis. Rather it suggests merely the *delusion* of self-perfection. This is, of course, what makes a person's pride "false," but how many readers are going to take the time to work all that out?

"Using *the net* of introspection." One thinks of introspection as incisive, not as something that gathers anything in. "Incisive" suggests a sword perhaps (the image Master often used), or a knife.

"**Using the net of introspection,** *he catches delusion and destroys it.*" How are we to visualize destroying something with a net? Nets are used for gathering in. Only after the gathering does any question of destruction arise. The reader is asked, however, not only to *catch* delusion with a net, but to use the same net to destroy it, for no other means are suggested to him to effect delusion's destruction. Thus, he may visualize himself trying to use the net to clobber delusion to death.

"**Forsake the slumber of ignorant habits and awaken wisdom by performing those good habits which alone can free life from danger and** *crown* **it with lasting happiness.**" First, an aside: One *performs* actions, but one *indulges* habits. A greater confusion results, however, from this reference to freeing life from danger and then *crowning* it.

One crowns kings. One crowns popes (I suppose). How does anyone merit a crown by merely forsaking slumber and awakening his wisdom? The reader needs somehow to be brought in on the secret: the glorious triumph, perhaps, before hosts of angels; victory after incarnations of struggle, and the final attainment of divine kingship in cosmic consciousness. All this would need to be explained, of course. Instead, all the reader is asked to do in order to merit his crown is "perform those good habits which alone can free life from danger." Somehow, it doesn't seem enough.

"**To be drunk with the daily round of haunting useless habits. . . .**" Here in a single phrase are encountered three unrelated images: drunkenness, a daily round (which implies a routine existence), and haunting habits, which— apart from that unpoetic repetition of "aitches"—conveys an image of ghosts. These habits, moreover, apart from being "haunting," are described as useless. The mind pauses to wonder, "What kind of 'haunting habit' would be *useful*?"

"**Your soul was not meant to be a prisoner of passion, sleeping behind bars of ignorance.**" If one is engaged in an act of passion of any kind, he is hardly asleep!—except maybe in some metaphysical sense that ought to be explained to the reader as quickly as possible. Better still, avoid mixing metaphors.

"**Jerk yourself from the stupor of sloth.**" It is not easy to imagine anyone in a stupor of sloth suddenly finding the inspiration or the energy to "jerk" himself from anything, let alone from sloth.

"**. . . sloth; race forward with progressive activities.**" This shift from sloth to racing forward requires a leap of faith. To "race forward with progressive activities" becomes, however, an impossibility. Progressive activities have nothing to do with racing forward. They are associated in the mind, rather, with the *quality* of the activities concerned, not with their spatial movement.

"**Catch success in the net of soul creativity.**" This fondness for nets, having now been indulged twice, becomes especially unfortunate. For the image works just as badly the second time as the first. To begin with, is success something anyone actually "catches"? The reader would have to ponder the point. Next, is it possible to catch success in a net? Again, further pondering. Third, the reader will wonder how soul creativity might be woven to form a net.

Soul creativity is itself not an easy image to bring to a focus. How does it differ from other kinds of creativity? And then, again, how does creativity of *any* kind—not only soul creativity—become a net with which to catch success—or anything else for that matter? As the mind does not easily pair discrimination with a net, so does it fail to couple nets with creativity.

In the next paragraph we have, again, the expression, "false pride"—the third use of this expression in as many paragraphs. In this case the expression is followed by "of material existence." Is there some true, or valid, pride in material existence to justify calling this particular form of pride "false"?

"Bask in the light of meditative peace and Self-realization, which destroys false pride of material existence and banishes inner soul gloom." The mind finds it difficult to form any clear image of how its soul gloom ever got started in the first place. First, why "inner" soul gloom? Is there some kind of "outer" soul gloom? Second, and more fundamentally, isn't contact with the soul supposed to make one happy? Gloom, surely, stems from the ego, not from the soul. In transcending ego we free ourselves from the ego's capacity to plunge us even occasionally into gloom. Surely it is cause for despair, and not for mere gloom, if banishment of the ego and reclamation of soul-consciousness leaves us as much as ever subject to delusion!

I should like to reiterate the importance of not confusing poetry with a profusion of images. Poetic images have to be few, apt, and well developed. Better one image developed over one or more paragraphs or stanzas, than dozens of images offered to persuade the reader that there's a whole barrel of them where those came from.

Alliteration, too, must be used sensitively and sparingly, else it becomes an object of humor (as Shakespeare demonstrated in some of his best comic scenes). Later on in SRF's edited commentaries one encounters the expression, "delusion drowsy devotees." Here again is an example of unpoetic alliteration. It fails to convey any clear image to the mind. People who are in delusion may be described as being asleep in it, but to call them "drowsy" with their delusion is something the reader needs to have explained on the spot, and not assumed from something he may have read several stanzas earlier.

If one simply hasn't the gift of poetry, it is the better part of valor not to try. Unfortunately, these *rubaiyat are* poetry. A commentary on them, therefore, should be poetic also. Master had the soul of a poet, and a great one at that. Though he left the process of refining his words to his disciples, we should appreciate in all its depth *and beauty* the treasure he left for us to work on.

Bliss-Avatar?

The purpose of this essay is, above all, to address the question implied in the title, which concerns my Guru, Paramhansa Yogananda, and his true mission in life. First, however, it will be necessary for me to lay a careful groundwork for my discussion, because most modern readers, even in India, have not the slightest idea what those ancient words, *avatar* and *guru*, really mean.

I must begin, therefore, by explaining certain basic aspects of the spiritual path. I'll try to keep it simple and lucid, as well as (I hope) enjoyable to read. At the same time, however, I must warn the unwary: We'll be swimming in deep waters!

Avatar and *guru* are, as I said, words of which the ancient meanings have changed—indeed, in popular understanding, beyond all recognition from their original and lofty purpose. To my astonishment, I have found these corruptions, at least in newspapers, almost *more* rampant in India than in the West.

Guru, properly speaking, means *spiritual* teacher. In the popular parlance of our day it has come to be applied to almost anyone with the slightest authority in any field. Thus, I can even imagine a Mafia hit man being described as the "guru" of his "hit-men-in-training"; or a seasoned spy being labeled the "guru" of the young men he is preparing to work in his "cloak and dagger" field. To someone who lived, as I did, under a great spiritual master who fully deserved the label "guru" in its original and true meaning, the modern corruptions are bizarre to the point of being laughable.

A true guru is one above all who knows God. He is the highest kind of saint, having consciously, in cosmic consciousness, attained oneness with God. This attainment means he is able to infuse into receptive disciples his own spiritualized consciousness, and thereby to raise those who are spiritually ready to the same exalted state as his own. This subtle transfer of consciousness is the true meaning of that important passage concerning Jesus Christ in the Bible: "As many as received him, to them gave he power to become the sons of God." (John 1:12)

The same debasement has occurred in the case of the word *avatar*. In the popular mind, this word has come—as nearly as I've been able to make out—to mean merely a role that one plays in life, as in the words, "Joe Sleaze, the businessman, in his *avatar* as social activist . . ." or, "Sally Pumpkin, the housewife, in her *avatar* as professional cook. . . ."

In its original, true, and forever lofty sense, the word *avatar* has a deeply inspiring meaning. If it is considered a "role" at all, the role is a purely divine one. *Avatar* means a "descent of the Supreme Spirit into human form," the idea being, "for the spiritual upliftment of mankind." There are not many Hindus even who understand the word rightly. According to classical thought among orthodox Hindus, *avatar* refers to the several incarnations of the god Vishnu, usually (but not always) to his descents into human form. According to popular belief, these incarnations include Rama and Krishna, another one being predicted for the future: Kalki avatar.

Paramhansa Yogananda, however, whose mission it was to bring the original and true teachings of India into modern language and understanding, stated that Vishnu is only a human personification of an aspect of the Cosmic sound, *AUM*, the three letters of which signify three distinct vibrations of the Cosmic Vibration: the creative (personified as Brahma), preservative (personified as Vishnu), and destructive or all-dissolving (personified as Shiva)

The true meaning of *avatar*, Yogananda explained, applies to the descent into human form of *any* fully liberated soul who is sent down by God for the upliftment of a whole society, and for the redemption of large numbers of earthly beings (a feat not possible for ordinary saints even after they become fully liberated).

The stages of spiritual freedom, as well as of sainthood, begin at the point of sincere commitment. Anyone who is deeply devoted to the spiritual search may rightly, whether married or single, be called a *sadhu*—the Indian word for "saint." A *sadhu* can still fall from his lofty calling, but if he perseveres in wholehearted dedication to the challenge before him, of rising out of separative, ego-consciousness, he must ultimately realize the state of oneness with God. As Paramhansa Yogananda often put it, "A saint is a sinner who never gave up."

Sadhus, however, are likely to encounter temptations that may never assail worldly people. One such pitfall is spiritual pride. A worldly egotist's pride can be crushed with relative ease in many ways: by material failure; by being bested in anything that has fed his pride; by the contempt of others; by social scandal. These are but examples that suggest the worldly person's fragility. The pride of a spiritual person, on the other hand, is founded on something more real. It is difficult, therefore, for him to overcome it, and may take even lifetimes before he realizes the degree to which that pride has been self-limiting—indeed, self-suffocating.

Self-giving devotion is the best way of escape from spiritual pride. And devotion itself dawns with the discovery of the truth inherent in these words by Paramhansa Yogananda: "Evil is the absence of true joy." One who nurses in himself feelings of pride discovers at last that pride obliterates the consciousness of joy, even as thick fogs obscure the sunlight.

There are many other psychological obstacles the *sadhu* must face. These include subtle doubts (whether intellectual or spiritual); fears (perhaps of the tests that lie ahead);

cowardice (perhaps in confronting those tests); missing the real point of the spiritual path (achieving oneness with God); and self-involvement (which may seem to him a spiritual attitude, if he superficially tells himself he is only trying to "live in the Self," even though in fact his inward focus takes him inward contractively upon his ego).

Another pitfall—indeed, the greatest of them all—is by no means mental only, but is in fact the resistance offered by the cosmic Satanic force to any effort man makes to escape the net of *maya*, or delusion. The more earnestly one tries to get out of *maya*, the more vigorously does Satan resist that effort.

Anyone who questions the existence of Satan will do well to ponder the words of Yogananda on the subject: "I used to think Satan was only a mental concept. Now that I have found God, however, I join my testimony to that of all who have gone before me: Satan is a conscious, cosmic force, working constantly to thwart man's efforts to achieve salvation." I have quoted these words variously in other contexts, as I am myself uncertain as to their exactness. (I read them in a transcript of one of his talks.) I am quite confident, however, as to their intrinsic meaning. An argument on this subject is well made also, I think, in my book *Revelations of Christ* in the chapter titled, "Does Satan Exist?"

Satanic temptation always comes to seekers at their points of special weakness: pride; sexual desire; the ego-reaffirming longing for romance; a desire for money or fame, for vengeance, or for worldly power and prominence. Again, these are examples, merely. Delusion can assume countless forms.

Satan also sees to it "kindly" that anyone who is wholeheartedly dedicated to serving God will have his full share of persecution. I don't use that word, "kindly," altogether in a spirit of sarcasm, though I know it must sound that way. For my own experience of life, though perhaps slight, has taught me that my greatest spiritual growth has always been the outcome of what others no doubt assumed was, for me, the very bitter taste of persecution. In fact, after the first blow I received of anger, condemnation, and utter rejection by those whom I considered my own nearest and dearest, I took on a certain ballast. Realizing, even if belatedly, that persecution would be the "name of the game," I resolved never again to let anyone's treatment or opinion of me affect my inner peace.

I don't at all mean to say I grew calloused, hardened, or numb. Such reactions are normal enough for the *samsari*, or worldly person, who bounces continually back and forth between one emotional extreme and the other. The *sadhu*, however, is hardly worthy of his calling if, knowing (as he ought to know) that he is on a path leading to eternal bliss, he doesn't try to find in every outward experience at least a kernel of that bliss. My Guru often said, "Experiences are essentially neutral. They seem either happy or sad, according to the attitude in the mind."

My duty as I saw it, in the face of that first and (to me, for a time) overwhelming tragedy, was to discover in myself the right attitude with which I might rise above it. This attitude I found in the understanding that *no one* can ever rob us of our ability to *give* love. In loving others, moreover—as I had always found—lies our true happiness. Thus, I resolved—indeed, it was far more than a resolution—to love others unconditionally. My happiness, once I'd arrived at this decision, became unshakable; indeed, it became joy undiluted. Moreover, when I encountered people who actually manifested evil, I could still love God, and therefore love *the God in them*.

Temptation comes to the *sadhu* in many ways. Always its purpose, being of course Satanic, is to draw him back again toward involvement in worldliness. For though he tries his best to clamber out of the pit of delusion, that upward slope is very slippery. He cannot get out by mere willingness to do so. Grace, ultimately, is the key to everyone's salvation. Many of the temptations one faces ought, for *samsaris* or worldly people, to be placed in quotation marks, for these involvements also provide the means by which they can actually be *helped to rise out of* the delusion of ego-involvement. Romantic human love, for example, offers most human beings a valid means of expanding their sympathies and, thereby, of loosening the hold ego has on them.

In fact, were it not digressing from the nub of our present discussion, I could, I think, make a good case for each of the so-called temptations I've listed above for the *sadhu*, and to show how each of them might prove a real spiritual help for many people who have not yet reached the point of becoming committed spiritually. The important thing to understand is that, from whatever point one has reached on his own upward journey, there is always a higher, as well as a lower, potential. For the true *sadhu*, anything that shrinks his consciousness inward upon the ego must be viewed as, ultimately, anathema.

When my Guru said, "A saint is a sinner who never gave up," he was referring to one who is not only saintly, but victorious in his saintliness. He once told me, "Remember, you won't be safe until you've reached *nirbikalpa samadhi*." Even the first stage of *samadhi*, known as *sabikalpa*, in which the soul realizes its oneness with God, is only a temporary exaltation from which one must return to "normal," ego-consciousness. It is still possible, therefore, even at this high stage, through some loophole in his spiritual defenses, to be seized once again by the power of *maya*. My Guru in fact told me of several cases of saints who had fallen spiritually after attaining the high state of *sabikalpa*.

Fortunately, one reaches the point on his spiritual journey when, after years of struggling, he finds himself sailing on relatively smooth waters. He is aware that Satan still hovers "in the offing," but that eternal enemy of the soul stands by now, not helpless, but perhaps a little discouraged. For the *sadhu* has become at last a "veteran of foreign wars"—the "foreign" aspect of those wars being the endless, niggling attractions toward outward desires and attachments—and is now firmly focused on attaining the highest goal of all: union with God. Such a person may justifiably be considered an "almost victorious saint," for though he still needs to be careful, it is also true that nothing in this world exerts any special appeal for him anymore. In his heart he knows that God is pleased with him, and his only desire, now, is to merge back into oneness with the Beloved. People's good opinion of him means nothing to him anymore other than, perhaps, the blessing of being able to serve them better because they are open to what he can share with them.

People's bad opinion of him, on the other hand, even their enmity and persecution of him, actually reinforce in him his natural feeling of friendship for all. This happens for two reasons: first, because such behavior toward him inspires him to analyze himself impersonally and see whether he might not benefit from their criticism; and secondly, it strengthens in him a growing awareness of his kinship with all mankind in the fact that he sees everyone striving to reach what is basically the same goal in life: perfection in ultimate bliss.

If there is any obstacle remaining for him, it is likely to be only the possible intrusion of complacency: a tendency to "fall asleep at the door." Thus, he may find himself increasingly content with being a merely *sattwic*, virtuous human being, filled with good qualities but, alas, so comfortable in them he may become spiritually lazy. Spiritual laziness does not, unfortunately, wholly lack a certain affinity for *tamasic* laziness. This fact suggests how people continue for countless incarnations, spiritually rising and falling like waves on life's ocean, until they finally develop the firmness of will never to rest again until they've attained union with God.

The best way out of the slough of complacency is always, like the wise virgins in Jesus Christ's parable, to keep the lamp of devotion burning.

The "fully victorious saint" is one, finally, who is what is known as "freed while living": a *jivan mukta*. Such a person has attained *nirbikalpa samadhi*, and final victory over the supreme—indeed, the only—obstacle he ever had: his self-created burden of self-identity, self-separative, ever self-divisive from others, which forms a yawning chasm between himself and God. When a person attains this highest state at last, he will never fall again. Satan will of course, perhaps with renewed vigor, oppose him in all his efforts to do good in this world of duality (which is Satan's domain), and to serve others in God's name.

A *jivan mukta* still has his incarnations of *past* karma to work out. Only from his state of inner freedom can that karma be dissipated. He himself remains untouched by the karma, however. If, then, let us say, he had a past life as a ruthless pirate, his job as a *jivan mukta* is to review that lifetime from his present state of inner freedom, and to see that it was God alone, through that private ego-dream, who acted in that capacity. Thus alone is it possible to release into the Infinite any hold he may still have on that past dream. All that will remain is the *memory* of ego-involvement in it, a memory that ties all his past lives together but that is no longer personal. That is to say, *in omniscience* he remembers everything that happened in that life, but is no longer in any way bound or defined by the memory.

I once asked my Guru, "Why can't the *jivan mukta* simply say, 'I am free,' and *be* free?" His answer surprised me: "He can if he wants to. In that state, however, you don't care. You are inwardly free anyway. Many saints see their need to work out that past karma as an excuse to come back and help their disciples." A *jivan mukta*, you see, is already one with God. In the Divine, no question can exist, among *jivan muktas*, of good, greater, and greatest. In God, all are equal.

Once a *jivan mukta* has finally been freed even from past karma, he is called a *param mukta*, a *siddha* (perfected being), or (in English) an "ascended master": a supremely free soul. Very few liberated souls return from the state of complete absorption in perfect, absolute bliss to the realm of *maya*. Having spent countless million incarnations not only wandering in delusion, but many afterward in seeking to get out of delusion, and having finally found God, they feel their laurels—won through much suffering during both those phases of outward existence—have been well earned, and may now be deservedly savored through eternity in *Satchidananda*: ever-existing, ever-conscious, ever-new bliss.

This brings us finally to the true meaning of *avatar*. An *avatar*—in English, a "descended master"—is one whose concern for others is so deeply rooted that he deliberately postpones the perfect bliss of complete immersion in God, returning to manifested creation for the salvation of as many as are receptive to his message and blessing of divine love.

A *jivan mukta* must, my Guru told me, according to the divine will, liberate a certain number of disciples. I asked him, "How many?" "At least six," was his reply.

Master told me of an event before his time, with which his father had been personally acquainted. A maharaja in Bengal had ordered a lake drained on his property. Workers found three men buried deep in the silt at the bottom of the lake, seated in a yoga posture, their bodies in a state of perfect preservation. Engineers working at the site estimated, by the depth under the silt at which the three men were discovered, that they must have been there at least three centuries.

These outwardly lifeless forms didn't respond to initial attempts at reviving them. Thereupon, the maharaja ordered more drastic measures to be applied. I don't know the nature of those measures, but I seem to remember, from Master's account, that they consisted of pressing hot coals into the soles of their feet.

At last, all three men were brought back to outward awareness. They were distressed at having their profound meditation so cruelly disturbed. "You will see the results of your sin," they told the maharaja. "They will affect yourself and your entire family. We had almost reached complete liberation from all karma. Now we shall have to be reborn to attain that end." The yogis thereupon left their bodies, and a short time later the maharaja and the members of his close family died.

My Guru, in telling this story, added an interesting footnote: "The Divine Mother didn't want those men to achieve freedom for themselves alone. That was why they were found, brought back to outward awareness, and obliged therefore to reincarnate in new bodies." (It was at this time, if my recollection is correct, that I asked my Guru how many one must free. He replied, as I've already stated, "At least six.")

The above story has more than one fascinating facet. First, one wonders why—if it was Divine Mother's will for the yogis to be revived—the Maharaja had to pay for the evident sin of reviving them. For it was not only his cruel manner of going about it that constituted his sin: it is also considered a sin to disturb anyone who is deeply immersed in meditation. In this case, however, I would say that the cruelty of method was the much greater sin.

The second intriguing aspect of the story is that all the Maharaja's immediate family had to pay for his sin. Why? The decision to apply those hot coals (or whatever they were) was his alone. Do an individual's actions have an effect on the karma of any group to which he belongs? Yes they do, but this effect is not so easy to explain. Still, let me try.

I must begin with a statement made by Swami Sri Yukteswar, quoted in *Autobiography of a Yogi*: "Reason is rightly guided only when it accepts the inevitability of divine law." There is no point in challenging the rightness of any spiritual law. We have no choice but to adjust our understanding to the actual ways karma works.

Thus, the Bible quotes the Jews of Christ's time—the "chief priests, and elders," and "the multitudes," as accepting the punishment (if such it had to be) for his crucifixion, assuming it for all their people: "His blood be on us, and on our children." (Matt. 27:25) Not a pleasant thought; indeed, the mind naturally rejects it out of hand! And yet—who can say that the Jews have not, for these two thousand years since that terrible event, undergone many exceptional hardships? They have shown themselves an extraordinarily gifted people, and yet, still, they have suffered. Will that karma change in our lifetime? Everyone must surely hope so.

When we are born into any group—a family, a nation, a people; perhaps, indeed, onto a particular planet—we must to some degree accept participation in its karma. Our own actions will aid or worsen that karma to whatever degree those actions are outstanding. In the case of the maharaja in that story, the immediate group had to pay for the sin of that one (though central) member. Such, indeed, is the law.

I mention this teaching because it has one very important ramification, pertinent to the subject of this essay. When a saint becomes fully liberated, seven generations of his family *in both directions* are freed also. "Such," as Yogananda put it, "is the glory of the crop." To what degree are those family members freed? Certainly not to the extent of becoming fully liberated themselves, for *that* degree of freedom, one must work individually. Every family member, however, may be granted a high level of realization, perhaps even freedom from the need for further earthly incarnations. At any rate, all of them will gain a sufficient store of good karma to be greatly blessed in their ongoing evolution, and stimulated toward the search for God if they have never, so far, set foot consciously on the path. Moreover, although most *jivan muktas* have no children of their own, this great blessing reaches out into "collateral" branches: cousins, nieces, nephews.

As an interesting sidelight on this issue, Dr. Lewis, Yogananda's first Kriya Yoga disciple in America, on hearing from the Guru about this great blessing for the family, quite naturally asked, "What about the disciples?"

"Oh, they come first," replied the Guru. Indeed, a guru's spiritual family is his strongest karmic bond. On the other hand, if he returns repeatedly to earth, it seems almost a surfeit of special grace for his direct disciples to receive that extraordinary blessing again and again over repeated incarnations. Also regarding the family of an *avatar*, though I am not able to speak with authority, I am inclined to believe that this blessing applies particularly to the first incarnation in which a soul attains final liberation.

Is there objective evidence for the truth in these last paragraphs? If so, I am not aware of it. Inasmuch, however, as there is "no new thing under the sun" (Ecc. 1:9), I cannot but think that *someone, somewhere*, has done the necessary research and found for it supportive statistics. For myself, the best I can offer is my own general, perhaps more-or-less-poetic impressions.

A wave consists of many drops of water. Only when the sweep of movement over an ocean's surface is able to raise enough water will it produce a wave of any great height. Similarly, though I am not in a position to offer statistics, I think we may safely state that groups of souls, whether nations or families within those nations, rise and fall *en masse*, as it were. Surely, then, one whose "wave of karma" is itself "on the rise," so to speak, will be born into a family in which the general movement, too, is upward.

My *impression*—it is only that—of saintly souls is that their families generally are strong willed (even if not spiritually inclined), for the most part morally upright, blessed with "success karma," and each of them in some particular way idealistic. Thus, their upward motion helps to give impetus to the saint's own spiritually upward rise. They are *participants in*, and not merely passive beneficiaries of, his own supernal blessings. (Otherwise one would have to say that the grace they receive from him seems, at least, to constitute a rent in the fabric of karmic law.)

Family members—descendants, in short—who come *after* that saint's lofty attainment are both drawn to his family by a natural affinity with him, and help to ensure that his attainments be of practical, outward benefit to the world, rather than only a tree that bears fruit in the wilderness.

I have also observed those generations of disciples who came both before and after a great saint's life. Surely those who came before helped to contribute to his ultimate sanctity— even if their "contribution" constituted only persecution of him! Those, on the other hand, who came afterward seem to have been particularly blessed with wisdom, devotion, and spiritual insight.

An *avatar*—to return to the next stage of spiritual freedom—is one who retains what my Guru called the "desireless desire" to continue helping to liberate others. There is in that desire no bondage, where he himself is concerned; it is only his deep love for humanity that brings him back to earth.

People who make distinctions of quality between one *avatar* and another are speaking in ignorance. In God, it is not possible for such relativities to exist. Thus, if Yogananda called Lahiri Mahasaya a *yogavatar*, Swami Sri Yukteswar a *gyanavatar*, and Babaji a *mahavatar*, he was referring to their outer roles, not to their inner realization.

To describe anyone, on the other hand, as a *purnavatar* (complete *avatar*) shows a misunderstanding, unless the description is meant poetically, rather than literally. The mistake lies in indicating that it is rare for such an incarnation to contain in himself all the divine qualities. Since all *avatars* are equal both in realization and in divine power—merely emphasizing, in their outward roles, some particular aspect of the divine in their specific missions on earth—it would, according to my own best understanding, be pointless to call any of them *purna*, or complete.

I once asked my Guru, in the context of the relativities of realization, "What about Mataji, the sister of Babaji? In your autobiography you state that she was 'nearly as highly advanced as Babaji.'" Master replied, "That means she hadn't yet reached complete freedom. But," he added, "she must have reached it by now." Not an altogether satisfactory answer, perhaps, but it shows that *everyone*, having once reached spiritual perfection, is as great as any other liberated master.

Rajarshi Janakananda, Yogananda's most highly advanced disciple, reached full liberation in this lifetime. Rajarshi himself declared that Paramhansa Yogananda qualified for the further title, *premavatar*: "incarnation of divine love." Certainly I would not presume to challenge that appellation. Yet I have asked myself, "Did Master himself fully endorse it?"

At Sister Gyanamata's funeral, Master said, "Sister got there [attained liberation in God] through wisdom. I myself got there through bliss."

On at least three occasions I was with the monks when he gave them an important piece of advice. I was alone with him on one other occasion when he said the same thing to me personally: "It is better to seek God primarily for bliss, and only secondarily for His love, for in love there is the possibility that one's feelings may become too personal, rather than expansive outwardly to infinity."

I've given careful "credentials" for this advice, showing it as having been truly what he said, because when I mentioned it to Daya Mata she replied, "I never heard him say *that*" — as if to imply that he could not have said it. Curiously, it seems that during his discussions with the monks he was more inclined to speak in terms that were spiritually impersonal. With the nuns, I believe he tended to speak of God more in His personal aspects, and of love for Him/Her, too, in a more personal sense.

I have mentioned on other occasions how Tara edited those words he addressed to me, "Wherever God is, there His saints come," changing them to read, "Wherever *a devotee* [italics mine] of God is, there His saints come."

Years after he'd addressed to me words I've quoted above, "Evil is the absence of true joy," Tara said to me she could make nothing of it, and therefore changed his words editorially to read, "Men turn to evil in the absence of true joy." What she'd missed in his meaning was that his words addressed, not men's *reactions* in the matter, but the nature of evil itself. To me, it was her version that lacked proper insight. It was too human, too personal. For indeed, Master's words as he spoke them were true: The farther one goes into evil, the less he has of true joy. Master's words explained specifically, therefore, what it is about evil that *makes* it evil: it obscures more and more completely the true bliss of the soul.

Tara showed this personal take also in her comment to me about my interest in the Bhrigu Samhita, a very ancient document that contains predictions about the future lives of individuals who would be born centuries in the future, relative to the time of that samhita's composition. What most interested me was that this document, if valid, gives proof of a level of greatness in ancient Indian culture that was far beyond anything remotely imagined about that culture by modern scholars. For one like myself, whose job it has been to present the high state of India's advancement in its ancient spiritual culture, the possibility that this ancient book of prophecies might be true was like stumbling upon a Rosetta stone. For someone again, like me, who wanted facts to support Sri Yukteswar's view of history which showed that mankind *descended* from a much higher culture, that "Rosetta stone" seemed to be, in addition, a diamond mine.

Tara's statement, "The ONLY reason for your interest in that book was that it said such glowing things **about YOU!**" left me utterly nonplussed. I couldn't plumb the depths of suspicion that must have given rise to such a charge. And yet Tara, of all the women disciples, was perhaps one of the *least* personal in her outlook.

Consider what my discovery consisted of: *two* books of prophecy, in two different parts of north India. The second began with the words, "I have already given him a reading in my *Yoga Valli.*" This second reading went back eight lives. Of this life it said I would be born in Romania and raised in America; that my father would name me James (my actual, though little-known, first name); that I would have two brothers, "but no living sister is possible, though one will die in his mother's womb." (I checked with my mother after my return to America, and she confirmed that she had in fact had a miscarriage.) This second reading said that my guru's name would be Yogananda; that I would become well known in the world as a teacher of *ashtanga* yoga (I was relatively well known then already). It gave me the fruits of my good karmas (former actions), and also those of my bad actions. It said nothing about my future that my Guru hadn't told me already. It added, however, that I would return to my own country within two months (a correct prediction), and that, upon my return, I would be "given a high position." (In fact, shortly after my return I was made the vice president of our organization and was placed on the board of directors.)

I did what I could to verify the antiquity of this old parchment, which was in any case said to be only a copy of the original. The best I could get was that it was "definitely not recent—much older than months, and written in a kind of script used about 150 years ago."

To me, even today after some fifty years, this document contains much more than Sherlock Holmes's customary statement about a case presenting "several points of interest."

Well, my purpose here is not to discuss the (perhaps) turgid depths of feminine psychology, but simply to point out, as Master did, the possible pitfalls of devotion when it is directed too personally. For there are many kinds of love. In English we don't even have an equivalent for *Prem*. *Prem* signifies infinite, divine love. It may be described as what Conscious, Absolute Bliss feels for Universal Creation. Divine love is only an *expression* of Bliss. Bliss, on the other hand, is higher than love, since love implies some object to be loved.

Because the very concept of impersonal, divine love is quite beyond the average person's capacity for understanding, added to the fact that the word *prem* doesn't even exist in the English language, I wonder how widely the classification *premavatar* is, or even *could* be, understood. Adding that question to Master's own words, and taking into account that the women disciples haven't shown much understanding of, and still less appreciation for, the deeper, more philosophical aspects of Master's teachings, makes me wonder whether he, himself, would not have preferred the term, *Blissavatar*.

Why not, instead of "Bliss," the Sanskrit equivalent: Ananda? Simply because "Ananda" alone doesn't do it. It should be *Satchidanandavatar*—hopelessly cumbersome to the modern ear. Ananda by itself carries rather the connotation of Joy, to which there are always contrasts: sorrow or suffering, for example. Only Divine Bliss is absolute. We can "cut to the chase" with it in English, so why not say, simply, *Blissavatar*?

Paramhansa Yogananda was certainly an incarnation, also, of divine love. I am not trying in any way to discount Rajarshi's appellation. At the same time, I think it must be added that, to be an *avatar* at all, divine love must be the inspiration behind the descent implied. What else would cause a completely free soul to come back from absolute bliss to this "vale of tears"? Yet Sri Yukteswar, whom Master described as manifesting God's love to him, was so distant in his outward expression of that love that, once when I said to Master, "I see deep divine love expressed in his eyes," Master chuckled at what could only be described as a regretful memory. His words to me were, "There was no love in those eyes!" So, all right, I accept that, comparing the two, what Master manifested *particularly* was indeed divine love.

Yet, to me, Bliss remains his main self-definition, and helps me better to understand that aspect of his personality which could have given rise, in others of his incarnations, to Arjuna and to William the Conqueror.

I therefore offer this suggestion humbly, and also somewhat hesitantly, as an appellation that covers what I might call the *whole* picture.

Why then *not* think of him *also*, as I've suggested, as a Bliss-*avatar*?

Part Four

SPIRITUAL LEADERSHIP IN THE NEW AGE

CHAPTER ONE
THE IMPORTANCE OF HIERARCHY

The basic guidelines for all organizations have been well stated by the U.S. Army, though I imagine the same ones exist in military organizations everywhere. I learned these principles many years ago from a former U.S. army colonel. He explained that in the army the lines of authority are set up to look like a genealogical chart:

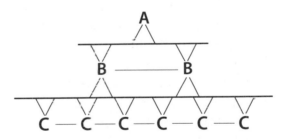

The basic principles, four in number, are as follows:

1. Always follow the lines of authority. In giving directives, *A* may deal only with *B*; never directly with *C*. *C*, in receiving directives, may deal only with *B*; never directly with *A*.

2. For every job that is given, as much power must accompany it as is necessary to ensure that the job can be carried out.

3. A man cannot have two masters, "for either he will hate the one, and love the other; or else he will hold to the one, and despise the other." (Matt. 6:24)

4. Organizations fail for one of two reasons: either too much power is delegated, or too much power is withheld.

These principles are in fact basic to all organizations. A hierarchical structure does not prevent a leader from taking a personal interest in those who are several steps below him in the ranks. Even in an army, a good general doesn't hold himself aloof from his soldiers. He talks with them, asks them about their families, shows concern over any wounds they may have received in battle, is interested in how they feel toward their superiors. At the same time, however, *he never gives direct orders except through the established channels.*

These lines of authority are necessary for the simple reason that it isn't possible for anyone to do everything. A leader must either delegate authority or fail to accomplish anything worthwhile. When he ignores these lines, he ends up, to all practical purposes, assuming onto his own shoulders the entire burden for decision-making.

Here is an example of how the demise of effective leadership often occurs:

A delegates to *B* a position of authority over *C*. *A*, then, not wishing to lose contact with *C*, doesn't hesitate to make certain recommendations to *C* directly.

C, quite naturally, prefers to have direct contact with *A*. Not only is his own status enhanced thereby: He also feels more confident of receiving his directives undiluted. *C*, therefore, begins going to *A* for certain instructions, especially in matters where, he suspects, *B* won't give him exactly the answers he desires.

A comes in time to develop a degree of confidence in *C* that he doesn't have in *B*. This is perfectly natural, considering that the mere fact of *B*'s being higher than *C* on the hierarchical ladder doesn't ensure his personal superiority to *C* in every, or even in any, respect.

Thus, *A* begins giving more and more orders directly to *C*. He may even entrust *C* with certain assignments about which he doesn't trouble to tell *B*, since these assignments don't concern work in which *B* is directly involved.

Now then, what is the effect on *B* of this circumvention of his normal authority? Naturally, he is expected in most situations to direct *C* as usual. The problem is that he cannot know when his orders might be contradicted by some order already given to *C* directly by *A*. *B* therefore hesitates to give *C* clear orders, and resorts instead to making hesitant suggestions on matters that he ought to deliver firmly and confidently.

Sooner or later, the contradiction he fears from above will actually occur. *B* asks *C* to do something, and *C* confronts him with a more authoritative order he has already received from *A*. Thus, *B* finds himself demoted, for the moment, to a level of equality with *C*. In the future, *B* quite naturally will tread all the more lightly when issuing a directive to *C*.

The time comes finally when *C*, having received a commission personally from *A*, is subsequently given a conflicting order by *B* and announces bluntly, "I'm sorry, I can't do it."

"Why not?" *B* asks.

"You'll have to ask *A*," replies *C*, not wishing to break the confidence he's had from their mutual superior. In this case, *B* finds himself for the moment demoted virtually to a level subordinate to *C*, for *C* is privy, however temporarily, to *A*'s counsel on a matter regarding which *B* has not been included.

Time may further direct circumstances toward the possibility—and, given the realities of human nature, the probability—that *C* doesn't always *like* an order he has received from *B*. In this case, since the habit of by-passing his immediate superior is already well established in him, his tendency will be to go to *A* and try to get the order rescinded. *A*, moreover, perhaps not realizing that *B* has actually given an order, or perhaps wishing to be strictly fair, may decide in *C*'s favor and tell him so directly.

Fair *A* may be. The effect, however, will be to strip *B* of all but the outer symbols of his position: his name on the door and in the organization's formal charts. *B* now, to save face, may never again on his own initiative issue orders to *C*, even if only to write a letter or stamp an envelope—without first clearing the matter with *A*.

Nor is this all. For suppose *B* does clear the matter before issuing an order, and suppose that even now *C* doesn't like the order, and thinks he has a chance of getting it rescinded: In this case, *C* will not accept that the order reached him *in toto* as *A* first approved it. He will assume, quite naturally, that it was *B* who added the unattractive features to the order, and will base his complaint to *A* on this assumption. If *A*—again, perhaps only from a wish to be scrupulously fair—is persuaded that those features really *aren't* necessary, the chances are better than even that *B* will be blamed for having added them.

In such an organization, the middle man becomes ineffectual. Nor is he, from time to time, seen only as a stumbling block to "progress": he becomes also the "whipping boy" for many of the mistakes that get made.

How, then, will *B* react? If he is willing to put up with the indignity of his present position, he will probably restrict himself in future to making only the tamest suggestions, to displaying to one and all the blank countenance of cautious diplomacy, seeking to propose and follow only the safest course. He may even look upon inactivity itself as that safest course. One thing is certain, however: he will let his superior make as many decisions as possible.

It is easy to understand the insecurity of *B*'s position. But what about that of *C*? Has it become secure? Far from it. It is no more so than *B*'s. For even though *C* now has a direct line to *A*, he can't very well go to the top every time a little problem arises. Nor is he confident enough of *B*, or of *B*'s confidence in him, to go to him more than he feels strictly necessary. He won't dare to make any but the most timid decisions himself, lest *B* take the opportunity to reassert his authority by reporting him to *A*. Thus, *C*'s position is quite as frustrating as *B*'s.

Meanwhile, then, what of *A*? One might suppose that he, at least, reigns securely. Such is by no means the case, however. True, *A* has both *B* and *C* depending on him to arbitrate every difference of opinion that arises between them. Unfortunately, the need to do so leaves *A* so overwhelmed with work, as he tries to control everything out of fear that he might lose his hold on the reins, that he can't really do anything effectively. *A* therefore finds himself, in time, making decisions at virtually every level of the organization, having little time left now for really constructive work. Whatever effectiveness he might have had, if he hadn't felt himself so over-burdened with "incompetent subordinates," is bogged down in a quagmire of petty decision-making, as he struggles bravely to keep things inching along. Such, he reflects wryly, is the price of being a conscientious leader.

In fact, he could not contribute more effectively to the demise of his organization were that his actual intention. For his mind, overwhelmed as it now is with the flood of internal problems, is no longer free to concentrate effectively on anything external to the problems themselves.

Of the three, *A* is probably the most lacking in self-confidence. For he at least knows he *ought* to be doing something constructive. The others aren't really expected to do anything responsibly, and so have little or nothing to feel guilty about. *A*'s insecurity can only increase, moreover, with the years; that is what generally happens to people who feel a need to mask their inability to cope. His hidden insecurity culminates in corrosive attitudes of suspicion, self-protectiveness, and fear.

This mental climate becomes widespread in organizations where too much authority is concentrated at the top. New influences become suspect *on principle*. The increasingly timid, self-enclosing spirit that develops in the whole organization becomes nurturing soil for the flourishing weeds of distrust. Petty issues become exaggerated, often to the point where they loom as major crises. Minor setbacks assume the dimensions of disaster. Fear and worry render constructive work increasingly difficult and dynamic action, impossible.

Self-protectiveness assumes, under such conditions, the dimensions of a primary principle. Workers come to view their output in terms of how busy they are, not of how much actual work they get done. Hours are wasted in writing interoffice memos (the brighter and funnier, the more applauded), re-arranging papers on their desks, "for greater efficiency," and chatting idly together.

I should add here that everything I've written so far is based not on theory, but on years of personal experience.

CHAPTER TWO
HIERARCHY DURING *Dwapara Yuga*

Now then, what does all this mean for *Dwapara Yuga* concerns, for Paramhansa Yogananda's mission on earth, and (my own immediate concern) for the Ananda communities I have founded to help fulfil his mission?

The organizational chart, hierarchical in nature, seems basically right and sound for all well-run institutions, whether in *Kali* or in *Dwapara Yuga*. There are further ramifications, however, that require a different application in each *yuga*.

Authority during *Kali Yuga* owes its power entirely to one's position. And that position—whether aristocrat, merchant, or farmer—is largely an accident of birth. Rarely does anyone in the middle classes change his place in the social structure. With the dawn of *Dwapara Yuga*, however, people see things increasingly in terms of equal rights, individual traits, and individual worthiness. Matter, as I've said before, is seen increasingly in terms of its subtle, underlying reality; outer forms are given *decreasing* emphasis. Art forms which, today, tend toward the grotesque (as though to mock form altogether) will be more normal again, but will emphasize more their inner, animating consciousness. People will be seen more in terms of their inner character than of their outward molding. Beauty, whether human or natural, will be seen in terms more of the consciousness it expresses.

Authority, in *Dwapara Yuga*, must still descend from above, but the concept, "above," will come increasingly to mean not mere physical positioning, but also higher understanding: the subtle essence, for example, beneath (or within) grosser realities. God Himself is not above us, literally. He constitutes the innermost reality of all superficial appearances. "Divine vision," Paramhansa Yogananda stated, "is center everywhere, circumference nowhere."

One difference between *Dwapara Yuga* and *Kali Yuga* is that, in *Dwapara*, institutional efficiency is brought about more by *enlisting* the interest, support, and cooperation of others than by coercion. In *Dwapara Yuga*, then, heart quality balances hierarchical authority and offsets the authoritarian command of the *"Kali Yugi"* who says, "Do as you're told. You are just a cog in the large institutional machine, doing your little part to advance the purpose for which the machine was created. Fulfill your function; keep to your position; don't try to be the brains of the outfit; stick to the function for which your job was designed."

The *Kali Yuga* mentality states, "In an institution, no one has a right *even to think* unless his job is to direct the entire enterprise." *Dwapara Yuga* mentality, on the contrary, states, "In an institution, the *conscious energy-flow* determines the outcome of an undertaking. As light has been proved to be both a particle and a wave, so the consciousness behind every energy-flow is centered at every point in its flow."

In practical terms, what that second statement proclaims is that every member of an organization is encouraged to think creatively—within bounds, of course, for there may always obtrude that "institutional sore thumb," the egotist, whose bluff and bluster require occasional "hosing off." The sort of creativity that deserves encouragement may not relate to the overall activity of the organization, but it can at least concern better ways of serving and improving the person's own function within the organization.

A janitor, for example, should be encouraged to think in terms of how to make as immaculately clean and shiningly beautiful as possible the sites for which he is personally responsible.

A secretary should be encouraged to think in terms not only of serving his or her immediate boss, but of how to improve the overall efficiency of that service: how to get out prompt, thoughtful responses to the letters received; how to find ways of making filed letters quickly available when needed; how to determine his or her priorities, with the boss's approval, but without burdening him with more decision-making than he needs. If the boss is unnecessarily fussy in attempting to control the department, a good secretary will accept the situation with good grace, but will then respectfully offer suggestions for improving his control—perhaps to the point of letting him see that he *can* relax a little! A good secretary may offer solutions, also, to whatever problems arise, or (s)he may ask the boss tactfully for solutions to the problems he raises, or suggest possible solutions when he (or she, of course) doesn't quickly come up with any. (Good humor is often the best way of handling a recalcitrant boss!)

Intelligent and creative efficiency on the part of a good secretary includes showing interest in the boss's concerns, and a desire to help relieve him for more creative activity. Usually, fussiness on the boss's part indicates a lack of trust in others and, ultimately, lack of faith in himself. Usually also, therefore, a secretary who shows super-ability, plus a sincere desire to be helpful, will reduce those fears and bring about the mental relaxation which nurtures trust. At any rate, an intelligent secretary can usually find ways of freeing a too-fussy superior from excessive anxiety and thereby help him or her to be more personally creative.

The essence of *Dwapara Yuga* is a combination of greater fluidity with more expansive energy, which leads to greater *self*-expansiveness.

The self-expansive janitor, then, in a *Dwapara* enterprise will not limit himself to thinking of how to improve his "domain" for his own sake, but will think also of the convenience his work provides to those for whom his work is a service. He will concentrate more also on the pleasure it gives them to see everything neat and clean, and will overlook the trouble it causes him every time someone enters his work space. He will seek ways of improving his work for *other people's* sake, and not only for his own. In this way also, he will take pride in adding to the overall harmony of the whole firm.

The self-expansive "*Dwapara*" secretary, similarly, will be more concerned with being useful than with using anyone toward his or her own selfish ends. In this way (s)he, too, will add to the overall harmony and productivity of the establishment.

So much, in both cases, for self-expansiveness. A janitor will also express greater *fluidity*, by his openness to new and more efficient ways of cleaning, waxing, or arranging and storing things. And a secretary will express fluidity by willingly embracing new and more efficient methods of working.

The kind of fluidity I really mean, however, in using that word, refers especially to creative *mental* output, though it may apply somewhat also to such matters as physical coordination. Athletic records, for example, are constantly being broken, whether in speed or in team sports. The fluidity of coordination, surely, may be counted also in this *Dwapara* category. Even increased speed demands better coordination. Paramhansa Yogananda, for example, when a young man was an extraordinarily fast runner. He also had an unusual style of running. I wasn't on the scene in those days, but I wonder if his style didn't reflect a new and better kind of physical coordination.

CHAPTER THREE
CREATIVE LEADERSHIP

It is in the area of leadership, of course, that the efficiency of a *Dwapara* institution differs most from leadership of the typically *Kali Yuga* sort. The top leader—CEO, president, chairman, or whatever his title—may at least intuit the truth, "Divine insight is center everywhere, circumference nowhere," for he will naturally separate the concept of creative insight from the more mechanical aspects of hierarchical authority. That is to say, he will follow the old system when making decisions, and passing them on to others, but he will also listen to and encourage creative suggestions from everyone on his staff.

If even the janitor has a new idea for how to improve his department, or even for how to improve a broader function of the whole company, even though his natural recourse will be to his immediate supervisor first, the president (let us, for convenience, call him that) should consider it a part of his job to let everyone know that he is open to suggestions from all levels of the organization. He will pass that suggestion on to others, as seems proper. If, however, he speaks directly with the janitor—and it would be a graceful act on his part to do so—he should say, "I like the idea. I'll discuss it with others, and if they agree, I'll see that you hear about it; we may even involve you in its implementation." In other words, the president will follow due process, but will never delude himself that only those in charge are qualified to have and to share creative ideas.

Interestingly, in more and more enterprises nowadays, a bonus is offered to those who come up with creative ideas, when they are accepted.

Apart from matters that concern the operation of an institution, there is no need for hierarchical formalities. To specify what I mean more clearly, let me present the process we follow at Ananda.

If someone asks me, for example, for spiritual advice, I feel free to give it to him directly no matter what his position in the "pecking order." On the other hand, if my advice concerns his activities for the organization—telling him, for instance, to keep silence for one hour a day (an unusual piece of advice, to be sure, but one which might affect his work with others), I will first consult his immediate superior, or get him and that superior to work it out together, while generally, of course, deferring to the superior's priorities. Sometimes, however, depending on circumstances, I will "go to bat" for the individual, if I feel his needs transcend other considerations.

I am glad to say that I've never had the problem, in such cases, of a superior resisting my efforts to help an individual. Always we've worked everything out to the satisfaction of all concerned.

CHAPTER FOUR
OF SPACE AND TIME

An interesting feature of *Dwapara Yuga*, according to what I have read, is that as this age progresses it will abolish the delusion of space. In this context, *Treta Yuga* (the next higher *yuga*) is said, again, to abolish the final delusion: time.

These two claims may seem, from the present vantage point, quite beyond even our most "cutting edge" perceptions. And yet, we've seen remarkable advances already in this general direction: through radio and television; through the speed of airplane travel and other forms of rapid transportation; through present means of instant communication. To voyage to other planets seems a future inevitability. Even so, what has been accomplished so far is only the reduction, not the elimination, of the seeming reality of space. Will space ever be eliminated altogether as an objective fact? That, I frankly believe, is not a possible outcome of mere astral influences. Such enlightenment can occur only through a combination of divine grace and free will. I would state only, then, that *Dwapara Yuga* will bring an increased awareness of the illusory nature of space, as most educated people today are aware of the illusory nature of solid matter. Today we know that material grossness is only an illusion. Still, don't space and time seem woven too deeply into the fabric of reality to be airily dismissed as nonexistent?

One hint as to the purely mental aspect of space may be seen in the discovery by modern science that space is, in fact, finite. Were we to ask a physicist, "If the material universe is, as you say, finite in size, what lies outside of it?" his answer would be, "Nothing. You are applying human concepts where they do not obtain."

There is one way, however, that I can imagine the universe as being finite with nothing outside of it whatsoever. Such would be the case were it a pure thought! For thought alone is completely self-contained. The moment we even ask ourselves the question, "What lies outside it?" we expand the thought. We human beings can of course have only a limited effect on matter, but if God, as the ancient teachings aver, dreamed the universe into existence, we may confidently state that His dream is only as large as the Dreamer Himself dreamed it.

A suggestion that time, too, is illusory may be inferred from a curious writing that has come down to us from very ancient times. It is a vast "manuscript," copies of which are said to be located at several places in India, purporting to predict the future lives of individuals born long after the manuscript was written—born this far, and even farther in the future. If this manuscript is valid, it could only, one supposes, have come down from the last descending *Treta Yuga,* when its subject matter, which deals with the delusion of time—was at least widely accepted in theory.

I myself found a page of this manuscript dedicated to my own life. It correctly predicted events that had not yet occurred in this life, but that did occur later.

I will not elaborate further, here, on this amazing (or at any rate fascinating) phenomenon, since modern understanding falls so far short of these possibilities as to be mired in complete incredulity. I will, however, say for those with the curiosity to ponder such matters, that apart from stating my monastic name, my birth name, my Guru's name, the country in which I was born (Romania), and the land where I later lived (America), it said things about my family that I myself had never heard, but was able to verify later, after my return to America.

It accurately predicted certain events in my immediate future, which at the time seemed impossible of fulfillment. It also made a reference to the more general future, which may prove true also for the whole world. Its reference was, "In the future in his country, when there will be weeping in every home. . . ." I share these words, though with some hesitation, in the hope that they may provide a timely warning of coming hard times—economic, and perhaps also such serious trials as global warfare and even widespread natural cataclysms. My Guru, too, warned of these things. I touch on them here because I do, in fact, believe we are approaching times of great trial.

A man I met years later told me of his own experience with this book—or, as I've called it, phenomenon—and found that it predicted both his visit and that of several other people in the room on that occasion, actually mentioning them by name. He told me also of a friend of his whose reading, as if to confirm its veracity, had stated, "As this is being read out, there will be a thunderclap." The sun was shining and the sky was clear of any clouds. Yet at that instant there came a loud thunderclap.

I know these things must strain the credulity of many readers; therefore I don't insist on them. I include this material here, extraneous as it is to the subject of this essay, to substantiate my claim, the validity of which is already apparent this early in *Dwapara Yuga*, that much of what we consider a fundamental reality is not at all so.

To bring that thought down into the context of this essay, it is timely to add that we are already seeing another aspect of man's awareness of shrinking spatial distances. We see it in his growing ability to control things from afar. Many companies today are international in scope. The *A-B-C* configuration is therefore rapidly losing some of its top-heaviness. Some decisions, of course, can and must be made at an institution's international headquarters. Many of them, however, can be made only in terms of circumstances that vary from place to place.

My own father represented ESSO for seven years in the south of France, where he'd been sent to find oil. He did find it and received, as a result, the French *Légion d'honneur*.

Someone (actually, it was a friend of his) visited him from the Board of Directors in New York. This man took a casual glance at a map of the area being considered, pointed a pencil at one spot, and said, "Why don't you drill there?" In fact, this wasn't where oil was eventually found. Such, however, is the arrogance one often sees among administrators who work at the headquarters of an organization, and who imagine themselves therefore specially qualified to judge matters even far from home.

About this same "infallible judge," a mutual friend in the company once remarked to him with an ironic grin, "You know, M— —, you must be just about the greatest geologist in the whole world."

"Oh, no," came the modest disclaimer; M— — then added self-deprecatingly, "In oil, maybe."

CHAPTER FIVE
PERSONAL EXPERIENCE

I must speak here once more of my own experience, not because Ananda ranks anywhere among the great business empires—far from it; it isn't even a business!—but because Ananda's history is my history, and Ananda's years of experience are my own.

Ananda at present has branch communities in several American states and elsewhere in the world. How Ananda is organized is due partly to a deliberate attempt on my part to tune in to the "rays" of *Dwapara Yuga*.

Before founding Ananda, I used to ask myself, What business had I in founding a community? The only thing I could see that I had going for me was my enthusiasm for the concept. I did, perhaps, have a certain ability to infect others with my enthusiasm. I had also been for some years in charge of a community of monks, and had had other relatively direct experience of group dynamics. Apart from that, however, I'd shown no noteworthy abilities. I'd had no business experience, no exposure to accounting and book-keeping practices, no training in hands-on skills such as carpentry or plumbing. Apart from a month spent on a farm after graduating from high school, I'd had no experience in agriculture. I'd never even worked for a living. I'd spent most of my adult life in a monastery, where my lack of practical know-how inspired a certain amount of good-humored chaff from others. Is it any wonder I used to ask myself what I was doing in founding a community?

In addition to all of the above, my besetting "sin" was self-doubt. It often made me deprecate my own abilities, both to myself and to others. This was a weakness, I admit, though perhaps in another sense it was also my strength. I've wondered sometimes whether my "accomplishments" haven't been more by default than due to any special talent of my own. Something needed to be done that hadn't been done yet, and no one else seemed interested in doing it. So—why not, myself, give it a try?

I must confess also to having had, for years, a deep personal interest in communities, in helping people, and also in inspiring them to help themselves. My solution to my peculiar sense of personal inadequacy was to think rather in terms of giving out to others than of worrying about what I myself could or could not do. What, I asked myself, did my abilities matter? The important thing was simply to pitch in and do my best.

I've written several tracts on leadership in which I have stated repeatedly that a secret of good leadership is to shun self-importance, and, instead, simply to forget oneself. It is much easier to rise above self-preoccupation when one doesn't think of the energy coming back to him from others, but concentrates on the energy he himself is giving out to them and to the world.

I lacked practical knowledge, but I was always ready to listen to others. Having heard their alternatives, I had faith in my choice of the best one, and even in my ability to come up with solutions of my own, for God has given me an ability to see, from almost any contemplated action, what the results will be even miles down the road, or years in the future. I was also very much dedicated to the ideal of communities, having dreamed of creating them since I was fifteen.

Well, I guess I had one further advantage: I wasn't afraid of failing. I firmly believed in the principle Krishna teaches in the Bhagavad Gita: *nishkam karma*, action without attachment to (or desire for) personal results. This belief freed me to commit myself completely to positive action. Listening to others kept me open also to creative suggestions and ideas.

Leaders who try to tune in to the rays of *Dwapara Yuga* must make an effort to sense the energies around the people they work with. When a truly *Dwapara* leader delegates authority, he neither concerns himself overmuch with all the details of what his delegate will do, nor turns that subordinate entirely loose to "do his own thing." I would describe the process as holding the delegate within the leader's own "energy field." A leader must be able to *feel* that person's realities. This may not be an easy skill to develop, but I would say this much with certainty: The more one tries to do a thing, the better he will become at doing it.

I once assigned a small group the job of starting a community in the north of Italy. It was a mere beginning, and I was obliged to leave them and return to other duties in America. My friends might have felt that I'd abandoned them, particularly since the circumstances for them proved, for a time, quite difficult. However, they and their situation remained very much an active concern of mine. I held them in my energy field, so to speak, phoning them often, revisiting them when I could, and constantly seeking ways of helping them. I don't think they ever felt unsupported by me.

The important thing, I have found, is to view people as individuals—indeed, as friends—never as statistics. In an institution with branch communities (or offices), moreover, it is important for each branch to have at least some autonomy. Especially in a *Dwapara Yuga* institution where quality is recognized as being more important than quantity, such autonomy is necessary.

High energy can lead also, of course, to concentration on high profits rather than on the quality that develops with individual freedom. Chain stores, the focus of which is entirely on monetary returns, may of course succeed better creating rubber-stamped images of themselves. My thought, then, is of *service*-oriented organizations, particularly those which render spiritual service. In such organizations, particularly, the needs of people may vary considerably.

In the Ananda church and community in Palo Alto, for instance, the surrounding area, known internationally as "Silicon Valley," is focused on high technology. Obviously, the energy there is different from that which exists in our Portland (Oregon) center, where the general consciousness is more "laid back." The consciousness in Portland, again, is different from that in Seattle (Washington), where the general tendency is to focus more on individual freedom. In Ananda's work in Italy, again, there is a more devotional energy than is found on the West Coast of America. And in India there is more general openness to the higher, more abstract spiritual teachings.

People everywhere, however, are basically the same. It would be a mistake to give too much credence to something one sometimes hears: an insistence, uttered with great emphasis, that "Our people are special." A leader must have the wisdom to see beyond superficial differences, and realize that certain guidelines must also apply universally. I say this because I have encountered people, especially among leaders of spiritual groups, who insisted that basic teachings needed to be "adjusted" (for that, read "diluted") in their own situation. I have never surrendered to this argument, nor have I ever found the slightest reason, later on, to regret what those people saw as my "recalcitrance."

CHAPTER SIX
PASSING THE BATON

The important thing is to be true to your basic ideas. The next is to develop a spirit of unity in your organization. The *A-B-C* configuration is necessary where it applies: to the structural aspects of an organization. However, just as the energy that manifests matter is more real and essential than any material form—this truth becomes ever more apparent to people as the earth advances into *Dwapara Yuga*—even so, a harmonious and uplifted spirit can be the best bond in a *Dwapara* organization.

The first requirement for this bond is universal respect, a spirit which must be engendered from the top down. The president—or, on a local level, one's immediate superior—must not only feel, but must *show*, respect for everyone under him. Without respect there can be no true harmony in an organization. If the president doesn't show respect for others, he will not tolerate gladly anyone who does show it; rather, he will view that person with (usually) unspoken disapproval. Most people know, after all, how they *ought* to behave. Someone working under a haughty boss, if the subordinate is, himself, respectful and polite to everyone, will find himself being slowly edged toward the door.

I used to think that there ought to be some system for bypassing the need of groups to depend for their spirit on that of the leader. I didn't want to accept such dependence as being a necessary aspect of group dynamics, for the organization I served in had, in many places, branch meditation groups where the leaders sometimes had to move away from there for reasons of their work, or who simply lost interest in the teachings. Certainly it would be ideal for the spirit, and even the existence, of the group to continue at the same level after its leader's departure or demise. Despite my best efforts, however, I was forced eventually to conclude that the spirit of a group always reflects the spirit of its leader.

We had a group in Oakland, California, which I considered to be the best of our meditation groups anywhere. Its leader, after many years of serving the group, was obliged to retire owing to problems of health. I made it a point, after she left, to visit that group regularly. I also did my best to devise a system that would enable them to keep their group spirit unaltered no matter who was leading them. After making what I considered my very best effort, I was forced at last to accept that this was one project in which I'd never succeed. A good leader was simply necessary to healthy group dynamics. Even today, I would like to be proved wrong. Perhaps even, as people progress into higher consciousness with the ascending *yugas*, outward leadership will no longer be necessary. Ideally it would be better if everyone, blessed with the right understanding, would come to compatible, and usually unanimous, conclusions.

Some years ago, a study was made of the life-expectancy of organizations after the death of their founders. Very few, it turned out, survived very long. Those who did so underwent fundamental changes, corresponding to the characteristics of the new leadership. These leaders needed, moreover, to be strong enough themselves to keep the ship floating.

Many leaders, unfortunately, whether the founders of anything or not, are jealous of strong leadership qualities in others under them. They view anyone who possesses such qualities as a potential rival. (In a spiritual work, they may accuse him of excessive pride and ambition.) In so doing they show remarkable short-sightedness, for it should be obvious to everyone that the leadership will in any case change someday. It should therefore receive priority attention now, while the ship is still able to tack left or right as the need arises.

What should one look for in a potential leader? The first two qualities, I would say, are an attitude of service, and a desire to help others. The third quality is an ability to inspire such attitudes in others. I've said this before: Never appoint anyone to leadership who betrays a desire for self-importance.

In a hand-written letter I received from Satnya Sai Baba, written on the first of January, 1971, he said, "It is easy to drive people but it is hard to lead them." Seek to develop leaders who understand instinctively that good leadership is the sort that can inspire others to *want* to do what is right. To find such representatives, of whom one will probably replace you someday, *be* first such a leader, yourself. Whatever qualities you want in others, set them first, yourself, an example of those qualities. What you *are* will always speak louder than any words you speak.

I have seen leaders make a show of respecting those under them. Such posturing quickly becomes transparent. I remember the president of a business in Italy who once, while I was visiting his office, called an assistant of his into the room and made a great show of camaraderie towards him. I shuddered for the poor man's sake, for it was clear to me that he knew his boss was showing him mere condescension, while in fact only insulting him—more so than if he'd spoken impersonally. It seemed to me the show was being put on for my sake, and I would very much have liked to apologize to the poor peon.

Clearly, then (I hope), respect must begin with a respectful *attitude*. It cannot be expressed as camaraderie unless it is accompanied by frequent invitations to one's home for dinner or to one's club for golf. One cannot express sincere camaraderie toward everybody, nor would it be desirable to do so. There should be a certain impersonal reserve in the way one behaves even toward his friends, lest excessive familiarity breed—not contempt, exactly, since contempt suggests an awareness of hidden faults and weaknesses—but forgetfulness of that nobler aspect of human nature which is best expressed and appreciated in silence. As Emerson put it in his essay on the Oversoul: "Men descend to meet."

The underlying delusion behind the desire for excessive familiarity is—perhaps not so strangely—the desire for a mate, and the forever-disappointed hope of achieving that degree of union which can occur only when the soul merges into God.

My Guru once said to me, "When I was young, I had many friends, and enjoyed their company. Then one day someone said to me, 'I once had many friends, but since my marriage I find I seldom see them anymore.'

"'Thank you very much,' I replied. 'You have taught me an important lesson.' Since then, I have always remained somewhat apart, in my inner Self."

Friendship, which of course is something in any case that no one can share equally with all (one human being simply cannot spread himself so thin), can be given universally only if it is friendship in God. For one *can* learn to see God in all, and to love Him in all. The first step to that universal love, however, is to *respect* God in everyone—to bow to

Him in one's heart. For He dwells in the heart of everyone
we meet.

This kind of respect is what I urge people to develop
toward their associates. They should try first to associate
with God, moment by moment, in their hearts. In that association they should visualize all men as participating. Later,
as one develops deep devotion to God, he should bow to
Him lovingly in all. And as devotion ripens to love, he will
find it natural to love God also in everybody.

It all begins, however, with respect: respect for the truth
above all, and for the truth we define as God.

Respect for one another should be actively encouraged
in every organization. As my Guru once said to the monks,
"I want you all to respect one another, as you respect me."
He knew that respect, at least, was a concept we could all
understand, appreciate, and adopt for ourselves.

To develop that attitude in your staff, defer to them as
often as seems feasible. Don't be the sort of leader who insists always on having the last word. If anyone under you
offers a suggestion, try never to reply, "I've tried that already," or, "I've had that same thought myself." If you let
others take the credit for having made a suggestion, they will
feel encouraged to make further ones, and perhaps even to
make better and better ones. But if you dampen their enthusiasm, you may find yourself needing to resolve even small
issues yourself.

Once people have been instilled with the right spirit, you
can fairly safely count on their making a right decision most
of the time. For understanding follows on the heels of right
spirit. A leader's primary job, then, is to instill that spirit in
others. His personal example, also, is of great importance.

It is important for him also to share his hopes and dreams
with those of whose understanding he feels confident.
It may be better for him not to share those dreams with

everyone, since those who have not yet reached his level of commitment may feel overwhelmed if he asks them to plunge into the waters too quickly. People need time to grow into a new idea. The loftier the idea, moreover, the longer the time needed to adjust to it.

I noticed that my Guru never tried to force people beyond their own capacity to understand. If anyone failed in this respect, he would simply drop the matter and ask less of him in future. To paraphrase Sathya Sai Baba, it may be easy to drive people, but even if you get them moving in the right direction, they'll only bleat like sheep, and require constant watching. Jesus Christ, though known as "the Good Shepherd," led those only who would follow him of their free will, rejoicing in his leadership and cooperating with it in heart, mind, and soul.

In working with others, encourage a certain interplay of lighthearted humor. My Guru could laugh with us joyfully without ever sacrificing his dignity. He owed his ability in this respect to the fact that he remained always centered in his Self within. Such, indeed, is the ideal leader. Certainly a *spiritual* leader should strive to act always from his own center.

King Henry I of England established a routine for his court that might to some extent be emulated by every business. He set the morning hours aside for serious matters. The afternoons he designated for play and recreation. I grant, of course, that very few businesses could follow such a plan literally. Nevertheless, if one reflects on the amount of time that gets spent—wasted would be an employer's term—by workers needing a little relaxation now and then, it might not be a bad idea to set aside definite periods for relaxation, as an accepted part of every workday. Certainly it seems unlikely that Henry's court, with a whole country to run, had nothing better to do than "waste" time in fun and games. There was sound reasoning behind this daily program.

Kindness is, of all things, what touches people the most closely. Alas, it is the one quality that is the most easily overlooked in the rush of getting things done. Here, then, I address presidents and all other leaders: please, take the time to show an interest in your subordinates! Think of them as people who have needs of their own. Respect those needs as you would your own. Reflect: To treat others kindly takes no more energy than to treat them indifferently! In the end, the support it will win you will save you a great deal of energy, worry, and anxiety. If ever you find yourself complaining about the "incompetence" of the people on your staff, ask yourself "Have I, perhaps, been feeding that incompetence?"

In a spiritual organization, it will help to bring all the branches more closely together in a spirit of harmony if special times of celebration are appointed throughout the year, occasions in which everyone is invited to participate. Isn't that something which, for all Christians, is accomplished by Christmas and Easter festivities? It helps in bonding a whole society.

I regret that printed cards nowadays say only, "Season's greetings." The intention is not to offend anyone, but I'd much rather be invited to share other religionists' festive days also. Why not? Isn't God the same one Father/Mother of us all?

Once mutual—indeed, universal—respect becomes ingrained in an organization, other wholesome spiritual attitudes will develop as a matter of course.

Alas, spirituality is discounted nowadays, even (believe it or not) in churches and other religious institutions. Oh, of course, they still get work done, and may even be abuzz with activity. But love for God? the desire to commune with Him, and to bring Him into every activity? You will find in such matters that He is a distant concern. St. John of the

Cross said that a single act of pure love for God is of greater value than all the pious activity of monks, nuns, and religious workers busily serving God in the field.

It would solve everything if people lived more for God in their hearts. Many people, instead, blame religion itself for half the disharmony in the world. It isn't religion they should be blaming: It is people's native bigotry, intolerance, condescension, and judgment of their fellow beings, attitudes that are too often labeled "religious." People make a religion of their small-mindedness, while squeezing their hearts tightly with their own egoism.

Love God. One often hears the advice, "You should love yourself, first." I don't agree. It depends on which self you are loving. If your love is for your own ego, you are giving love to the very source of all your suffering and misery. You should love the soul: the presence of God within you. As for your ego, you should (again) *respect* it—if only for its amazing ability to lead you ever further into delusion! Respect its cleverness in confusing you as to the true value and meaning of life. And then, respect it for its *potential* to reach out toward higher and nobler ideals in life, by opening yourself to God's grace. For in your higher potential lies the promise of God Himself to every soul: eternal fulfillment— not in grubby money-making, nor in equally squalid passions, nor in self-debasing desires for mere tinsel wealth and possessions—no, but in *Satchidananda*: Eternal, Conscious, Ever-new Bliss in union with God.

INDEX

ABOUT THE AUTHOR

"Swami Kriyananda is a man of wisdom and compassion in action, truly one of the leading lights in the spiritual world today."

—Lama Surya Das,
Dzogchen Center,
author of *Awakening
The Buddha Within*

SWAMI KRIYANANDA

A prolific author, accomplished composer, playwright, and artist, and a world-renowned spiritual teacher, Swami Kriyananda refers to himself simply as "a humble disciple" of the great God-realized master, Paramhansa Yogananda. He met his guru at the young age of twenty-two, and served him during the last four years of the Master's life. And he has done so continuously ever since.

Kriyananda was born in Rumania of American parents, and educated in Europe, England, and the United States. Philosophically and artistically inclined from youth, he soon came to question life's meaning and society's values. During a period of intense inward reflection, he discovered Yogananda's *Autobiography of a Yogi*, and immediately traveled 3,000 miles from New York to California to meet the Master, who accepted him as a monastic disciple. Yogananda appointed him as the head of the monastery, authorized him to teach in his name and to give initiation into Kriya Yoga, and entrusted him with the missions of writing and developing what he called "world-brotherhood colonies."

Recognized as the "father of the spiritual communities movement" in the United States, Swami Kriyananda founded Ananda World-Brotherhood Community in 1968. It has served as a model for a number of communities founded subsequently in the United States and Europe.

In 2003 Swami Kriyananda, then in his seventy-eighth year, moved to India with a small international group of disciples, to dedicate his remaining years to making his guru's teachings better known. To this end he appears daily on Indian national television with his program *A Way of Awakening*. He has established Ananda Sangha, which publishes many of his ninety literary works and spreads the teachings of Kriya Yoga throughout India. His vision for the upcoming years in India includes founding cooperative spiritual communities, a temple of all religions dedicated to Paramhansa Yogananda, a retreat center, a school system, and a monastery, as well as a university-level Yoga Institute of Living Wisdom.

FURTHER EXPLORATIONS

If you are inspired by *Religion in the New Age* and would like to learn more about the teachings of Paramhansa Yogananda and Swami Kriyananda, Crystal Clarity Publishers offers many additional resources.

PARAMHANSA YOGANANDA

Autobiography of a Yogi
Paramhansa Yogananda

Autobiography of a Yogi is one of the best-selling Eastern philosophy titles of all time, with millions of copies sold, named one of the best and most influential books of the 20th century. This highly prized reprinting of the original 1946 edition is the only one available free from textual changes made after Yogananda's death.

Yogananda was the first yoga master of India whose mission was to live and teach in the West. His account of his life experiences includes childhood revelations, stories of his visits to saints and masters in India, and long-secret teachings of Self-realization that he made available to the Western reader.

In this updated edition are bonus materials, including a last chapter that Yogananda wrote in 1951, without posthumous changes. This new edition also includes the eulogy that Yogananda wrote for Gandhi, and a new foreword and afterword by Swami Kriyananda, one of Yogananda's close direct disciples.

PRAISE FOR *Autobiography of a Yogi*

"In the original edition, published during Yogananda's life, one is more in contact with Yogananda himself. While Yogananda founded centers and organizations, his concern was more with guiding individuals to direct communion with Divinity rather than with promoting any one church as opposed to another. This spirit is easier to grasp in the original edition of this great spiritual and yogic classic."

—David Frawley, Director, American Institute of Vedic Studies, author of *Yoga and Ayurveda*

THIS TITLE IS ALSO AVAILABLE IN:
52-Card Deck and Booklet
Audiobook (MP3 format)

Revelations of Christ
Proclaimed by Paramhansa Yogananda,
Presented by his disciple, Swami Kriyananda

Over the past years, our faith has been severely shaken by experiences such as the breakdown of church authority, discoveries of ancient texts that supposedly contradict long-held beliefs, and the sometimes outlandish historical analyses of Scripture by academics. Together, these forces have helped create confusion and uncertainty about the true teachings and meanings of Christ's life. Now, more than ever, people are yearning for a clear-minded, convincing, yet uplifting understanding of the life and teachings of Jesus Christ.

This soul-stirring book, presenting the teachings of Christ from the experience and perspective of Paramhansa Yogananda, one of the greatest spiritual masters of the 20th century, finally offers the fresh understanding of Christ's teachings for which the world has been waiting. This book presents us with an opportunity to understand the Scriptures in a more reliable way than any other: by learning from those saints who have communed directly, in deep ecstasy, with Christ and God.

PRAISE FOR *Revelations of Christ*

"This is a great gift to humanity. It is a spiritual treasure to cherish and to pass on to children for generations. This remarkable and magnificent book brings us to the doorway of a deeper, richer embracing of Eternal Truth."

—Neale Donald Walsch, author of *Conversations with God*

"*Kriyananda's revelatory book gives us the enlightened, timeless wisdom of Jesus the Christ in a way that addresses the challenges of twenty-first century living.*"

—Michael Beckwith, founder and Spiritual Director, Agape International Spiritual Center, author of *Inspirations of the Heart*

THIS TITLE IS ALSO AVAILABLE IN:
Audiobook (MP3 format)

The Essence of the Bhagavad Gita
Explained by Paramhansa Yogananda
As remembered by his disciple, Swami Kriyananda

Rarely in a lifetime does a new spiritual classic appear that has the power to change people's lives and transform future generations. This is such a book.

This revelation of India's best-loved scripture approaches it from a fresh perspective, showing its deep allegorical meaning and its down-to-earth practicality. The themes presented are universal: how to achieve victory in life in union with the divine; how to prepare for life's "final exam," death, and what happens afterward; how to triumph over all pain and suffering.

PRAISE FOR *The Essence of the Bhagavad Gita*

"The Essence of the Bhagavad Gita *is a brilliant text that will greatly enhance the spiritual life of every reader.*"

—Caroline Myss, author of *Anatomy of the Spirit* and *Sacred Contracts*

"*It is doubtful that there has been a more important spiritual writing in the last 50 years than this soul-stirring, monumental work. What a gift! What a treasure!*"

—Neale Donald Walsch, author of *Conversations with God*

THIS TITLE IS ALSO AVAILABLE IN:
Audiobook (MP3 format)
This title is available as a paperback book without commentary, titled *The Bhagavad Gita*.

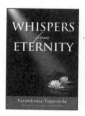

Whispers from Eternity
Paramhansa Yogananda
Edited by his disciple, Swami Kriyananda

Many poetic works can inspire, but few, like this one, have the power to change your life. Yogananda was not only a spiritual master, but a master poet, whose poems revealed the hidden divine presence behind even everyday things.

Open this book, pick a poem at random, and read it. Mentally repeat whatever phrase appeals to you. Within a short time, you will feel your consciousness transformed. This book has the power to rapidly accelerate your spiritual growth, and provides hundreds of delightful ways for you to begin your own conversation with God.

This title is also available in:
Audiobook (MP3 format)

The Wisdom of Yogananda series

This series features writings of Paramhansa Yogananda not available elsewhere. These books include writings from his earliest years in America, in an approachable, easy-to-read format. The words of the Master are presented with minimal editing, to capture his expansive and compassionate wisdom, his sense of fun, and his practical spiritual guidance.

How to Be Happy All the Time
The Wisdom of Yogananda Series, Volume 1
Paramhansa Yogananda

Yogananda powerfully explains virtually everything needed to lead a happier, more fulfilling life. Topics covered include: looking for happiness in the right places; choosing to be happy; tools and techniques for achieving happiness; sharing happiness with others; balancing success and happiness, and many more.

Karma and Reincarnation
The Wisdom of Yogananda Series, Volume 2
Paramhansa Yogananda

Yogananda reveals the truth behind karma, death, reincarnation, and the afterlife. With clarity and simplicity, he makes the mysterious understandable.

Topics covered include: why we see a world of suffering and inequality; how to handle the challenges in our lives; what happens at death, and after death; and the origin and purpose of reincarnation.

Spiritual Relationships
The Wisdom of Yogananda Series, Volume 3
Paramhansa Yogananda
    Topics include: how to cure bad habits that spell the death of true friendship; how to choose the right partner and create a lasting marriage; sex in marriage and how to conceive a spiritual child; problems that arise in marriage and what to do about them; the divine plan uniting parents and children; the Universal Love behind all your relationships.

How to Be a Success
The Wisdom of Yogananda Series, Volume 4
Paramhansa Yogananda
    This book includes the complete text of *The Attributes of Success*, the original booklet later published as *The Law of Success*. In addition, you will learn how to find your purpose in life, develop habits of success and eradicate habits of failure, develop your will power and magnetism, and thrive in the right job.

SWAMI KRIYANANDA (J. DONALD WALTERS)

The Path
My Life with Paramhansa Yogananda
Swami Kriyananda (J. Donald Walters)
    This is the moving story of Kriyananda's years with Paramhansa Yogananda, India's emissary to the West and the first yoga master to spend the greater part of his life in America.

When Swami Kriyananda discovered *Autobiography of a Yogi* in 1948, he was totally new to Eastern teachings. This is a great advantage to the Western reader, since Kriyananda walks us along the yogic path as he discovers it from the moment of his initiation as a disciple of Yogananda. With winning honesty, humor, and deep insight, he shares his journey along the spiritual path through personal stories and experiences.

Through more than 400 stories of life with Yogananda, we tune in more deeply to this great master and to the teachings he brought to the West. This book is an ideal complement to *Autobiography of a Yogi*.

Praise for The Path

"This book let me see inside the life and teaching of a great modern saint. Yogananda has found a worthy Boswell to convey not only the man but the spirit of the man."
—James Fadiman, author of *Unlimiting Your Life* and *Essential Sufism*

This title is also available in:
Audiobook (MP3 format)

In Divine Friendship
Swami Kriyananda

This extraordinary book of nearly 250 letters, written over a 30-year period by Swami Kriyananda, responds to practically any concern a spiritual seeker might have, such as: strengthening one's faith, accelerating one's spiritual progress, meditating more deeply, responding to illness, earning a living, attracting a mate, raising children, overcoming negative self-judgments, and responding to world upheavals.

Connecting all of these letters is the love, compassion, and wisdom of Swami Kriyananda, one of the leading spiritual figures of our times.

The letters describe in detail his efforts to fulfill his Guru's commission to establish spiritual communities, and offer invaluable advice to leaders everywhere on how to avoid the temptations of materialism, selfishness, and pride. A spiritual treasure that speaks to spiritual seekers at all levels.

Meditation for Starters
Swami Kriyananda

Have you wanted to learn to meditate, but just never got around to it? Or tried "sitting in the silence" only to find yourself too restless to stay more than a few moments? If so, *Meditation for Starters* is just what you've been looking for, and with a companion CD, it provides everything you need to begin a meditation practice. It is filled with easy-to-follow instructions, beautiful guided visualizations, and answers to important questions on meditation such as: what meditation is (and isn't); how to relax your body and prepare yourself for going within; and techniques for interiorizing and focusing the mind.

Awaken to Superconsciousness

Meditation for Inner Peace, Intuitive Guidance, and Greater Awareness

Swami Kriyananda

This popular guide includes everything you need to know about the philosophy and practice of meditation, and how to apply the meditative mind to resolving common daily conflicts in uncommon, superconscious ways. Superconsciousness is the source of intuition, spiritual healing, solutions to problems, and deep and lasting joy.

Praise for *Awaken to Superconsciousness*
"A brilliant, thoroughly enjoyable guide to the art and science of meditation. [Swami Kriyananda] entertains, informs, and inspires—his enthusiasm for the subject is contagious. This book is a joy to read from beginning to end."
— *Yoga International*

Affirmations for Self-Healing

Swami Kriyananda

This inspirational book contains 52 affirmations and prayers, each pair devoted to improving a quality in ourselves. Strengthen your will power; cultivate forgiveness, patience, health, enthusiasm, and more. A powerful tool for self-transformation.

Praise for *Affirmations for Self-Healing*
"[This book] has become a meditation friend to me. The inspiring messages and prayers, plus the physical beauty of the book, help me start my day uplifted and focused."
—Sue Patton Thoele, author, *Growing Hope*

This title is also available in:
Audiobook (MP3 format)

AUDIOBOOKS AND MUSIC

Crystal Clarity Publishers has available online many of our titles in unabridged MP3 format audiobooks. To purchase these titles and to see more music and audiobook titles, visit our website www.crystalclarity.com. Or look for us in many of the popular download sites.

Metaphysical Meditations
Swami Kriyananda (J. Donald Walters)
Kriyananda's soothing voice guides you in thirteen different meditations based on the soul-inspiring, mystical poetry of Paramhansa Yogananda. Each meditation is accompanied by beautiful classical music to help you quiet your thoughts and prepare for deep states of meditation. Includes a full recitation of Yogananda's poem *Samadhi*, which appears in *Autobiography of a Yogi*. A great aid to the serious meditator, as well as to those just beginning their practice.

Meditations to Awaken Superconsciousness
Guided Meditations on the Light
Swami Kriyananda (J. Donald Walters)
Featuring two beautiful guided meditations as well as an introductory section to help prepare the listener for meditation, this extraordinary recording of visualizations can be used either by itself, or as a companion to the book, *Awaken to Superconsciousness*. The soothing, transformative words, spoken over inspiring sitar background music, creates one of the most unique guided meditation products available.

Relax: Meditations for Flute and Cello
Donald Walters
Featuring David Eby and Sharon Nani
This CD is specifically designed to slow respiration and heart rate, bringing listeners to their calm center. This recording features 15 melodies for flute and cello, accompanied by harp, guitar, keyboard, and strings.

Bliss Chants CD

Ananda Kirtan

Chanting focuses and lifts the mind to higher states of consciousness. *Bliss Chants* features chants written by Yogananda and his direct disciple, Swami Kriyananda. They're performed by Ananda Kirtan, a group of singers and musicians from Ananda, one of the world's most respected yoga communities. Chanting is accompanied by guitar, harmonium, kirtals, and tabla.

Other titles in Series:

Divine Mother Chants   Power Chants
Love Chants   Peace Chants

Crystal Clarity Publishers

When you're seeking a book on practical spiritual living, you want to know it's based on an authentic tradition of timeless teachings, and that it resonates with integrity. This is the goal of Crystal Clarity Publishers: to offer you books of practical wisdom filled with true spiritual principles that have not only been tested through the ages, but also through personal experience.

We publish only books that combine creative thinking, universal principles, and a timeless message. Crystal Clarity books will open doors to help you discover more fulfillment and joy by living and acting from the center of peace within you.

Crystal Clarity Publishers—recognized worldwide for its bestselling, original, unaltered edition of Paramhansa Yogananda's classic *Autobiography of a Yogi*—offers many additional resources to assist you in your spiritual journey including over ninety books, a wide variety of inspirational and relaxation music composed by Swami Kriyananda, Yogananda's direct disciple, and yoga and meditation DVDs.

For our online catalog, complete with secure ordering, please visit us on the web at:

www.crystalclarity.com

Crystal Clarity music and audiobooks are available on all the popular online download sites. Look for us on your favorite on-line music website.

To request a catalog, place an order for the products you read about in the Further Explorations section of this book, or to find out more information about us and our products, please contact us:

Contact Information	mail:	14618 Tyler Foote Road
		Nevada City, CA 95959
	phone:	800.424.1055
		or 530.478.7600
	fax:	530.478.7610
	email:	clarity@crystalclarity.com

ANANDA SANGHA

Ananda Sangha is a fellowship of kindred souls following the teachings of Paramhansa Yogananda. The Sangha embraces the search for higher consciousness through the practice of meditation, and through the ideal of service to others in their quest for Self-realization. Approximately 10,000 spiritual seekers are affiliated with Ananda Sangha throughout the world.

Founded in 1968 by Swami Kriyananda, a direct disciple of Paramhansa Yogananda, Ananda includes seven communities in the United States, Europe, and in India. Worldwide, about 1,000 devotees live in these spiritual communities, which are based on Yogananda's ideals of "plain living and high thinking."

"Thousands of youths must go north, south, east and west to cover the earth with little colonies, demonstrating that simplicity of living plus high thinking lead to the greatest happiness!" After pronouncing these words at a garden party in Beverly Hills, California in 1949, Paramhansa Yogananda raised his arms, and chanting the sacred cosmic vibration AUM, he "registered in the ether" his blessings on what has become the spiritual communities movement. From that moment on, Swami Kriyananda dedicated himself to bringing this vision from inspiration to reality by establishing communities where home, job, school, worship, family, friends, and recreation could evolve together as part of the interwoven fabric of harmonious, balanced living. Yogananda predicted that these communities would "spread like wildfire," becoming the model lifestyle for the coming millennium.

Kriyananda lived with his guru during the last four years of the Master's life, and continued to serve his organization for another ten years, bringing the teachings of Kriya Yoga and Self-realization to audiences in the United States, Europe, Australia, and, from 1958–1962, India. In 1968, together with a small group of close friends and students, he founded the first "world-brotherhood community" in the foothills of the Sierra Nevada Mountains in northeastern California. Initially a meditation retreat center located on 67 acres of forested land, Ananda World-Brotherhood Community today encompasses 1,000 acres where about 250 people live a dynamic, fulfilling life based on the principles and practices of spiritual, mental, and physical development, cooperation, respect, and divine friendship.

At this printing, after forty years of existence, Ananda is one of the most successful networks of intentional communities in the world. Urban communities have been developed in Palo Alto and Sacramento, California; Portland, Oregon; and Seattle, Washington. In Europe, near Assisi, Italy, a spiritual retreat and community was established in 1983, where today nearly one hundred residents from eight countries live. Ananda also has a rapidly expanding work in India where it operates a number of centers and meditation groups. Swami Kriyananda currently lives in Pune.

Contact Information　　mail:　　14618 Tyler Foote Road
　　　　　　　　　　　　　　　　Nevada City, CA 95959

　　　　　　　　　　　phone:　　530. 478.7560
　　　　　　　　　　　online:　　www.ananda.org
　　　　　　　　　　　email:　　info@ananda.org

THE EXPANDING LIGHT

Ananda's guest retreat The Expanding Light, is a guest retreat for spiritual studies visited by over 2,000 people each year. We offer a varied, year round schedule of classes and workshops on yoga, meditation, and spiritual practices and studies. We also offer personal renewal retreats where you can participate in ongoing activities as much or as little as you wish.

The beautiful serene mountain setting, supportive staff, and delicious vegetarian food provide an ideal environment for a truly meaningful, spiritual vacation.

Contact Information　　mail:　　14618 Tyler Foote Road
　　　　　　　　　　　　　　　　Nevada City, CA 95959

　　　　　　　　　　　phone:　　800.346.5350
　　　　　　　　　　　online:　　www.expandinglight.org
　　　　　　　　　　　email:　　info@expandinglight.org